- 3.4.87 -

For Saffie and Charlie
with thanks -
Fredly [signature]

THE
"POLYTYQUE CHURCHE"

FOR
C A R O L Y N

"Quella che imparadisa la mia mente"

THE
"POLYTYQUE CHURCHE"

Religion and Early Tudor
Political Culture,
1485–1516

PETER IVER KAUFMAN

ISBN 0-86554-211-2

The paper used in this publication meets
the minimum requirements of American National Standard
for Information Sciences—Permanence of Paper
for Printed Library Materials, ANSI Z39.48-1984.

Library of Congress Cataloging-in-Publication Data
Kaufman, Peter Iver.
The "polytyque churche."
Includes index.
1. Great Britain—Church history—16th century.
2. Great Britain—Politics and government—1485-1603.
I. Title.
BR750.K38   1986   282'.42   86-12812
ISBN 0-86554-211-2 (alk. paper)

CONTENTS

PREFACE

I owe the title to John Bale. His estimate of late-medieval English
Christianity as "rather a polytyque churche than a christen churche,"
seemed something of a goad, yet my interest in religion and early Tudor
political culture dates from my previous work on the soteriologies of several Catholic reformers. I had been preoccupied then with their practical
spirituality, but I wondered from time to time whether their criticisms of
clerical worldliness (of "secularitie") were valid. Now, by juxtaposing
fresh evaluations of the critics with reinterpretations of several areas they
criticized, I hope to add to the stock of recent reappraisals that makes the
study of late-medieval Christendom so lively.

Thanks are due to several scholars whose encouragement trans-
formed an ordeal into a truly gratifying challenge: from afar, Gary Dick-
son, Richard Trexler, Francis Oakley, John Wilson, Jerald Brauer, and
Bernard McGinn; and my colleagues at the University of North Carolina,
Grant Wacker, Giles Gunn, John Headley, Anne Hall, Ritchie Kendall,
and Darryl Gless. On separate occasions three wise and valued friends,
Robert Pozen, Marcia Colish, and Mark Rose, put me back on track when
I seemed hopelessly derailed.

This small book has acquired these and so many other debts principally because its maker, at the time of its making, was a historical theo-
logian struggling to understand something about political history, civic
pageants, early Tudor administration, and the church's institutional life.
A generous grant from the National Endowment for the Humanities enabled me to take my questions and confusion to Cambridge. Professor G.
R. Elton and members of his seminar were hospitable, patient, and im-
mensely helpful. Stretching toward their high standards has been an ex-
hilarating experience, yet they will know that there must be more
stretching before the job is done. Whether working quietly in my rooms
or rattling on in commons, I was mindful of and grateful for the kindness
of the president and fellows of Wolfson College. Lively and learned conversation at Wolfson made Cambridge an enchanted place. The Coopers
of Long Reach Road—Dick, Deanne, Adrian, and Frances—made Cambridge a second home.

I have leased information from several libraries and archives. Colleagues at the University Library, Cambridge, at the Public Record Office
in London, and at the Davis Library in Chapel Hill merit special mention
and thanks. I am also indebted to J. B. Trapp and Brigitte M. Urswick
Boardman for material on Christopher Urswick, and to Jane Fowles of
Longleat House for correspondence concerning the *Objectiones et argu-*

menta . . . Westmonasterii. Richard Rose saved me from committing several blunders with reference to jurisdictions in Northumberland. John S. Henderson provided perspective on lay confraternities and popular piety. Had Brendan Bradshaw not listened so tolerantly and argued so cogently for his alternative readings of Erasmus and More, I could not have pondered as profitably the issues presented here in part two. Mark Rose's comments on several chapters in parts one and three chased some mistakes from the manuscript and made my thoughts on pageants and popular culture less of a muddle. John O'Malley, Carolyn Wood, and Winthrop Hudson read the whole book in typescript and coaxed or cudgled me to reconsider and demystify. Without such good friends and kind critics, I could not have derived so much enjoyment from setting and resetting these bones. That "the thing" stands at all is due to all of them. But now that it has ambled into their libraries, they may wish that they had been less kind. I hope that the customary disclaimers will suffice, for I am certainly responsible for a rather inflexible attachment to the style that has survived gentle prompting to dress *The "Polytyque Churche"* differently. And I am responsible as well for the errors that remain.

I acknowledge with thanks the permission to reprint material that appeared in several journals. My interpretations of Polydore Vergil's *Historia* were first presented in the pages of *The Historian* (1985) and in those of *The Sixteenth Century Journal* (1986). *The Journal of British Studies* (1982) published the assessment of John Colet that is distributed throughout part two. The study of sanctuary in part three was originally composed for *Church History* (1984).

INTRODUCTION

This is a book about the interpenetration of religion and political culture in England from the accession of Henry VII in 1485 to the appointment of Thomas Wolsey as the realm's chancellor thirty years later. It is not a book that busies itself with the biographies of churchmen who entered government service. Neither is it an exhaustive analysis of three decades of parliamentary initiatives and statutes. The *"Polytyque Churche"* is an interpretative essay on Christianity's coalition with the new dynasty and an attempt to retrieve conditions that made possible the redistribution of power and influence within the church and in political culture.

For nearly five centuries readers have been treated to a one-sided view of the late-medieval English church, and that one, uncomplimentary side has been permitted to stand for the whole. The first chapter, a history of the history of earliest Tudor religion and politics, chronicles the deception. The second chapter takes another look at late-medieval complaints about ecclesiastical improprieties and clerical worldliness—complaints that were often emphasized and exploited by historical literature. It finds that many of the most damaging accusations say more about the critics' uncompromising idealism than about the "polytyque churche's" political realism. Fresh perspectives on the religious dimensions of public service and on the political characters and consequences of ecclesiastical administration develop through the first two chapters but fully crystallize in the third, with scenes from clerical life that offer illustrations of the interpenetration of religion and political culture.

To the extent that omissions in the historical literature have minimized clerical contributions to the Tudor dynasty's first and formative years, what follows is a step toward restoration. To the extent that idealistic critics' censures have been mistaken for the fruits of impartial, accurate, investigative reporting, what follows is also a reconsideration of the rhetoric of discontent as well as a suggestion for the Tudor church's rehabilitation. Obviously, this requires that some discussion of the Tudor usurpation and of the trajectories of Tudor policy be incorporated into these chapters. But for readers unfamiliar with late-medieval English history, the remainder of the introduction reviews developments.

* * *

Ah, was it not enough, that mutuall rage,
In deadly battels should this race ingage,
Till by their blowes themselves they fewer make,

and pillers fall, which France could never shake?
But must this crooked Monster now be found,
to lay rough hands on that unclosed wound?
His secret plots have much increast the flood,
He with his brothers, and his nephews blood,
Hath stain'd the brightnesse of his Fathers flowres,
and made his owne white Rose as red as ours.
This is the day, whose splendour puts to flight
Obscuring clouds, and brings an age to light.

Medievalists have been accustomed to quincentennial celebrations. The anniversary of *this day*, however, is unlikely to cause much of a stir. Summer 1985 will have arrived and passed by the time this introduction reaches readers and few persons, save for a scattering of specialists, will recall that much of the summer and autumn of 1485 was spent completing the transition from York to Tudor that was effected on 22 August by the battle near Market Bosworth. *This day* is Bosworth.

The bard was John Beaumont, who reduced the clash between rival nobilities to a great cluster of couplets more than a century after the battle. The "mutuall rage," which he deeply deplored, refers to decades of civil war—"obscuring clouds" that made the end of the Middle Ages seem as barbaric as their beginning. England was sparsely populated in the fifteenth century: slightly more than two million inhabitants worked the land or wandered the streets of the realm's few cities. Many citizens were only dimly aware of the baronial quarrels and wars, the fallout from Henry VI's long minority and ill-fated reign (1421-1471). Nonetheless, Beaumont was probably right about the aristocracy's devastation: "and pillers fall, which France could never shake." Henry VI (the final Lancastrian and unquestionably the least competent) and his councilors dissipated Crown lands, squandered wealth, lost control of most continental possessions, and provoked many leading proprietors. Their indignation set the territory on the road to Bosworth.[1]

Things fall apart when the center does not hold. In Henry VI's realm, "things" not only fell apart, they fell into competing parties that disrupted political culture for two generations. Edward IV twice wrested power from the Lancastrians, but divisions in the nobility prevented him

---

[1]Excerpts from Beaumont's "Bosworth Field" are taken from Roger D. Sell's critical edition, *The Shorter Poems of Sir John Beaumont* (Åbo: Åbo Akademi, 1974) 66-83. John Gillingham's analysis of Bosworth is among the most penetrating; see *The Wars of the Roses* (London: Weidenfield & Nicholson, 1981) 233-46. Elsewhere in the volume, Gillingham shows some disdain for familiar landmarks, and his remarks on "cosy" England and fifteenth-century conflicts (1-31, 51-75, 136-55, 256-57) are best checked against received opinion. For example, review J. R. Lander, *The War of the Roses* (London: Secker & Warburg, 1965); and K. B. McFarlane, *The Nobility of Later Medieval England* (Oxford: Clarendon Press, 1973).

from finally consolidating his family's authority; indeed, during the last years of his own reign (1480-1483), Edward himself hastened the renewal of civil war. His wife's relations, the Woodvilles, were unpopular. Older and more established families were distressed when the king appeared particularly solicitous of Woodville fortunes. Henry Stafford, duke of Buckingham, was all but ostracized from court, perhaps at the Woodvilles' prompting, for Stafford was their chief rival for authority in Wales. The queen had also marked William, Lord Hastings, as an enemy because she resented his orchestration of the king's whoring.

An anti-Woodville faction had taken definite shape by the time Edward IV died and partisans realized that custody of the young heir, Edward V, would give their adversaries an insuperable advantage. Fortunately for Stafford, Hastings, and their allies, Richard, duke of Gloucester, the king's only surviving brother, was named protector. Richard had not been at court for years, and his return as protector may have been engineered for the sake of reconciliation. But he swiftly sided with the Woodvilles' enemies, placed Edward V in the tower, teased his other nephew from the queen, disputed the legitimacy of both boys, and apparently had them murdered. Had Beaumont's "crooked Monster" been granted a longer reign, his accomplishments might have overshadowed his crimes. Richard III demonstrated administrative talents and instincts that surpassed those of his immediate predecessors. Within thirty months of Richard's coup d'etat, however, Henry, earl of Richmond, had landed at Milford Haven, marched through Wales, and made his way to Bosworth where the last York would give way before the first Tudor king of England.

*   *   *

See what a guide these Fugitives have chose
who bred among the French our ancient foes
Forgets the English language and the ground
And knows not what our drums and trumpets sound.

Royal proclamations against Henry were freighted with charges that the would-be king had sold England to France in order to finance his invasions. Thus the lines that Beaumont scripted for Richard III have some basis in late-medieval Francophobia. Henry, of course, had been "bred" across the channel. He and his uncle fled to Brittany soon after Lancastrian fortunes collapsed for the final time in 1471. Several years later Edward IV promised to treat Henry handsomely should he return and his host, Duke Francis II, be persuaded to release him. But the Tudors feared the worst and prevailed upon the Bretons to rescue their candidate for the Crown before Edward's agents were able to escort him back to England.[2]

Nine years later Henry Tudor did set sail. Stafford, the duke of Buckingham, had betrayed Richard III and raised troops to unseat the king and to prepare a warm welcome for Richard's rival. Edward and Peter Courtenay collected an army in Cornwall and Devonshire for the same purposes. But, in this instance, Richard proved more cunning than the rebels, and before the Tudor fleet reached the English shore, he had mastered the situation. Moreover, the weather was uncooperative, and Henry had only two ships under his command when he was within sight of Plymouth. Yorkist loyalists pretended to be rebels and tried to get the cautious commander to disembark, but Henry smelled a rat and returned first to Normandy and then to Brittany. Duke Francis received his disappointed guests, who were consoled only by the fact that the abortive revolution had increased the number of refugees who might soon be assembled for a second assault. The fugitives were summoned to Rennes where plans were sealed on Christmas day, 1483, in the cathedral. Henry vowed to marry Edward IV's eldest daughter and thereby to resolve dynastic controversies once he had removed Richard III.[3] Breton officials, for their part, promised to subsidize another expedition. The final thrust, however, was delayed for fifteen months, during which time Richard naturally conspired to have the earl of Richmond delivered into his hands.

Richard's navy harassed Breton shipping. Eventually the king offered to trade peace in the Channel and support against France for the Tudor fugitives. Henry heard that he was soon to be surrendered, so incognito he left for France. In England, precautions against a second invasion amounted to general commissions of array, for Richard's chances rested principally on his ability to raise an army rapidly and proceed against intruders before they could attract local troops to their cause and their "king." But on 7 August Henry landed at Milford Haven and advanced unchallenged for two weeks. Welsh recruits joined his forces, which Charles VIII, the king of France, had previously augmented with Norman soldiers. Richard's company still outnumbered his opponent's, but Richard suffered defections before and during the battle at Bosworth. The loss of Stanley's support at a crucial moment cost him the contest and the Crown; a rather reckless charge at Henry cost him his life. Suddenly En-

---

[2]The rescue was imaginatively reconceived by Rosemary Anne Sisson in her recent, clever staging of Henry VII's early career, *The Dark Horse* (London: French, 1979). Stanley Bertram Chrimes, *Henry VII* (Berkeley: University of California Press, 1972) will remain for the foreseeable future the definitive biography, but also note J. D. Mackie, *The Earlier Tudors, 1485-1558* (Oxford: Clarendon Press, 1952); and Michael Van Cleave Alexander, *The First of the Tudors* (Totowa NJ: Rowman & Littlefield, 1980).

[3]Ellis, *Three Books*, 203.

gland had a new dynasty. Yet a king by conquest can hardly be considered secure unless his claim stands on more solid ground.

Yorkists had effectively cleared the field of Lancastrian candidates: no serious challenge was expected from that quarter. Still, Henry's pedigree left something to be desired. His great-grandfather was illegitimate, and thus technically his connections with Edward III were impeachable. Marriage to Edward IV's daughter, Elizabeth, would fortify his claims to the Crown, though it doubtlessly occurred to Henry that his rule would be questioned should his wife predecease him. Fulfillment of the wedding pledge made at Rennes in 1483 would therefore have to be postponed until Henry was himself crowned. In the last analysis, Henry VII's right to rule would depend on his exercise of rule—on his government's ability to reconcile countrymen to the Tudor regime. The challenge would be to leave Henry's heir a more harmonious and prosperous realm than the one taken from Richard.

*   *   *

For Richmond boldly doth himselfe oppose
Against the King, and gives him blowes for blowes,
Who now confesseth with an angry frowne,
His Rivall not unworthy of the Crowne

The "blowes for blowes" account of individual combat is fictional. Beaumont nevertheless used Richard to foreshadow an appraisal of the first Tudor that became commonplace soon after the king's twenty-five-year reign concluded.

To be sure, there was dissent. During Henry's last years his deputies' single-minded pursuit of royal advantage led to strict enforcement of subjects' obligations to the Crown, and this led to resentment. Penalties and forfeitures enriched the government and some of its most vigorous agents. But this was not a radical deviation from the policy pursued for the first fifteen years after Bosworth, which witnessed "an enormous enlargement of prerogative rights."[4] The barons' jealousies and ambitions, which ignited and perpetuated the civil wars, were to be extinguished. Along the borders or "marches," aristocratic control was tempered by the appointment of churchmen to survey the king's prerogatives and to oversee local affairs. William Smyth, the bishop of Lincoln, dominated the king's council for Welsh affairs after the death of Henry's uncle. Smyth was succeeded in 1512 by the bishop of Coventry and Litchfield. In the north the bishops of Carlisle and Durham shared authority with one another and with several laymen nominated from time to time for special purposes. Conciliar government *in remotis* was nothing new, though as-

----

[4]Elton, *Studies*, 1:45-65.

signments awarded to "new men" reflected Henry VII's desires to keep the peace and to reduce the threat of insurrection. Disorder generally favored the prospects of the proprietors, whose armed retainers prosecuted their particular territorial interests. While the government often had to rely on the goodwill of these powerful nobles, greater advantages to the king followed if commissioners directly responsible and responsive to him and his council were placed in charge. This strategy along with the manipulation of attainders and their reversals, a shrewd form of intimidation, assured that most of the aristocracy remained relatively tractable and tame.[5]

For a time, however, the persistence of pretenders enlivened the possibility that England might again be rent by civil war. Lambert Simnel posed first as one and then the other of Edward IV's slain sons, and nearly all the nobility and higher clergy of Ireland conspired in the trick. Walter Fitzsimmons, archbishop of Dublin, presided over Simnel's coronation in 1487. But Simnel and his chief sponsor, Richard Simon, were quickly captured and within five years England's territories in Ireland were largely purged of Yorkist sentiment. Perkin Warbeck was a more serious rival. He also posed as Edward IV's true heir and received considerable encouragement from Yorkists in Burgundy. It is incomprehensible that the imposture fooled anyone, yet James IV, king of Scotland, welcomed Warbeck in November 1495, selected a Scots noblewoman as a bride for his "royal" guest, and allocated him a generous pension. Not long after Warbeck's arrival, guest and host invaded England.

The invasion ended badly for Warbeck and James, who retreated when they learned that an army had quickly gathered to oppose them. Soon thereafter, James either tired of his English king-in-residence or coaxed him to open a second front. Warbeck was sent to Ireland in the summer of 1497 to collect fresh troops for a landing in the southwest of England. He must have had little success with recruitment since only two vessels sailed for Land's End in Cornwall. Warbeck expected that the region would welcome him, and his numbers increased during the month that he roamed through the territory. Citizens in Cornwall had earlier objected to taxes, the revenue from which was earmarked for defense against Scotland, and they carried their protest to London. The king had little difficulty crushing this makeshift rebellion, but Warbeck imagined that he could fan hostilities still smoldering in Cornwall into a more serious offensive.

He was wrong. Exeter denied him entry, and though his company of followers had grown, it was still too risky to attempt battle in October,

---

[5]See especially J. R. Lander, "Attainder and Forfeiture, 1453-1509," *HJ* 4 (1961): 121, 134-41; Wilhelm Busch, *England under the Tudors: Henry VII*, trans. Alice M. Todd (New York: Burt Franklin, 1895) 291-304; and Alexander, *First of the Tudors*, 126-28.

when Henry VII appeared ready for the engagement. Warbeck himself deserted and sought sanctuary in Beaulieu, a few miles from the Channel. Henry wanted to prevent Warbeck's escape, yet he preferred not to violate sanctuary. The king promised clemency, and Warbeck voluntarily surrendered and made a full confession of the hoax. Two years later, after escape and recapture, Warbeck was executed along with the last bona fide Yorkist heir, Edward, earl of Warwick, who had been imprisoned since Bosworth.

What is most impressive about Warbeck's adventures is not the impostor's stubborn pursuit of the Crown, but rather the nobility's reluctance to get involved. For the most part, leading proprietors joined without hesitation against James in the north and against Warbeck in the south. Allusions to the realm's new order and to the hard-won tranquility were not without foundation.

The aristocracy's acquiescence to this new order, such as it was, did not depend exclusively on intimidation and on emergency or counterinsurgency measures. Political influence of the realm's leading families steadily eroded when it became clear that Henry meant to govern from the center. The government's appeals to the king's prerogative rights were, in essence, a programmatic reassertion of Henry's "personal rule" in most every policy decision. Intensely interested in revenues and disbursements, the king became very much his bookkeepers' keeper, as a robust chamber system, under his auspices, drained considerable business from the exchequer. This was akin to taking the country's treasury into the sovereign's household. Possibly haunted by the specter of Lancastrian insolvency, the first Tudor left little to chance, and the consensus is that "the deliberate intent to ferret out and exploit to the full the financial rights of the king arising from tenurial obligations was unquestionably a major feature of Henry VII's financial policy."[6]

Parliamentary subservience reflected general acceptance of centralization. Legislation endorsed and facilitated government regulation of the realm's economic life. For his part, the king relied less and less on his assemblies' imprimaturs. Once the threat of foreign war had subsided and Warbeck was in custody, he let seven years pass before calling legislators back into session. No interval since the middle of the thirteenth century was as long as the one between Henry's sixth (1497) and last (1504) parliaments. One can be forgiven, then, for suggesting that the king and his closest advisers ruled "absolutely," notwithstanding the fact that evidence for conciliar deliberations falls far short of what would be necessary to corroborate this (or any contrary) conclusion. A glance at foreign affairs adds little, for with respect to most negotiations, Henry VII seemed in complete control of his closely watched advisers and, quite in charac-

---

[6]Chrimes, *Henry VII*, 129. Also consult B. P. Wolffe, *The Royal Demesne in English History* (Athens: Ohio University Press, 1971) 202-203, 214-16.

ter, he seemed always in pursuit of objectives that would give his realm decided commercial advantages in Northern European markets and that would increase the Crown's customs revenues. The king's greatest diplomatic feat can best be phrased negatively: English armies were not mired in continental conflicts. Trade agreements and marriage contracts marked England's reentry into Europe after decades of civil wars had virtually guaranteed the island's isolation.

Of course, there were some conspicuous failures. Proprietors had so caged certain privileges that the Crown could not get at them. Landholders nominally alienated their property in order to spare their heirs the medieval equivalent of inheritance taxes, and they resisted Henry's efforts to close the loophole. The government enlarged the role of local justices of the peace and tried to discipline their performance, but the proliferation of regulatory statutes confirms that the problem of law enforcement was complex and that the regime was unable to solve it with sweeping gestures. Nevertheless, G. R. Elton's verdict on earliest Tudor administration stands without considerable qualification: Henry VII's government was more energetic and more efficient than that of Henry VIII before 1530.[7]

*   *   *

Henry VIII was an adventurer, a cautious father's somewhat reckless son. "Overseas" initiatives during the second Tudor's reign, as J. J. Scarisbrick has pointed out, amounted to a "forward continental policy" and a virtual renewal of the so-called "Hundred Years' War" with France.[8] At first, Henry VIII retained his father's appointees. When Bishop Fox and Archbishop Warham retired, Fox's apprentice, Thomas Wolsey, emerged as the king's closest adviser and, some have said, the king's master. Wolsey is certainly the late-medieval church's most notorious statesman. Wrapped snugly by Polydore Vergil in a villain's cloak, Wolsey has come to epitomize clerical greed, self-indulgence, and worldliness. Vergil insisted that the church paid a high price for Wolsey's political successes and influence, and it should be noted that the earliest Tudor church continues to pay inasmuch as the stain easily spread from Wolsey to his predecessors.[9] Did those predecessors victimize the church? Were leading ecclesiastical civil servants wholly self-serving and hopelessly corrupt? And if the "polytyque churche" was something less loathsome and more complex than a den of thieves, what is to be made of the chorus of earliest

---

[7]Chrimes, *Henry VII*, 166-71, for the judicature; Joel Hurstfield, "The Revival of Feudalism in Early Tudor England," *History* 37 (1952): 137-39, for feudal incidents of inheritance. For Elton's pronouncement, see *Studies*, 1:65.

[8]See Scarisbrick's *Henry VIII* (London: Eyre & Spottiswoode, 1968) 40-64.

[9]*AH*, notably 195, 209, 225, 257.

Tudor criticisms and complaints? For now, one may remove Wolsey's condemnation and the prospects for his rehabilitation from the docket. I shall not go beyond 1516, the year of Fox's resignation and the year that Thomas More published his *Utopia*, an excellent summary and a reevaluation of the idealistic critics' case against clerical worldliness. Between 1485 and 1516 the English church underwent no significant changes. It was dominated by no single person. Still, there are interpretative problems to transcend and discoveries to be made about the abiding coalition between church and government and the hybrid passions this generated. This introductory sketch of late-medieval and earliest Tudor political culture adds nothing to received opinion, yet it should prepare one to reassess some of those passions, to ponder the eclipse of the "polytyque churche," and to attempt a partial recovery.

• Part I •

THE
HISTORIANS

Chapter 1

THE ECLIPSE
OF THE EARLY TUDOR CHURCH:
ANDRÉ, FABYAN,
AND POLYDORE VERGIL

Bernard André, a blind poet and chronicler from Toulouse, accompanied Henry Tudor to England. His acquaintance with Henry in France, his participation in the triumphant return, and his presence in the new government as its official censor might lead one to expect accurate reporting. After all, he was within earshot of the new king and his trusted confederates as the path to the throne was charted and the new regime installed. Though blind, André had advantages denied to the most vigilant eyewitnesses, that is, he shared the vision of his patrons. He knew of their aspirations, their early conspiracies, and their maturing faith in the new Tudor monarchy. So if one expects accurate reporting from André, "accuracy" must refer to the correspondences between his remarks and the new government's self-image. His *De vita atque gestis Henrici Septimi* reached suspiciously epic proportions because the new dynasty saw itself and its achievements in that way. England's civil wars had not produced just another pretender or usurper; Tudor partisans believed that the island kingdom had embarked on an authentically new and different course, charted by a prudent and virtuous king. They hardly wanted their successes buried beneath a layer of historical causes and effects. The blind poet obliged. His *Twelve Triumphs* reflected Henry VII's sense that the rescue of England from tyranny and the subsequent imposition of law and order on his previously lawless kingdom were herculean tasks, rehearsals of which required operatic excesses. André's king and client could not have wished for a modest court historian.[1]

---

[1] André's *De vita* and *Les douze triomphes* are printed in *Memorials*, 3-75, 133-53. Eduard Fueter holds a low opinion of André (*"die schattenseiten der humanistischen Historiographie"*), but William Nelson approached André and other "humanists" at Henry VII's court more sympathetically. Fueter, *Geschichte der neueren Historiographie*, 2d ed. (Munich: R. Oldenbourg, 1925) 160-61; Nelson, *John Skelton, Laureate* (New York: Columbia University Press, 1939) 14-38.

André made the first Tudor a second Solomon and, like Solomon, Henry VII was said to enjoy the invincibility imparted by God's counsel and protection (*"nulle ne peult a qui Dieu veult aider"*). On this point as well as others, André's involvement and partisanship irredeemably compromised him. "Accuracy," which refers at this moment to correspondences between reports and events, has been deliberately sacrificed. Yet André's reports of his king's divine mission and majesty are tremendously valuable as early dramatizations of the new dynasty's own articles of faith: God prompted Richmond's return, pulled the army back to France when the enterprise was placed in jeopardy, prepared the ultimate success of those same forces, and preserved the new king from his rivals once the Crown had been taken in battle. André's narrative of the decisive campaign against Richard III, punctuated by his detailed restoration of Henry's prayers, leaves no doubt that the king possessed a direct line to God. Henry himself proclaims as much to soldiers who had been watching his supplications. "God is a just judge," he assures his comrades, "and he will punish the crimes of our enemies by our hands." He tells them that his right to rule, like that of Moses, has been acknowledged and established in heaven long before its manifestation in history. Then Henry and those loyal to him depart—their commission and success guaranteed—though not before the would-be king directs the clergy present to pray earnestly for a favorable outcome. Henry's valedictory leaves one uncertain whether the churchmen joined his troops or remained behind. It is clear, however, that his instructions did not privilege their part in the adventure. Their prayers follow his own. Unless one assumes that André detected a hollow center in his king's confidence, that is, suspected that Henry was less sure of divine sanction than he would think wise to disclose to his soldiers, the solicitation of the clergy's prayers was a mere formality. Henry had been designated by God as England's savior, so the oracles, counsel, and mediation of the church were hardly necessary. The clergy fade into the background as André's narrative catches the tide and carries his protagonist to his divinely appointed destiny.[2]

The next time Henry is overheard speaking with his God, he is making his last confession and, it appears, stipulating his own penance. The "true tournynge of his soule from this wretched worlde unto the love of almighty God" was not accomplished for Henry, but by him. Bishop John Fisher's account mentions the king's confessor, yet the story permits the king his self-reliance, even in self-effacement. Little can be learned of the church, which is introduced only briefly as one of several beneficiaries of Henry's final, apportionable kindnesses. The first Tudor might have been a generous patron of, or a thorny problem for, the English church, but readers of encomiastic memorials and vitae will know him exclusively as

---

[2]André, *De vita*, 22-27.

an agent of God's will for England. Larger than life, the king could reach to the heavens, pretty much without the assistance of his clergy.[3]

Larger than life, the king and the royal family tower above all other citizens. It was particularly expedient for certain of them to emphasize precisely this exaltation in the civic pageants composed to greet their new monarch and subsequently to welcome a bride for his firstborn son. Inhabitants of northern cities, who were indifferent and sometimes openly hostile to Henry before the issue of his succession had been settled, swarmed to his side and were inordinately obsequious in their tributes during his first tour of the kingdom. His "progress" north began soon after the victory over Richard III, for he was as interested to win the allegiance of subjects notoriously loyal to his predecessor as they were to win his goodwill. God's judgment on victor and vanquished alike was then a matter of record, so the receptions arranged for Henry were made worthy of a divine emissary. They were significant parts of each town's penance and special pleading. After Bosworth, previous political miscalculations were tantamount to sins against God's will for England. Nevertheless, with the magnanimity befitting an instrument of divine will, Henry would forgive them. If the towns' pulpits were used at all, they served to proclaim the papal bull supporting Tudor sovereignty. The initial pageants assume that a partnership had been effected between their new monarch and their God. The pope confirmed, and local clergy proclaimed, a judgment that had been rendered and a pact that had been sealed quite independently of the institutional church's loyalties.

The most intemperate aspect of the early pageants' theme appeared years later to celebrate the arrival of Aragon's Princess Catherine, betrothed to England's Arthur, Henry VII's son. Costumed characters in London gave encomiastic accounts of the foreigner's virtues and of their own royal family's accomplishments. The most flattering speech was reserved for Prelacy, who identified the Tudors with heaven's holiest family. Steadfast in the faith, Henry was said to resemble God in his prudence, wisdom, and liberality. By some mysterious logic, this made Arthur a second Christ. Prelacy exploited the allegory and seized every opportunity to be agreeable. The king had not masterminded the pageants and praises, but their public-relations value was surely not lost on him. Here Prelacy restated the conviction "accurately" represented in Bernard André's accolade. Chroniclers like Fabyan, the London draper, who had a demonstrable fondness for spectacles, spread the word in their towns and across the centuries that God endorsed and protected Tudor succession and that the Tudors might justifiably play the part of gods on earth.[4]

---

[3]John Fisher, "Sermon Sayd in the Cathedrall Chyrche of Saynte Poule within the Cyte of London," *The English Works of John Fisher*, ed. John E. B. Mayor (London: Early English Text Society, 1876) 271, 278-79.

[4]*GC*, 308. Also see below, ch. 7.

The part required considerable subsidies, so chroniclers, along with their fellow citizens, were taxed to support spending at their king's court. This should not be overemphasized, but dissent did erupt occasionally and antagonisms seem never far beneath the surface of those rehearsals of royal pageantry composed by literate artisans. Like the leaders of the Cornwall tax revolt in 1497, late-medieval chroniclers were less likely to blame the king than to censure his money-obsessed councillors, and Henry's episcopal advisers were favorite targets. Fabyan, whose chronicles widely circulated in the early sixteenth century, hastened to add to a generally complimentary epitaph the observation that Cardinal Morton "lyved not withoute the greate disdayn and great haterede of the Comons of this land."

The chroniclers' own disdain was subtly expressed. Church architecture often received more attention than the administrators it sheltered. News of the weathercock atop the steeple of St. Paul's cathedral, its initial repairs, and its destruction by "the hidyous wynd" of 1506, passed from one chronicler to another, whereas hardly a word about the deans of the cathedral reached parchment or print. Obscure and frequently unnamed critics were considered more newsworthy than the leading prelates they berated. Fabyan reported the abjurations of numerous dissidents, but he allotted only one line for an obituary for Richard Hill, the bishop of London. And lest mourning break the cadence of the journal, the chronicler appended a short notice on the prices of herring and almonds before turning swiftly from the dead bishop to another accused heretic.[5]

The chroniclers were fascinated by the Lollards. The chronicles leave the impression that the church was besieged by critics, and occasionally a reporter would join the assault. One compiler exchanged the title "cardinal" for "carnoll" in several references to Thomas Wolsey. The same document collapses an account of Wolsey's death in 1530 with the details of a particularly gruesome execution that same year. Poor Wolsey ended his days and entered this one history as an archfiend "boylled in smythefyld," a penalty actually decreed for the culprit convicted of trying to assassinate Bishop John Fisher of Rochester. On the whole, however, chroniclers were cautious. They let few remarks directly critical of their church seep into their journals—too few anyway to suggest their kinship with persecuted malcontents. Yet they reduced the stature of church officials by strictly budgeting the roles awarded them in historical literature. Bishops and abbots, "all mitred and croysed," were present at the

---

[5]*CL*, 208; and, for Morton's epitaph, 232. Stories of the ill-fated weathercock (222, 261) reached Lynn and were snatched up by that town's reporter, *Six Town Chronicles of England*, ed. Ralph Flenley (Oxford: Clarendon Press, 1911) 189.

pageants, for example, but they were invariably in the background, part of the staging but only rarely part of the action.[6]

When the chroniclers glanced at internal church affairs, quarrels usually caught their attention. Fabyan was intrigued by the murder of Shene's prior and the assault on another monk who "was alsoo slayn or in grete jupordy of lyff." The report identifies the criminal, "a munk of the same cloystre," and suggests that he had accomplices, "adherentis which were temporall men and artyficers of the cyte." But Fabyan concluded the entry, suddenly, dispassionately, and more or less arbitrarily, without providing a clue to motive or consequence. The search for confirmation and elaboration in official registers has turned up only a brief reference to the absolution of one monk for the murder of another, yet this is a considerable gain when compared to the futile search launched to corroborate another chronicler's brief-but-tantalizing remarks about Archbishop Rotherham's disgrace. Chroniclers simply have economized too well. They may provide complete and reliable accounts of the court's ceremonial life, but they cannot be counted on to transmit faithfully and fully news of the early Tudor church. The single exception in the London chronicles, a rehearsal of the dispute between the bishop and the prior of Christ Church, is a model of obfuscation.[7]

Nothing, then, in the early sixteenth-century chronicles dispels the illusion, inherited from André, that the church was inconsequential. Victimized, in a sense, by the chroniclers' deletions, condensations, and confusions, the early Tudor church must appear to readers as an institution all but broken by scandal and general mayhem and plagued by incessant Lollard criticism. Whether chroniclers intended this is still debatable, for their "method" must be held partly responsible for readers' inferences. Chroniclers spliced together previous records and personal observations of ostensibly unrelated events and commonly omitted editorial comments on cause and consequence. Then and now, the chronicles can be maligned as imperfect histories, but it would be more appropriate to say that they expressed an altogether different concept of history from the one that inspired narrative accounts. Chroniclers were devoted to successions more than resolutions. They typically left most matters, secular as well as ecclesiastical, unfinished and unconjugated as they moved rapidly from episodes in their towns' commercial lives, to weather, to foreign wars, with hardly a care for transitions. They presented events in the order of their occurrence, and reports broke off when

---

[6]*Six Town Chronicles*, 193, 196. My assessment differs quite radically from Kingsford's opinion of chroniclers' "ecclesiastical prepossessions," *English Historical Literature in the Fifteenth Century* (Oxford: Clarendon Press, 1913) 43.

[7]*CL*, 199-203, and *GC*, 250-56. For the Shene incident, *GC*, 323; and E. Margaret Thompson, *The Carthusian Order in England* (London: S.P.C.K., 1930) 297-98; and, for Rotherham, *Six Town Chronicles*, 80, 165.

fatigue, boredom, or death overtook their authors. The chronicles had no narrative purpose; their running accounts had no principal end in view, save running. Crowded with detail, their journals were relatively uninterested in personality and policy, and they often were more narrowly concerned with town rather than with Crown. Even then, reconstruction of civic life from the chroniclers' records is unlikely unless the juxtaposition of bishops, Lollards, herring, and homicide reveals secrets that the very nature of the documents seems so well disposed to protect.

With all this, it is easy to forget the chroniclers' virtues. Their frugality may reflect indifference to causal connections, but it also exhibits an admirable restraint. Fabyan had no tolerance for hearsay, and when his information on overseas affairs was obtained "by wynd and not by wrytyng credyble," he preferred silence.[8] Bernard André scattered superlatives and caricatures through his account of the king's capture of Perkin Warbeck (the capstone of early Tudor campaigns against pretenders), but Fabyan only knew for certain and bluntly wrote that "cam a messanger [to London] from the kyng unto the mayer assertaynyng hym that Perkyn was takyn." Economy, in this instance, is hardly lamentable.[9] Yet the chronicles are persistently judged by standards more applicable to the Renaissance revival of historical narrative, and they are usually shelved as "rude and artless compilations." One is tempted to forget that chroniclers were often keen observers of their time, even if they were reluctant to penetrate behind appearances and to impute meanings to, and predict outcomes for, the events they recorded. They were patently unwilling to make an Armageddon of every battle and a Versailles of every truce. Perhaps most important in the context of this study, town chroniclers prefigured the *Landesgeschichte* that decisively ordered world history around the biography of a place rather than around the church's place in God's providential arrangement of world affairs. Town chroniclers took history out of the cloisters where it had long been written from an ecclesiastical point of view. They chronicled and celebrated civic life, invaluable fragments of which survive largely because of their enterprise. Pageants and commodity prices were preeminent parts of their environment. One gets the impression, however, that prelates were not.

The few prelates who were taken to the printers were lost in the clutter of names, events, and statistics that chroniclers stuffed into their journals. So many subjects were crowded together that the privileged role of place was often obscured; therefore, it is commonly and justifiably thought that civic chronicles have no central subject. It is quite another matter when one turns to narrative history, for a single, central subject is the very organizing principle of narrative, "the fixed reference point," according to Hayden White, "by which the flow of ephemeral events can be endowed

[8]*GC*, 283.

[9]Ibid., 258; cf. André, *De vita*, 72.

with specifically moral meaning." Renaissance humanist historians have been accused of losing their own "fixed reference points" in the swirl of anecdotes and aphorisms they drew into their work from antiquity, classical and Christian. But the best narrators among them self-consciously used examples and illustrations from the past in their report of some central subject's passage through time.[10]

The origin of narrative history is not fixed in observation or in the sifting of earlier observations found in civic chronicles. The process of shaping a narrative begins with the selection of a central subject and with the decisive determination of its thematic unity. The narrative's unity is derivative, in that narrative becomes a historian's effort to direct the passage of a central subject toward its preselected outcome and through time and crisis, which are themselves made meaningful as elements of the narrator's dramatic and persuasive effect. Successive stages of the central subject's career can be plotted as such only after the subject and the nature of its endurance have been identified. Although the endurance of the institutional church enchanted previous generations of scholars, most humanist historians were unlikely to advance the tradition of church history. It was not that they were especially influenced by chroniclers' relative disregard for prelates and ecclesiastical policy. While they studied non-Christian literature, humanist historians were not insensitive to the profound impact of the medieval church on European culture. And they were certainly not irreligious. Northern European humanists believed that the revival of antiquity's literature heralded a renewal of piety and fresh interest in the serious study of sacred scripture. But the humanist historians generally looked upon religious formalism as an abnormality.[11] Rites, penances, pilgrimages, and indulgences had proliferated and obstructed

---

[10]Hayden White, "The Value of Narrativity in the Representation of Reality," *Critical Inquiry* 7 (1980): 15-17, 25; cf. J. G. A. Pocock, "The Origins of the Study of the Past: A Comparative Approach," *Comparative Studies in Society and History* 4 (1962): 226-27, 244-45. For what follows, consult W. B. Gallie, *Philosophy and the Historical Understanding*, 2d ed. (New York: Schocken Books, 1968) 22-125; W. H. Dray, "The Nature and Role of Narrative in Historiography," *History and Theory* 10 (1971): 153-71; Seymour Chatman, "Toward a Theory of Narrative," *New Literary History* 6 (1975): 295-318; and Hayden White, "The Historical Text as Literary Artifact," in *The Writing of History*, ed. Robert H. Canary and Henry Kozicki (Madison: University of Wisconsin Press, 1978) 55-58.

[11]See the final chapters of my *Augustinian Piety and Catholic Reform: Augustine, Colet, and Erasmus* (Macon: Mercer University Press, 1982); and Rudolph Padberg's discussion of cisalpine "humanistic Catholicism," in *Erasmus als Katechet* (Freiburg: Herder, 1956). For the contours of Northern renaissances, see the essays by Sem Dresden, Jozef Ijsewijn, Denys Hay, and Lewis W. Spitz in *Itinerarium Italicum: The Profile of the Italian Renaissance in the Mirror of Its European Transformations*, ed. Heiko A. Oberman and Thomas A. Brady, Jr. (Leiden: E. J. Brill, 1975).

primitive and pure Christian piety. Though they were little better than superstitions, they had become enshrined in the church's institutional practices. Why should early-sixteenth-century narrative historians choose as a central subject an institution encumbered by pernicious or, at best, obsolete practices?

Another central subject suggested itself to Polydore Vergil. Vergil had been deposited at the Tudor court in 1502, ostensibly to oversee the collection of Peter's Pence, but the king hinted that his guest, whose *Adages* and *De rerum inventoribus* had already earned him a considerable reputation, might be profitably employed as well in the composition of his realm's history. The story of England's rescue after decades of civil war was especially worth retelling, at least to the sovereign who wished to be honored and remembered for having engineered the rescue. The invitation was accepted. Though he approached the task by investigating Roman Britain and by challenging rather recklessly the historicity of popular legends retailed by native chroniclers, Vergil more than conformed to Tudor expectations in the final chapters of his *Anglica Historia*.

The narrative culminated with a historical rationalization of Tudor rule. The land's prosperity came to depend on the Crown's security. Henry VII's part in God's plan for England, proleptically present in Vergil's account of fifteenth-century unrest, was completely realized and comprehensible when the historian could predict with confidence "the most quiet and flourishing condition of state" after Henry had mastered his rivals. Anglo-Norman chronicles were peculiarly adept at alerting citizens to the value of their territorial identity, so much so that they were imitated on the Continent. Later, fifteenth-century chroniclers were more provincial. With Vergil, history was again manipulated and exploited to rekindle something like *Nationalgefühl* and to associate it with the new dynasty. The late-medieval vicissitudes and the heroic redemption of the Crown, Vergil's central subject, gave meaning to history and a marketable myth to the Tudors.[12]

---

[12]Details of Vergil's career can be gathered from Denys Hay's *Polydore Vergil: Renaissance Historian and Man of Letters* (Oxford: Clarendon Press, 1952). Hay has edited the manuscript of Vergil's final chapter (in 1513) on Henry VII and has printed as well the author's revisions for the early printed editions (1534, 1546, 1555). For the "flourishing condition of state," see *AH*, 149. For the influence of Anglo-Norman chronicles, consult Paul Joachimsen, *Geschichtsauffaßung und Geschichtßchreibung in Deutschland unter dem Einfluss des Humanismus* (Aalen: Scientia-Verlag, 1968) 6-8. An early English translation of Vergil's reigns of Henry VI, Edward IV, and Richard III, *Three Books of Polydore Vergil's English History*, ed. Henry Ellis (London: Camden Society, 1844), should be reviewed in connection with the arguments presented here. Also see Antonia Gransden, *Historical Writing in England*, vol. 2 (London: Routledge & Kegan Paul, 1982) 435-43. As for the marketability of Vergil's Tudor myth, with special consideration of his influence on Edward Hall and William Shakespeare, see Irving Ribner, *The English History Play*

In Vergil's *Historia*, the Crown's passage from civil war to Tudor tranquility generated the coherence and suspense that chroniclers failed to coax from or inject into their material. Vergil did draw upon Fabyan's London chronicles, but he apparently rated them well below earlier and more melodramatic presentations. Fabyan had been too cautious. His note on Perkin Warbeck's capture ("cam a messanger . . . that Perkyn was takyn") showed judicious restraint, but Vergil wanted eyewitness testimony to the momentous Tudor victory. If unsupplied by chroniclers, it must be found elsewhere or freshly created.

> Although the king had thus subdued the rebellious mob, nevertheless he considered he had not removed all occasion of sedition until he had got the head of the conspiracy, Peter Warbeck, into his hands. Since he could not achieve this by force, he attempted to achieve it by a subterfuge. Accordingly, he first completely surrounded the sanctuary at Beaulieu with armed men so that no chance of flight would be open to Peter. Then he sent trustworthy messengers to the young man, promising to pardon and forget all his offenses if only he would surrender himself to royal grace. Peter, realizing his affairs had fallen into a most critical state and that (so often had his projects been abortive) no further hope of making good remained, when he heard he was promised pardon he thereupon put his trust in Henry's official clemency, left the sanctuary of his own will, and surrendered himself to Henry.

Vergil's narrative opens with a safe inference. It is quite likely that the king would have been unable to rest until the opposition's figurehead had been taken into custody. The second supposition is somewhat suspect. Warbeck had so often rebounded from defeat and disappointment that the imputation of hopelessness is not completely credible. Vergil's interpolations, however, breathe life and drama into the chronicles' accounts.

---

in the Age of Shakespeare (Princeton: Princeton University Press, 1957) 15-16, 104-105, 157-58. It makes little difference that E. M. W. Tillyard, among others, jealously guards Hall's purported preeminence, for it is clear, as G. R. Elton noted, that Hall is "almost unadulterated Vergil" when he reports early Tudor affairs. Tillyard, *Shakespeare's History Plays* (London: Chatto & Windus, 1961) 42-51, 59-61, 69, 237, 242, 304-305, 320-21; and Elton, *Studies*, 1:58. The fact that Henrician and Elizabethan chroniclers were deeply indebted to Vergil and that they, in turn, provisioned Shakespeare with motifs for his tetralogies would appear indisputable; but legitimate as well as silly questions persist and, in some instances, they have been transformed into doubts and objections—e.g., David Frey, *The First Tetralogy: Shakespeare's Scrutiny of the Tudor Myth* (The Hague: Mouton, 1976); and A. L. French, "The Mills of God and Shakespeare's Early History Plays," *English Studies* 55 (1974): 313-24. In any event, it makes no sense whatsoever to scold Shakespeare for exaggerations and historical inaccuracies (John Gillingham, *The Wars of the Roses* [London: Weidenfield & Nicholson, 1981] 1-14). As I have argued elsewhere, he splendidly amplified Vergil's themes, however he came by them. Given his sources, Shakespeare did quite well. Given ours, perhaps we may be faulted for credulity.

Undeniably, one has passed from the chronicles' clutter to a history in which narrative decorum often dictates the shapes and significances of "facts," and in which contemporary reports (and silences) could not obstruct the development of plot and purpose.[13]

Bernard André's colorful mix of superlatives also differed from the town chroniclers' journals, but Vergil was not about to copy uncritically the poet's endless affirmatives. To Vergil, André must have seemed overly fond of adjectives and thin on action. The *Historia*'s Henry VII was neither infallible nor omnicompetent, but rather a shrewd and deliberate statesman. Enemies and diplomatic difficulties were not overcome instantaneously and with ease, as André lyrically implied, but by careful and complex planning. Peace with Scotland, for example, deprived dissidents of an accessible asylum and might therefore guarantee greater obedience (*"facilius in fide continerentur"*), so Vergil took considerable pains to report accurately the progress of early Tudor negotiations.[14] André seemed to think that charisma of nearly mythic proportions resolved everything, but Vergil appealed to policy as well as to personality. Henry VIII apparently agreed more with André, and Vergil dutifully noted the king's conviction that his royal presence was the condition for military conquest. Vergil even granted that there was something admirable, valorous, and inspirational about Henry's self-esteem.[15] Yet Vergil remained conspicuously more concerned with office, and it may have been with some satisfaction that he concluded his narrative of the wars of 1513 and his own manuscript with an account of the most spectacular English victory—achieved without benefit of the proud sovereign's presence. While Henry VIII stormed France and was rewarded only modestly for

---

[13]*AH*, 109-11. To demonstrate the point, compare *The Chronicle of Calais in the Reigns of Henry VII and Henry VIII*, ed. John Gough Nichols (London: Camden Society, 1846), where king and councillors "landyd" and left with little comment, and Vergil's frequent efforts to learn or to invent reasons for the passages and to identify the chief contenders for royal favor and largess (*AH*, 208-11). For Vergil's sources and informants, see Francis Aidan Gasquet, "Some Materials for a New Edition of Polydore Vergil's *History*," *TRHS*, n.s. 16 (1902): 9-11; and Hay, *Polydore Vergil*, 85-88, 93. With respect to the undaunted Warbeck, review "The Story of Perkin Warbeck," appended to James Gairdner's *History of the Life and Reign of Richard III* (Cambridge: Cambridge University Press, 1898) 263-335.

[14]*AH*, 28; see Vergil's request for information directed to James IV and printed in *Polydore Vergil's English History . . . The Period Prior to the Norman Conquest*, ed. Henry Ellis (London: Camden Society, 1846) xii-xiii.

[15]The relevant passage runs thus: "Impleret homines certae spei, illisque fidem faceret, se omnium suorum majorum laudes facile exuperaturum esse. Hac igitur Regis cura et industria breviter classis octo et quadraginta magnarum navium ante omnia, rebus omnibus tam hominibus quam bello necessariis instructa parataque est" (*AH*, 198).

his efforts, his agents at Flodden convincingly repelled an invasion by France's ally, James IV of Scotland.[16]

The effect of Vergil's preoccupation with the Crown in his profiles of earliest Tudor Catholicism is not difficult to detect. The *Historia*'s printed editions paraded Henry VII's rather unpretentious ecclesiastical reforms, quite possibly to call into question Henry VIII's more startling and ruthless abrogation of traditional prerogatives and immunities.[17] Though Vergil had once joined the chorus that complained loudly against clerical nepotism, simony, greed, popular superstition, and papal arrogance, nothing of this echoed in the *Historia*'s manuscript.[18] But if silence, prima facie, seems symptomatic of the historian's friendship for the church, qualified only by his later enmity for Wolsey, it must be said that Polydore Vergil was to prove an unreliable partisan. Study of revisions that Vergil made in preparation for publication brings this to light. The manuscript recorded provisions, translations, political appointments, and deaths of several prominent episcopal civil servants with some kind remarks on each subject's qualifications for office. Richard Fox rapidly climbed from poorer to wealthier dioceses and endeared himself to Henry VII, *"ob ejus singularem fidem, integritatem, ac prudentiam."*[19] John Morton, in Vergil's judgment, was one of the chief architects of England's peace and Tudor security and thus richly deserved the benefits conferred on him as archbishop of Canterbury and chancellor of the realm.[20] William Warham, Morton's successor on both counts, was "praiseworthy"; and though his extraordinarily rapid rise in the church and at court during the first few years of the sixteenth century doubtlessly sent gossip cascading through the regular channels of Westminster's harridans to disappointed "time-servers," Vergil considered Warham a gentle, generous, and scholarly prelate and never whispered a reservation.[21] By the time he un-

---

[16]Ibid., 214-20.

[17]Ibid., 116-17.

[18]See, e.g., Vergil's *De inventoribus rerum*, first published before his visit to England, but cited here from the 1521 Basel edition, book 6, ch. 13; and book 7, chs. 3-4 (73r-74r; 77v-80v).

[19]*AH*, 55-57, 98-99. Keeper of the Privy Seal from 1487 to 1516 and bishop successively of Exeter, Bath and Wells, Durham, and Winchester, Fox—along with Morton—was regarded as "all powerful" in the king's council. This was in 1489 and presumably for some time thereafter. *CSP, Venice*, 1:177.

[20]*AH*, 121; *Three Books*, 180-82, 194. Despite Claude Jenkins's brief but penetrating study ("Cardinal Morton's Register," in *Tudor Studies*, ed. R. W. Seton-Watson [London: Longmans, Green & Co., 1924] 26-74), the present century has seen little of Morton. One expects a change in the next decades, especially from Christopher Harper-Bill. Consult his "Archbishop John Morton and the Province of Canterbury, 1486-1500," *JEH* 29 (1978): 1-21, and below, ch. 8.

[21]*AH*, 69, 121, 130.

dertook to publish the *Historia* in 1534, however, England's political climate was quite different from what it had been twenty years earlier when the manuscript had been completed. A court historian could not be overly courteous or complimentary to previous Catholic principals without risking royal displeasure.

Vergil himself counseled historians to tell no lie and conceal no truth. It must have been perfectly well understood at the time that narrative historians were hired, more often than not, to moralize the social system to which they owed their leisure and to celebrate the virtues of its custodians, to whom they owed their commissions.[22] The *clientis causa* was at stake. Though God had apparently delivered power to historians' patrons, historians' dramatizations were solicited in order to reassure providence's beneficiaries and to keep their prospective adversaries aware of the enormity of their own crime should they tamper with divinely ordained rule. When Polydore Vergil turned redactor in 1534, his client's cause had been transformed by a series of quarrels over the legitimacy of the royal marriage. Compliments lavished on Warham and Fox, who had only recently left the stage, were either reduced or deleted from the manuscript. Whereas Vergil had noted that Henry VII gave Fox, then bishop of Durham, complete power in delicate negotiations with Scotland because Fox enjoyed the king's full confidence, he printed only a short statement that attributed the bishop's assignment to convenience.[23] Had Fox and Warham not protested Thomas Wolsey's expanding authority, which Vergil resented, perhaps they would have been scrubbed altogether from the fabric of the *Historia's* Tudor history.[24]

Growing antipathy toward the Catholic clergy seems to be implied in Vergil's narrative. Christopher Urswick's disappearance from the text confirms that what had happened to Warham and Fox was no accident

---

[22]For Vergil's admonition, see the addition to his early *De inventoribus rerum*, reprinted in *Polydori Vergilii Urbinatis de rerum inventoribus* (Louvain, 1644) 45. Also see the adage on flattery and duplicity included in Vergil's second edition of aphorisms, *Polydori Vergilii Urbinatis adagiorum liber* (Basel: Frobenii, 1521) 74 (no. 169, incorrectly paginated as p. 82); "Honorare labiis proverbialiter dicitur, qui dissimulanter . . . ac blandicule quempiam commendat, utope, aliud loquens aliquid sentiens, cum ea laus de corde non proficiscatur." Some later critics took a harder line and equated flattery with mendacity. In this connection, see Julian H. Franklin, *Jean Bodin and the Sixteenth-Century Evolution in the Methodology of Law and History* (New York: Columbia University Press, 1963) 92-94; but for a more sympathetic reading of the renaissance narrators' dilemma, consult "Some Afterthoughts," in Charles Edward Trinkaus, *Adversity's Noblemen: The Italian Humanists on Happiness* (New York: Columbia University Press, 1940) esp. 145-46.

[23]"Qui in propinquo erat" (*AH*, 100-101).

[24]Apropos of Vergil's blistering attack on Wolsey's despotism in the *Historia's* third edition, see Frank V. Cespedes, "The Final Book of Polydore Vergil's *Anglica Historia*: Persecution and the Art of Writing," *Viator* 10 (1979): 375-96.

or oversight.[25] From the first, Urswick was at the center of the conspiracies to take the Crown from Richard III. He was sent to the Continent to warn exiles of Richard's efforts to have Breton officials return the earl of Richmond to England. Familiarity with Breton diplomacy and treachery made Urswick the obvious choice years later, when the earl had become Henry VII, to arbitrate—in Henry's name—the dispute between Brittany's Duke Francis and the French king, Charles VIII. Vergil's manuscript reported the complicated mission, but the *Historia*'s printed editions summarily replaced *"Christoforus"* with *"legati."*[26]

Urswick's later assignment in Calabria, which involved meetings en route with the French king, by then at peace with England, was completely removed from Vergil's printed text.[27] When Charles of France sent agents to Dover in 1497, in order to transact business related to the precarious peace, Urswick, something of a specialist in Anglo-French affairs, was rushed to the coast. Vergil noted that the English statesman was to delay the French and to make certain that they heard nothing of the Cornish rebellion just then destabilizing the realm's government, and the manuscript concluded the story with praise for Urswick's performance: *"Quae Christoforus diligenter executus est."* The printed text, however, awarded him with anonymity. According to the 1534 edition, Henry sent not his faithful *"Christoforus,"* but *"aliquot heroes,"* and the final remark had been changed from active to passive voice, *"id quod diligenter factus est."* Urswick had vanished, leaving behind only his diligence.[28]

In one instance, the manuscript had recorded a personal account of yet another of Urswick's assignments, which could only have come directly from Urswick. True to form, the printed editions of the *Historia* pared down the narrative and substituted a squadron of horsemen for the historian's informant (*"dimiserat per oram aliquot equitum turmas"*).[29] Compared with his virtual purging of Urswick, Vergil's manipulation of the manuscript's record of Richard Fox's climb to power was minimal and superficial. His bone-rigid determination to do away with Urswick is quite baffling, though until some probable cause can be coaxed from the evidence, the disappearance can hardly be catalogued as confirmation of the *Historia*'s eclipse of the early Tudor church.

---

[25]To complete the sketch of Urswick presented here (for quite narrow purposes), it will be necessary to review, in addition to Emden, Thomas A. Urwick, *Records of the Family Urswyk, Urswick, or Urwick* (privately printed, 1893) 81-140; and James Kelsey McConica, *English Humanists and Reformation Politics* (Oxford: Clarendon Press, 1965) 70-72.

[26]*AH*, 35-37.

[27]Ibid., 66-67.

[28]Ibid., 95.

[29]Ibid., 22.

But Urswick was very much a churchman as well as an active and reliable diplomat. Along with Fox and Morton, he was prominent among
the prelates to whom Henry VII entrusted his government, presumably
to break the grip of baronial power and to end the competition among the
aristocracy that had perpetuated England's civil war. Urswick and Fox
were present in the small chamber of the Hospital of St. John's of Jerusalem on the March morning in 1486 when Morton was handed the Great
Seal.[30] Urswick was himself appointed almoner, master of King's Hall,
Cambridge, and dean of York by 1488. During the next decade he accu-
mulated other ecclesiastical livings, among them preferments to the arch-
deaconries of Wiltshire and Richmond, though, as noted, he was
frequently abroad representing his king.[31] Francis Bacon was sufficiently
impressed with Urswick's ubiquity and influence to have gauged each
mission's importance by Urswick's participation.[32] Urswick's career,
nonetheless, seems to have stalled. He was busy entertaining on the king's
behalf in 1506 when Erasmus urged him to find greater leisure, but his
work did not propel him to positions of authority in the church's hierarchy.[33] In fact, Urswick was nearly bolted to his parish church in Hack-
ney from 1502 until his death twenty years later. He had probably not yet
lost royal favor by 1513, for Vergil's manuscript, completed that year,
lauded the veteran statesman. In 1519, however, Vergil failed to include
him in an inventory of learned Englishmen, a preposterous omission insofar as Urswick was a close companion and correspondent of many others classified there. Urswick's estrangement was apparently a matter of
record, even before Vergil so amended his *Historia* to give it definitive
expression.[34]

---

[30]*Rerum Britannicarum Medii Aevi Scriptores: Materials for a History of the Reign of
Henry VII,* 2 vols., ed. William Campbell (London: Longman & Co., 1837-1877)
2:133.

[31]In this connection, see a neglected objection to Urswick's absenteeism in J.
Armitage Robinson, "Correspondence of Bishop Oliver King and Sir Reginald
Bray," *Proceedings of the Somersetshire Archaeological and Natural History Society* 60
(1914): 6.

[32]See Bacon's *The History of the Reign of King Henry the Seventh,* ed. F. J. Levy
(New York: Bobbs-Merrill, 1972) 103, 147, 151, and esp. 185.

[33]Allen, *OE* 1:426. For Urswick's hospitality to Castiglione in 1506, see Julia Cart-
wright, *The Perfect Courtier,* 2d ed., 2 vols. (London: J. Murray, 1927) 1:182-87.

[34]The list is appended to Denys Hay's "The Life of Polydore Vergil of Urbino,"
Journal of the Warburg and Courtauld Institutes 12 (1949): 150-51. The document casts
some doubt on Hay's explanation of the *Historia*'s subsequent elimination of Urswick. Hay had argued that several deletions, including that of Urswick, were at-
tributable to the lack of interest in the 1530s in "the tittle-tattle of Henry VII's reign."
Urswick was forgotten because he was so forgettable. "The Manuscript of Polydore Vergil's *Anglica Historia,*" *EHR* 54 (1939): 246-47. My argument, that the case
for later disfavor is stronger than that for later lack of interest, is corroborated, to
some extent, by the fact that the former accounts as well for the 1519 omission.

One cannot completely rule out the possibility that Urswick had alien-ated Vergil, that a single jest or blunder or insult split diplomat from his-torian. Tenants who cross their landlords are sure to see their places given to others, and in the *Historia* of 1534, squadrons of horsemen and faceless ambassadors occupy the spaces reserved for Urswick in the manuscript. Suspicions that the vexing redactions are signs of something more than a personal quarrel, which has left no other traces, must remain suspi-cions, yet they are deepened when an undated and neglected letter from Urswick to Thomas Goldstone is used to mine Vergil's enigmatic editorial tactics. The letter places Urswick and Goldstone, prior of Christ Church, Canterbury, in the front ranks of clerics who resented the dynasty's in-choate efforts to deprive the church of its prerogatives and properties. Polydore Vergil hesitated to report on the culmination of those efforts in 1534, and he must certainly have thought it untimely to remind Thomas Cromwell and his sovereign of the limits to Urswick's dedication to the Crown.

The limits were probably reached after Henry VIII pressed his de-mands for unprecedented taxation in 1512 and after the parliament of that year agreed provisionally to deprive clergy *in minoribus* (in lower orders) of immunities from secular penalties after criminal prosecutions. This generated a lively debate that resulted, two years later, in the reinstate-ment of the clergy's privileges. However, the uncertainty and the Crown's levies presumably prompted a nostalgia, like Urswick's, for the time when English Christians were more respectful and steadfastly generous from the cradle to the grave and "dying wished to leave no heirs, save their churches." "Our times have so deteriorated," Urswick wrote to Gold-stone, "that churches have no hope of such donations and must think themselves fortunate if nothing has been snatched from them. A detest-able greed (*rapacitas*) and sacrilege has dislodged from its honored place old-fashioned liberality."[35]

Prior Goldstone was familiar with that "old-fashioned liberality," or at least with its residuum. In 1499 Henry VII's queen obliged herself to support the prior "in any of your reasonable desires concernynge the wele

---

[35]BL. Add. MSS. 15.673, ff. 113v-114r: "Morientes non alios heredes relin-quere quam ecclesias vellent. . . . At nostra aetate eo deventum est: ut non modo nihil sibi donari sperent ecclesiae; sed praeclare secum actum putent si nihil illis eripitur. [A]deo in prisce liberalitatis locum detestanda pluri morum repacitas: immo verius sacrilegium successit." This may very well refer to the Crown's re-luctance to grant mortmain licenses and to the imposition of steep fines assessed, from 1505, against the estates of persons who *sub rosa* alienated properties in fa-vor of intercessory institutions. See, *inter alia*, Alan Kreider, *English Chantries: The Road to Dissolution* (Cambridge: Harvard University Press, 1979) 83-84, 238; and Sandra Raban, *Mortmain Legislation and the English Church, 1279-1500* (Cambridge: Cambridge University Press, 1982) 190. For the 1512 dispute, see below, ch. 4.

of you or your place hereafter."[36] Yet the vastness and wealth of Goldstone's "place" made it a most tempting target. The priory itself, with
seventy-nine resident monks in 1511, was the largest religious community in England. Goldstone had undertaken an ambitious program of
renovation and new construction that made the cathedral priory more
conspicuous in Canterbury and improved the appearance and the pro-
ductivity of the priory's numerous Kentish estates. What share in all this
redounds to the archbishops—who were titular abbots—is arguable, but
the fact that the cathedral church, during Goldstone's tenure, "had
reached the zenith of its splendour" seems beyond dispute.[37] At court,
where the cost of armaments was a constant concern, the splendor was
unlikely to go unnoticed. The considerable rents that Goldstone collected
and directed toward impressive custodial work could rather easily be diverted to the royal treasury, should Henry VIII continue to flex his mus-
cles abroad and at home. Moreover, the ancient privileges that freed
monks, tenants, and possessions of the Canterbury priory from secular
services and jurisdictions seemed increasingly in jeopardy.[38] Goldstone,
it appears, asked Urswick to copy and forward the *Dissuasoria, ne Christiani Principes ecclesiasticos usurpent census*, written late in the previous
century by Maffeus Celsus to convince Venetian senators that church
revenues and properties were inviolable. The treatise was known to, and
perhaps circulated by, Urswick before this, and he enthusiastically com-
plied, encouraging Goldstone to use Celsus's protests as "a shield."[39]

Enemies were everywhere, Urswick reminded the prior, but there can
be little question that Urswick believed the government to be the principal adversary. He waved Becket's defiance of Henry II as a banner before
introducing the *Dissuasoria*'s *post hoc, propter hoc* reading of Venetian history that was alleged to contain as powerful an argument against royal
taxation and aggressiveness as Becket's immortality.[40] To Celsus, the lesson of history was simple and irrefutable: Venetians had rifled their
churches' properties and then, as a result, suffered through a nightmare

---

[36]*Christ Church Letters*, ed. J. B. Sheppard (London: Camden Society, 1877) 64.

[37]*Historia decanorum et priorum ecclesiae Christi Cantuariensis*, printed in *Anglica
sacra*, pars prima (London: Richard Chiswell, 1541) 146-49. The appraisal is that
of W. Woolnoth, *A Graphical Illustration of the Metropolitan Cathedral Church of Canterbury* (London: T. Cadell & W. Davies, 1816) 35; but also see Francis Woodman,
The Architectural History of Canterbury Cathedral (London: Routledge & Kegan Paul,
1981) 207-17.

[38]For the privileges, see R. A. L. Smith, *Canterbury Cathedral Priory* (Cambridge: Cambridge University Press, 1943) 83-99.

[39]Regarding Urswick's fondness for the *Dissuasoria*, see J. B. Trapp, "Notes on
Manuscripts Written by Peter Meghen," *The Book Collector* 24 (1975): 92-95.

[40]BL. Add. MSS. 15.673, f. 113v.

of economic and military calamities. The republic's humiliation in the Aegean was ascribed to the "insolent taxation" of the church (*"propter insolitam vestram sacrarum rerum ac vexate religionis injuriam"*). A spectacular series of Ottoman assaults on the Venetian stronghold of Negropont (1470) not only cheated the republic and all of Latin Christendom of the easternmost expanse of their empire but also, to no one's surprise, created the need for fresh subsidies. This, in turn, stirred the temptation once again to dispossess the churches. Turkish aggression must yet be contained and revenues lost by the restriction of commerce must be replaced. Celsus feared further taxation. A native of Verona, he feared most for the prosperous churches and religious orders in Venice's Terraferma provinces.[41] If Venice could be persuaded of the causes of its misfortune, ideally, compensation for the Aegean tragedy could be sought elsewhere. Apparently Urswick and Goldstone expected the formula for divine reprisal to dissuade their own monarch, whose ambitions for foreign conquest were notorious. And yet Polydore Vergil had already assured the Crown that providence had delivered power and wealth into Tudor hands. Who was Celsus, and who were his English importers, to tie those hands? Vergil had unquestioningly identified divine retribution with the collapse of the dynasty's enemies. To insinuate that God's continued partisanship was contingent upon the prosperity and independence of the church—that is, to insert the church between a Tudor and his God—must have seemed presumptuous and was almost certainly unpopular with Vergil's patrons after 1530 and probably by 1519.[42]

---

[41]Celsus, *Dissuasoria*, BL. Add. MSS. 15.673, f. 83v. For the provinces' fifteenth-century *"risanamento economico"* and religious foundations, consult Aldo Stella's two thorough studies, "La crisi economica veneziana nella seconda metà del secolo XVI," *Archivo Veneto* 58-59 (1956): 48-50; and "La proprietà ecclesiastica nella Repubblica di Venezia del secolo XV e XVL," *Nuova Rivista Storica* 42 (1958): 54-58, 63-65.

[42]Problems that Henry VIII encountered when he tried to collect his taxes (reported by Venetian visitors) were unlikely to increase royal receptivity to the *Dissuasoria*'s protests. Charlotte Augusta Sneyd, ed., *A Relation or Rather a True Account of the Island of England* (London: Camden Society, 1847) 41; *CSP, Venice*, 2:182; and Sebastiano Giustiniani, *Four Years at the Court of Henry VIII*, vol. 1 (London, 1854) 320. Celsus's caveat and its appeal should be evaluated along with other complaints about the Crown's strategies, from which sentiments tantamount to a siege mentality may be inferred. See, e.g., *Conv.*, 297-98; and John Tayler's 1514 convocation sermon, BL. Cott. MSS. Vitellius B ii, f. 81r. To these expressions of clerical anxiety, one may add Thomas More's trenchant reflection on how easily money could come between a sovereign and his subjects, *The History of King Richard III*, ed. Richard S. Sylvester. *CWTM* 2:5, 162. But if the *Dissuasoria*'s lesson made Tudor authorities apprehensive, a careful reading of the case would have calmed them. Celsus had an uncanny talent for reducing world history to a single law. He added an explanation of Pisan adversities to his narrative of Venetian troubles

Vergil took his revenge in the printed editions of his *Historia*. Urswick's disappearance was the most extreme modification in a text that otherwise minimized the Catholic church's auxiliary role in the dynasty's establishment. By 1534 there could be no comparison between England and Venice. The English needed no pontiff to protect their church and to interpret God's will to their sovereign.

Such substantive modifications were tailored for an English readership. Vergil's stylistic revisions for the *editio princeps*, however, were probably made with the author's continental, humanist friends in mind. They comprehended more readily than we do that historical narrative was a commodity created for a prince and for a price, and they would have been quite tolerant of the Tudor "pitchman's" hyperbole. Stylistic barbarisms and inadequacies, however, were unpardonable offenses. Vergil's message for the Continent was a welcome and altogether credible one, for the Tudors were widely perceived as friends of learning. Henry VIII's accession inspired predictions of a golden age and promises of preferment that brought Erasmus back to England from Italy, notwithstanding his fastidious tastes in climate and wine.[43] To stress the promise of Tudor rule, Vergil cut four years from the *Historia*'s manuscript, which had concluded with the English victory at Flodden in 1513, and elected to supply a short excursus, for the year 1509, on the prosperity of St. Paul's gram-

---

(BL Add. MSS. 15.673, f. 91) and, to give his warnings to greedy governments a canonical and timeless quality, he sedulously gathered anecdotes from ancient and from biblical histories (ff. 98r-100r). The tensions that occasioned this relentless anthologizing, however, had been superseded before Urswick had the *Dissuasoria* copied for Goldstone. Venice's defeat and humiliation enabled Pope Julius II to restore Venetians' ecclesiastical immunities. But the same Julius was disposed to grant English monarchs the license denied Venetian senators, if only to keep the Tudors indifferent to France's efforts to reanimate the previous century's conciliar dissent. In this connection, see Federico Seneca, *Venezia e Papa Giulio II* (Padua: Liviana editrice, 1962) 144-47; Alessandro Ferrajoli, "Breve inedito di Giulio II per la investitura del regno di Francia ad Enrico VIII d'Inghilterra," *Archivo della R. Società Romana di Storia Patria* 19 (1896): 425-27; and William E. Wilkie, *The Cardinal Protectors of England* (Cambridge: Cambridge University Press, 1974) 42-44.

[43]See Thomas More, "In suscepti diadematis diem Henrici octavi, illustrissimi ac faustissimi Brittaniarum regis. . . . ," in *The Latin Epigrams of Thomas More*, ed. Leicester Bradner and Charles Arthur Lynch (Chicago: University of Chicago Press, 1953) 16-21; and Allen, *OE* 1:451: "Ad opus tuum revertor, quod summis omnes laudibus in coelum tollunt. Sed prae ceteris D. Cantuariensis [Warham] ita probat et admiratur ut ex ejus manibus illud extorquere nequam. At dices, Nihil adhuc praeter laudes? Idem D. Cantuariensis sacerdotium tibi, si redeas, pollicetur, ut modo libras quinque pro viatico ad nos tibi mittendas dedit; quibus ego [William Blount, Lord Mountjoy] tantumdem adieci, non quidem muneris loco, alia enim appellanda sunt munera, sed ut ad nos properes et tui desyderio diutius ne torqueas." Also consult below, ch. 5.

mar school, which was founded in the first Tudor's final year.[44] Continental humanists, Vergil suggested, could be optimistic about the successes of their English counterparts, *"bonas literas propagandi."* But here, too, another sign of the church's eclipse in historical literature surfaces in Vergil's closing remarks. John Colet, the grammar school's great patron, had stipulated that the mercers rather than the church oversee his school's affairs, and Vergil duly recorded this break in the ecclesiastical monopoly of school supervision.[45]

By the time Henry VIII and his agents presided over the more complete absorption of ecclesiastical affairs into the commercial and political life of the land, there was hardly a need to suppress gratitude for Catholic contributions to the rescue of culture, Crown, and country. There seems not to have been any. The few traces in Polydore Vergil's manuscript had been doctored or removed by the historian himself. The literature of Tudor apology, from that point on, was not about to recover or to create any record of thanks. It was politically more prudent to infer from the lack of any such record the lack of any contribution and to perpetuate the sense of ingratitude cultivated during the promulgation of anticlerical legislation, just prior to Henry's divorces from Catherine and Rome.

---

[44]*AH*, 146-47.

[45]See "The Mercer's Charge," in Colet's *Statuta Paulinae Scholae*, printed in J. H. Lupton's *A Life of Dean Colet* (London: George Bell & Sons, 1909) 280-81. Also review Joan Simon, *Education and Society in Tudor England* (Cambridge: Cambridge University Press, 1966) 19-34, 72-74, 125, 153.

Chapter 2

ANATOMIES OF AUTHORITY: EARLY TUDOR POLITICAL CULTURE

The early Tudor church was not to recover fragments of its political preeminence until the seventeenth century. Even then, the almost inconceivable complexity of religion's relationships to political culture was irretrievable. Polydore Vergil had been too thorough. For the sake of narrative decorum, he traded much of what was or could then be known of the church's contributions to the dynasty's successes for a more limited perspective on the Crown's late-medieval peril and prosperity. Political change dictated revisions that further obscured clerical participation in early Tudor triumphs. Predictably, after 1534 Henry VIII's historians and polemicists painted with a wide brush and, disclosing the defects of all that savored of papism, they blackened the reputation of English Catholicism. John Bale, a Carmelite antiquarian who came quickly to preach royal supremacy, named Joseph of Arimathea the founder of England's church, and he asserted that Joseph had unconditionally given governing powers to the laity. Rome and her representatives, notably Augustine of Canterbury, usurped those very powers, which champions of Arimathean Christianity, King John in their vanguard, had ever since been eager to regain.[1] According to Bale, Augustine, assisted by his devilish monks, had prepared "antechrist a seate here in England" by the seventh century and the papists refused to be evicted. Rome always had her agents on English soil, or so it seemed to Bale, but the monarchy was able to pre-

---

[1]E.g., see Bale's *King Johan,* ed. Barry B. Adams (San Marino: Huntington Library, 1969) 108-12. In the same text Bale signaled his impatience with colleagues who had not made common cause with him against Vergil (134): "Yes! Therfor, Leylonde out of thy slumbre awake, and wytnesse a trewthe for thyne owne contrayes sake." If John Leland was too timid or reserved to divulge Vergil's "Romish lies and other Italish beggarys," John Bale certainly was not. Cf. the dedicatory epistle to Leland's *Assertio inclytissimi Arturi 1, regis Britanniae* (London: Joannem Herford, 1544); and Bale's "A Brief Chronicle Concerning the Examination and Death of the Blessed Martyr of Christ, Sir John Oldcastle," in *Select Works of John Bale,* ed. Henry Christmas (Cambridge: Parker Society, 1849) 8-9.

serve and exercise a few prerogatives that were reminiscent of pre-Augustinian Christianity and that distinguished the English church from continental Catholicisms. But it required Henry VIII, Bale's great protagonist of independence, to complete his remote predecessors' confiscations, to end Roman hegemony and clerical tyranny, and to vindicate English apostolic (that is, Arimathean) practices.

Bale was not altogether confident. He suggested with a hint of panicky suspicion that Arimathean recovery demanded more of the second Tudor than he seemed willing to give. One thing, nonetheless, was quite clear. Henry VII and early Tudor Christianity, "rather a polytyque churche than a christen church" and still bound nominally to Rome, could be classified with the perverted prelatical order that was rapidly passing away.[2] Bale's optimism, in this regard, echoed through much of sixteenth-century polemical and historical literature. Henry VII might be remembered by later Tudors for erupting in one isolated instance with "very great severity against the pope," but his son's more far-reaching and disruptive disagreements with Rome heralded the real redemption of English Christianity.[3]

Tudor Catholic apology quite naturally concentrated its attack on Henry VIII's impetuosity. Earliest Tudor ecclesiastical policy, popular piety, and prelates seldom entered the controversies that orbited principally around competing royal and papal supremacies. William Allen, for example, conceded that Henry VII had defied the pope's demands for the return of a shipment of alum confiscated by English seamen, but he could see no "great severity" in the defiance. Only a "grosshead," growled Allen, could claim the incident as a precedent for the Henrician schism and for Elizabeth's stubborn resolve to exacerbate it. On another matter, however, Allen found the first Tudor a most congenial model, and he took pleasure in noting some symmetry between the aspirations of exiled Elizabethan Catholics and those fugitives who surrounded Henry of Richmond in Brittany and who subsequently and "honorably" deposed their

---

[2]See, in this connection, Bale's muted complaint that the Henrician reformation had not satisfactorily undone damages done by "Romysche monkes," *The First Two Partes of the Actes or Unchast Examples of the English Votaryes* (London: Thomas Raynalde, 1548) xxix(v)-xxx(v). Compare Bale's discomfort with William Turner's position, competently redrafted by Ranier Pineas, "William Turner's Polemical Use of Ecclesiastical History and His Controversy with Stephen Gardiner," *Renaissance Quarterly* 33 (1980): 599-608. Of Pineas's many other papers on early Tudor polemical history, see esp. "William Tyndale's Influence on John Bale's Polemical Use of History," *Archiv für Reformationsgeschichte* 53 (1962): 79-96.

[3]William Cecil, *The Execution of Justice in England*, ed. Robert Kingdon (Ithaca: Cornell University Press, 1965) 28.

sovereign, Richard III.[4] Yet, for all this, sixteenth-century Catholics had few good words for their colleagues who labored in concert with the dynasty before it had repudiated Rome. Possibly they resented the first Tudor prelates for having bungled their commissions as agents of the church universal and for having permitted one wave after another of late-medieval England's turbulent history to erode the church's putative independence from the Crown.

Much of this is speculative and must remain so, for the silence yields few clues. But a glance at two biographies printed during the brief Marian interlude renders the imputation of resentment or, at least, of embarrassment more plausible. In 1553 Henry VIII's first daughter inherited the Crown and restored Catholicism to public life and privileges. George Cavendish seized the opportunity to answer charges leveled against his former employer, Cardinal Thomas Wolsey, by Henrician historians, but he gave ground and conceded the probability that Wolsey's public service ("worldly diligence and pains") interfered with his service to God. Cavendish, it seems, had little taste for the clergy's involvement in political life, perhaps because political life had ultimately been so unkind, and Henry VIII so ungrateful, to his master. From Cavendish's account of Wolsey's fall, one can easily form a legalistic hypothesis to explain the precipitous decline of English Catholicism: ecclesiastical officials who simultaneously served the state necessarily forfeited the impartiality that made them ideal arbiters of the realm's spiritual and moral life. Even Bishop Fisher, lionized for his later opposition to Henry VIII, was criticized by Cavendish for unseemly political partisanship.[5]

William Roper, another Marian biographer, indicted Bishop Fox on related charges. Roper's life of Thomas More charged that Fox became so attached to the Crown's interests that he engineered a conspiracy to deprive More of his freedom. Fox purportedly feigned friendship in order to trap "the beardless boy" into damaging disclosures that could be used to justify measures that would have amounted to nothing more than petty

---

[4]William Allen, *A True, Sincere, and Modest Defense of English Catholics*, ed. Robert Kingdon (Ithaca: Cornell University Press, 1965) 202, 210-11, 234. Also review Kingdon's "William Allen's Use of Protestant Political Argument," in *From the Renaissance to the Counter-Reformation*, ed. Charles H. Carter (London: Cape, 1966) 164-78. For Allen's general thoughts on the obligation to overthrow apostate magistrates, see Thomas H. Clancy, *Papist Pamphleteers: The Allen-Persons Party and the Political Thought of the Counter-Reformation in England, 1572-1615* (Chicago: Loyola University Press, 1964) 51-53. Kingdon's introduction to the *True, Sincere, and Modest Defense* (xxiii-xxxv) briefly chronicles Allen's translation of such thoughts into practice.

[5]George Cavendish, *The Life and Death of Cardinal Wolsey*, in *Two Early Tudor Lives*, ed. Richard S. Sylvester and Davis P. Harding (New Haven: Yale University Press, 1962) 17-30, 84, 122, 183, 186.

vindictiveness.[6] Fox's many contributions to political life vanished with
the rest of early Tudor Christianity. What is left is a doubtful story of be-
trayal deposited on the surface of Roper's narrative, as if only a crude me-
teorite remained from a remote and once-luminous galaxy. Marian and
Elizabethan Catholics were no better friends of the "polytyque churche"
of Morton, Fox, Warham, and Wolsey than were the Henrician historians
and Protestant polemicists.

The Tudor composition of history ended as it began, with hardly a desire to track or to treasure the church's leadership in the development and
implementation of the dynasty's policies. Leadership itself, however,
fascinated nearly everyone. Authority in a neofeudal political culture
constantly had to be salvaged from baronial competition that all too easily
degenerated into a chaotic and violent free-for-all. Insofar as historians'
attention was fixed on this process and on the question—and questionable virtue of—early-modern absolutisms, there was bound to be some
small recovery of the part played by prelates.

The recovery came early in the seventeenth century. Emphasis on
secondary causes and reluctance to decipher the designs of providence,
not to mention the new dynasty's self-interest, combined to disconnect
the Tudor's direct line to God. It was not only that history was written
then for the Stuarts, but that history was written to give Stuart politics—
and politics in general—a firm foundation in fact, not in mythologies of
origins but in studies of experience and in anatomies of political culture.[7]
In this Francis Bacon took the lead, though his own foundation in fact is,
in places, flimsy rather than firm. Bacon invented speeches for his leading characters. His fictions are easy to spot and easier still to criticize, yet
he peopled his *History of the Reign of Henry the Seventh* with councillors who
might otherwise have remained lifeless in subsequent histories. It seems
to have been more important to Bacon to make learning true to life than
to copy, without interpolation, the anecdotes that survived in Tudor narratives. He had grand plans to animate history and to prepare a special
place for history in the advancement of learning. Moral philosophy was
to be delivered from the baffling yet shabby abstractions in which speculative philosophers had clothed it, and dressed instead with historically
illustrated exhortations and admonitions addressed to those responsible

---

[6]William Roper, *The Life of Sir Thomas More*, in Sylvester and Harding, *Two Early Tudor Lives*, 199-200.

[7]W. H. Greenleaf, *Order, Empiricism and Politics* (London: Oxford University Press, 1964) 206, 214, 230; and Arthur B. Ferguson, *Clio Unbound* (Durham: Duke University Press, 1979) 76.

for Stuart policy and written in language that courtiers could understand.[8]

The lengthy speech attributed to Archbishop Morton is an imposture, remarkable because Bacon had no sympathy with the oration's objective.[9] Bacon staged the spectacle, however, to showcase Morton's virtuosity rather than to explain or to discredit policy.[10] He had persuaded himself that Henry VII warred more for profit than for honor, yet he obligingly permitted the chancellor to go on about the Crown's preference for war rather than dishonor in order to demonstrate how Morton would have exploited religious imagery and overstatement to present his sovereign's case in the best possible light. Bacon believed that Morton actually moderated Henry's tyranny, that he shrewdly mitigated the conceits of power without undermining the canons of *Realpolitik*. For the connoisseur of court life, then, here was a model statesman and, to the extent that Morton was that, he was a model churchman as well.[11]

Bacon was particularly impressed by Morton's apparent willingness to "screen" the king, that is, to take upon himself the blame for Henry VII's miscalculations and to endure the curses of overtaxed citizens. Bacon turned unpopularity, in this instance, into a political virtue.[12] The technique applied equally well, he must have thought, to his own career at court, which had come unraveled before he had written a word of his *History*. He had personal reasons for maintaining that the sturdy, selfless public servant bears reproach and suspicion with sphinx-like silence. Bacon had been compelled to retire from political life, but in Morton he found a way to have the last word without necessarily rehearsing the charges that led to his own ostracism and without recourse to recriminations. He observed, nonetheless, how Morton's sovereign had protected his maligned councillor, and, by extolling Morton, he drove home the lesson that there was nothing more valuable than an accomplished, loyal lieutenant, despite the ill will and envy that unflinching loyalty might occasion.

When the focus shifted from Morton, Bacon still wished to underscore how wisely Henry VII selected, used, and rewarded his advisers. Bishop Fox surfaces here and there in Bacon's biography, and Fox is in-

---

[8]Consult, in this connection, George H. Nadel, "History as Psychology in Francis Bacon's Theory of History," *History and Theory* 5 (1966): 281-87; and Mary Faith Schuster, "Philosophy of Life and Prose Style in Thomas More's *Richard III* and Francis Bacon's *Henry VII*," *PMLA* 70 (1955): 474-87.

[9]Bacon, *History*, 107-12.

[10]Cf. a somewhat different approach to Bacon's aims, *The Works of Francis Bacon*, ed. James Spedding, Robert Leslie Ellis, and Douglas Dennon Heath, vol. 6 (London: Longmans & Co., 1858) 75 n. 1.

[11]Bacon, *History*, 214.

[12]Ibid., 115, 187.

variably busy, arranging (and mending) treaties, marriages, and pageants, all with consummate skill. Henry VII was finally responsible for Tudor destiny, Bacon would have granted, but the coterie of councillors that drafted his legislation, received and disbursed his funds, and filled the diplomatic corps shaped the dynasty's successes from day to day and from crisis to crisis.[13]

To feature the power and planning behind the throne was to give considerable "court time" to Henry's episcopal civil service. Bacon ushered ecclesiastical statesmen back on the stage from which they had been rudely escorted by Tudor apologists during the previous century. When the king erred and injudiciously invested authority in two ruthless laymen, Empson and Dudley, the court preachers, "doing their duty," Bacon added parenthetically, encouraged royal remorse and atonement (though Henry VII died before the hangman was asked to dispatch the offenders).[14] Bacon's point may have been that the church was not simply at court to advise and consent but that, *in concilio* and from the pulpit, prelatical public servants monitored and directed the king's conscience. But there were limits to the biographer's enthusiasm. One must not assume that Bacon did more for the recovery of early Tudor public religion than to reintroduce several of its principals. He was satisfied to have confirmed the debts political culture owed to dutiful and diligent public servants, many of whom just happened to have been the church's helmsmen.

From Bacon, the image one gets of Henry VII's court is that of a bustling firm where everyone was youthful and energetic and instinctively inclined to adapt (and to legislate) creatively as circumstance and common sense required. Bacon thought that Henry VII presided expertly and was conspicuously better as a lawmaker than all the English kings who preceded him. He was plainly a notch above his son, Henry VIII, who, Bacon insinuated, regularly and habitually subordinated policy to impulse. But Bacon lavished little time on such comparisons and generalizations, which were patently imprecise and better left to those who composed histories at their leisure. He knew his *History* to be serious business *and* science. If his remarks on methodology are any measure of the matter, *The History of the Reign of Henry the Seventh* was intended as the first stride toward a science of court life. By following natural history's inductive procedures, civil history could tease from the data incontestable laws of social and political behavior. But the *History*, in this respect, was something of a disappointment. Bacon's early Tudor court is more an aggre-

---

[13]Ibid., 50-54, 194, 207-208, 217, 242.

[14]Ibid., 237-38. For the questionable character of Henry VII's remorse, see G. R. Elton, "Henry VII: Rapacity and Remorse," *HJ* 1 (1958): 21-39; J. P. Cooper, "Henry VII's Last Years Reconsidered," *HJ* 2 (1959): 103-29; and G. R. Elton, "Henry VII: A Restatement," *HJ* 4 (1961): 1-29. Elton's papers were reprinted in *Studies*, vol. 1.

gate of examples than a coherent program. The recondite "laws" governing court life remained recondite, despite the ambitious plans with which Bacon papered his scheme for the advancement of learning.

In another respect, Bacon's *History* and methodology are quite compatible. Once Bacon had understood ecclesiastical history to have been a discipline parallel to civil and natural history, but as his studies progressed he theorized that ecclesiastical history was generally a branch of civil history.[15] This about-face is clearly reflected in Bacon's narrative of court life from 1485 to 1509. Indeed, from his history of Henry VII's reign, one could infer that he considered civil history the only ecclesiastical history worth telling. He presumably stumbled across religious imagery, pageantry, stunning episcopal palaces, and inspired preachers as he sifted state papers and previous accounts. But Bacon held his course. He wrote principally about the political miracle performed by Morton, Fox, and several of their colleagues. They had fashioned some semblance of unity from territories and factions that, "like waters after a tempest, were full of working and swelling."[16] Other aspects of religious life must have seemed to Bacon pallid when compared with this achievement. Parish priest and pious pilgrim were never summoned to Bacon's court history, for political intrigue was an exclusively patrician drama.

The rise of Enlightenment anticlericalism assured that there would be no concerted effort to map the religious dimensions of the patrician political culture, which Bacon left unexplored. Clerics were summarily dismissed as either fools or flatterers.[17] If they held high office in church or government, it was because their king was their puppeteer. Bacon's admiration for administratively competent and loyal prelates was not enough to save them. He had not garrisoned his impressions and inventions with sufficient evidence to intimidate scholars disposed to think of religion as politically naive superstition (when it was not hideously rapacious and obstinately Roman). Bacon's discoveries did not sway successors who were eager to transform episcopal civil servants into sycophants and parasites at court. But he had fortified his special concern with Henry VII in such a way that subsequent historians were compelled to focus on the first Tudor's place in political history. Sandwiched between Richard III and Henry VIII, more controversial figures by any measure, Henry VII and earliest Tudor political culture might easily have gotten lost. Yet they did not.

David Hume's *History of England* vividly displays the eighteenth century's debts to and departures from Bacon's account. Upon completing

---

[15]See Nadel, "History as Psychology," 278-79.

[16]Bacon, *History*, esp. 185-87, 238-39.

[17]See, e.g., Peter Gay, *The Enlightenment: An Interpretation*, vol. 1 (New York: Knopf, 1968) 210-12.

two volumes of Stuart history, Hume set aside his promises to advance the narrative from 1688 to his own time. Instead, he turned back to Henry VII and his heirs. Hume never fully explained what he called his "retrograde motion," and his order of composition (from the last Stuart to the first Tudor) still generates scholarly controversy.[18] It is most often ascribed to Hume's growing dissatisfaction with the Whig mentality. Whigs considered the Stuarts authors of an oppressive and wholly un-English absolutism and they looked nostalgically upon the Tudors as defenders of ancient liberties. It is said that Hume shattered the Whig consensus by demonstrating that generations of "arbitrary" Tudor rule shaped Stuart conceits, that Stuart absolutisms were rooted in Tudor autocracies.

Hume's correspondence can be quarried for some support for this conclusion. He declared to William Robertson that his Tudor chapters "effectually stopped the mouths of those villainous Whigs." Most remarks of this kind, however, were ventured after Hume had finished with his Tudors. It is unsafe to read them as statements of intent. Moreover, the presumption of Hume's prior attachment to some anti-Whig or Tory program is beset by two further difficulties. In the first place, historiography and politics had become so tangled by the time Hume turned historian that there is no sure way to infer historiographical bias from political commitment. Robert Brady's seventeenth-century Tory rendering of England's past had been wrapped in the rhetoric of Walpole's Whig government. The Whig concept of England's "ancient constitution" was exploited by Bolingbroke, who opposed Walpole. Hume generally remained indifferent to squabbles of this nature. Ernest Mossner calls him a political misfit who earnestly hoped to lift his *History of England* above partisan politics. Hume's apparent neutrality, in fact, is the second difficulty that received opinion faces.[19]

---

[18]Hume, *Letters* 1:251. Neither Hume nor his contemporaries questioned the division of history into periods that corresponded to reigns or dynasties. The characters of kings and of governments, and changes therein, were still considered primary "moral causes" of developments in a nation's social and economic affairs. See Hume's "Of National Characters," in *Essays Moral, Political, and Literary*, ed. Thomas Hill Green and Thomas Hodge Grose, 2 vols. (Darmstadt: Scientia-Verlag, 1964) 1:244, 249-50. As we shall see, however, Hume indirectly repudiated this approach. Of the many editions of his *History of England*, the four volumes published in Philadelphia (1821-1822) seem most widely accessible in American libraries. Citations below, therefore, refer to that edition.

[19]For Hume's remarks to Robertson, see Hume, *Letters* 1:294. For the supposed anti-Whig strategy and its application to the *History's* order of composition, see Victor G. Wexler, *David Hume and the* History of England (Philadelphia: American Philosophical Society, 1979) 57, 98; John J. Burke, Jr., "Hume's *History of England:* Waking the English from a Dogmatic Slumber," *Studies in Eighteenth-Century Culture* 7 (1978): 235-50; and Guiseppe Giarrizzo, *David Hume, Politico e Storico* (Turin: G. Einaudi, 1962) 271. For Augustan politics and historiography, see Isaac

Hume's stipulations that his *History* was nonpartisan appear in his correspondence as often as his expressions of indignation at scurrilous Whig reviews of his Stuart volumes.[20] The two can be reconciled by assuming that Hume was irritated both by Whig prejudices and by the Whigs' failure to credit his own impartiality. To an extent, Hume could have argued that he had distributed his insult equitably. He had indeed located the origins of Stuart absolutism in Tudor history, where Whigs would not have wanted them. But he also deprived the Tories of their cherished illusion that Stuart absolutism had celestial origins. Conservatives planted the origins of their absolutisms in the very nature of political culture that derived from God and reflected divine government of the heavens (and earth). Hume traced origins to historical circumstance.[21]

From the outset, then, before approaching Hume's influential depiction of the church's contributions to late-medieval government, it is important to see that the theory that Hume returned to Henry VII exclusively to break the Whig grip on historical consciousness is unacceptable. It projects a single predisposition upon a configuration of attitudes and pressures, among them the self-imposed requirement to remain impartial, and it undervalues Hume's fascination with early Tudor political culture.

Long before Hume contemplated his *History* and pondered his "retrograde motion," Henry VII had acquired a considerable, if not an immaculate, reputation for suppressing baronial factions that held fifteenth-century England hostage to their feuds. In this respect, the theme of Polydore Vergil's final chapters had become the realm's anthem to its Tudor redeemer. If Hume truly wished to place history and, ideally, political culture above party, he could have asked for no better protagonist. The immediate task, then, was to correct some of the bruising assessments of

---

Kramnick, *Bolingbroke and His Circle* (Cambridge: Harvard University Press, 1968). Mossner's two articles should be consulted in conjunction with more recent attempts to controvert Giarrizzo: "An Apology for David Hume, Historian," *PMLA* 56 (1941): 671, 680-81; and "Was Hume a Tory Historian?" *JHI* 2 (1941): 225-36; also see Duncan Forbes, *Hume's Philosophical Politics* (Cambridge: Cambridge University Press, 1975); and J. G. A. Pocock, *The Machiavellian Moment* (Princeton: Princeton University Press, 1975) 486-87, 502-504. For all this, however, it must be conceded that Hume was inclined to couple Stuart and Tudor absolutisms (*History* 3:282-84, 684) and that conservatives across the Channel agreed with those "villianous [sic] Whigs" about the consequences, if not about the character, of that pairing. For Hume's "tremendous hold over French conservative opinion," see Laurence L. Bongie, *David Hume: Prophet of the Counter-Revolution* (Oxford: Clarendon Press, 1965).

[20]Hume, *Letters*, e.g., 1:180, 217-18, 470, 491.

[21]Cf. Giarrizzo, *Politico e Storico*, 158.

early Tudor authority advanced by Paul Rapin de Thoyras.[22] Once Nicholas Tindal furnished a translation, English readers enthusiastically adopted this Frenchman's *History of England*.[23] Given that Hume wished to commemorate Henry VII's "watchful policy and steady government," which, fused with "the intrepidity and courage of his [Henry's] temper," silenced "the very murmurs of faction," Rapin-Thoyras's indictments of the first Tudor's conduct, left unamended, would surely find their way into angry reviews.[24]

Rapin-Thoyras was outspoken. Bacon had implanted a banker's heart in Henry VII's breast, but Rapin-Thoyras insisted that greed was Henry's "predominant passion." Every policy that was formulated at court, without exception, was "frivolous" and aimed narrowly and selfishly at increasing the king's wealth. Hume agreed that Henry's purse had too often dictated policy, but he objected that the king's "ruling passion" was frugality that only by degrees "degenerated into avarice." What is more, Hume was disposed, and Rapin-Thoyras was not, to scold parliament, the church, and the aristocracy for the greed that made them all easy prey to their king's schemes to turn foreign conquest into profit. Rapin-Thoyras's constant drumming on the first Tudor's "covetous temper" found no significant place in Hume's narrative.[25]

According to Rapin-Thoyras, the king's way with money was an embarrassment to his partisans and a political liability as well. The more closefisted the Crown, the more likely Perkin Warbeck was to attract support.

> [Henry's] covetous temper had alienated several of the firmest friends to his person and the house of Lancaster. William Stanley, Lord Chamberlain . . . Sir Robert Clifford, Sir Simon Montfort, Sir Thomas Thwaites, William Barley were the leaders of the conspiracy. The lord chamberlain had greatly contributed to his victory of Bosworth by declaring for him in so critical a

---

[22]For Rapin Thoyras's interests in England, see Nelly Girard d'Albissin, *Un précurseur de Montesquieu: Rapin-Thoyras* (Paris: Klincksieck, 1969) 32-42, 96-126. If Hume had been encouraged to think that the work of an esteemed foreigner might be balanced and uncontaminated by party prejudice, he was quickly disillusioned. His disenchantment found expression in his correspondence as well as in his *History*. See Hume, *Letters* 1:179, 258.

[23]Forbes, *Philosophical Politics*, 233-34. But England's endorsement did prompt criticism. Forbes appears to have overlooked a particularly bitter protest composed for (and perhaps by) J. Wilford, who was scandalized that a foreigner should pronounce negative and, in Wilford's opinion, inaccurate verdicts on English affairs. *A Defense of English History against the Misrepresentatives of M. de Rapin Thoyras* (London: J. Wilford, 1734) esp. 3-8, 37, 74, 119-20.

[24]Hume, *History* 2:238, 246-47, 251.

[25]Cf. Paul Rapin de Thoyras, *The History of England*, trans. Nicholas Tindal, 4th ed., vol. 5 (London, 1759) 218, 302; and Hume, *History* 2:216, 233-34.

moment. The king owned it but thought him well rewarded with the spoils of Bosworth field and the office of lord chamberlain. But Stanley, thinking that too mean a recompense, was not satisfied. Sir Robert Clifford was son of him that murdered the young earl of Rutland, and afterwards lost his life in fighting for the house of Lancaster. Probably Henry had forgot the constant attachment of that family to his house and neglected to give him a share in his favors.[26]

The addition of Henry's forgetfulness (with reference to Clifford) to the account of Stanley's grievance (borrowed from Bacon) places the blame squarely on the king. Bacon had supposed that Stanley's "ambition was so exorbitant and unbounded" that the king was incensed by his chamberlain's "intemperate desires." Rapin-Thoyras omitted this extrapolation, but Hume restored it. He granted that Henry had so "depressed" the nobility by consolidating his personal hold on government after Bosworth that the danger of faction increased. The king's bright idea was possibly a bad idea, but Hume (and perhaps Henry) saw no alternative, save incessant civil war. On the whole, Hume thought Henry's the wisest possible policy, formulated to assure that baronial disputes ended not merely with a temporary truce but with a permanent resettlement of the Crown and reassertion of its rights. Hume allowed that discontented barons were prone to believe a pretender's fables should such credulity seem to provide opportunity for their reemergence, but in the final analysis, Hume attributed Perkin Warbeck's popularity and the credulity that braced it to the nobles' "restless ambition." If "covetous" were to be applied to any party at this point, Hume implicitly questioned whether the insatiable aristocracy had a greater claim to it than had their king.[27]

Once captured, the hapless Warbeck was paraded before the kingdom that he had hoped to rule, then imprisoned beside the earl of Warwick, whom he had impersonated, and finally executed upon the discovery of another conspiracy against the king's life. Henry VII used the episode to dispatch the authentic earl along with the counterfeit, thus ridding himself of the last genuine Yorkist heir. Rapin-Thoyras seized the occasion for his most gratuitous slap at the king's "covetousness." In part to cover his crime, Henry had argued that Ferdinand of Aragon would refuse consent for the planned marriage between his daughter Catherine and Arthur, Henry's heir apparent, until Warwick had been eliminated and the dynasty's future thereby secured. Rapin-Thoyras was persuaded that Henry was only dodging responsibility for the earl's murder, either by fabricating Ferdinand's ultimatum or by inflating the marriage's importance for England. Had no other advantage presented itself, Rapin-Thoyras concluded, Henry would have killed Warwick for Catherine's dowry. Hume, on the other hand, was again reluctant to reduce dynastic

---

[26]Rapin-Thoyras, *History*, 296.

[27]Hume, *History* 2:228.

policy to personal greed. Warwick's execution was "the great blemish of Henry's reign," yet Ferdinand's demand appeared to Hume sufficiently reasonable to have been real. Undeniably, with the disappearance of Warbeck and Warwick, "foreign princes, deeming his throne now entirely secure, paid [Henry] greater deference and attention." The dowry, in Hume's judgment, had nothing to do with the murder, though he suspected that Henry's promises to marry his next son to Catherine after Arthur's untimely death may have been prompted, in part, by his wish to keep Ferdinand's wealth in his own realm.

Hume's Henry VII relished a good bargain. But Hume could not bring himself to agree with Rapin-Thoyras that, for personal gain, the first Tudor frequently and "frivolously" mismanaged public affairs.[28] Quite the contrary, during the reign of Henry VII, royal authority was extended, obstinate nobles were "curbed," and the people seemed well and honorably served, at home and abroad. At least this was how Hume perceived things. He granted that Henry's government was oppressive, but he insisted that "it was so much the less burdensome" than oppression decentralized. Better one despot than dozens of petty baronial tyrants. Hume was persuaded, moreover, that the citizens of early Tudor England enjoyed "if not entire liberty . . . the most considerable advantages of it."[29]

Problems posed by the concurrent developments of liberty and law in English history fascinated Hume. His *Essays* pitted the principles of royalists against those of republicans.[30] His *History* ranged about for case studies. As a historian, Hume was like an eager consumer in a vast warehouse crammed with merchandise. After debating the perils and profit of Stuart absolutisms and the Cromwellian reaction, he shopped for another government that might illustrate historically the interplay between liberty and authority. He was drawn to Henry VII by Bacon, "a very unbiassed historian" who, in Hume's judgment, "lay the colors of blame more faintly than the very facts he mentions seem to require." Hume found that Rapin-Thoyras stretched Bacon's tale. If Bacon blamed too little, Rapin-Thoyras certainly appeared to blame the monarch too much. Hume probably believed that he could restore some sense of proportion.[31] But on two counts Hume swerved from the course that Bacon had charted. He made ecclesiastical civil servants victims rather than architects of the king's program. Moreover, ultimately the king himself was a

---

[28]Cf. Rapin-Thoyras, *History*, 333; and Hume, *History* 2:243-45.

[29]Hume, *History* 2:256-57.

[30]See Hume's *Essays*, particularly "Whether the British Government Inclines More to Absolute Monarchy or to a Republic," 1:122-27; and "Of the Parties of Great Britain," 1:133-44.

[31]Hume, *History* 2:607.

pawn in a larger game, which socioeconomic forces and "manners," by manipulating liberties and laws, play upon the surface of history and political culture.

Hume and Bacon agreed that Henry VII's "constant scheme" to declaw English barons involved staffing his administration with "new men," prelates prominent among them. Bacon admired the way those prelates used their opportunities; Hume was impressed, to a degree, by the way the king used the church. In essence, Hume added an edge to Bacon's remarks and, with it, sliced churchmen at court to the size of sycophants. Allowing that men like Morton and Fox were "persons of industry, vigilance, and capacity" who had shared Henry's early distress and dangers and who had every right, therefore, to share in his good fortune, Hume nonetheless turned their dedication into a somewhat scandalous dependence.

> Henry, as lord Bacon observes, loved to employ and advance prelates; because, having rich bishoprics to bestow, it was easy for him to reward their services: and it was his maxim to raise them by slow steps, and make them first pass through the inferior sees. He probably expected that, as they were naturally more dependent on him than the nobility, who, during that age, enjoyed possessions and jurisdictions dangerous to royal authority; so the prospect of further elevation would render them still more active in his service, and more obsequious to his commands.

The key term is *obsequious*. Early Tudor clerics, in Hume's estimation, were not their sultans' khedives and commissaries, but more their eunuchs. Wolsey, though, was enigmatic. The flood of obloquy that had all but engulfed his record as chancellor by the time Cavendish composed his biography had not abated, and Hume had trouble fitting Wolsey into his account of servile clerical complaisance. Wolsey's humility, he gathered, was false, yet his quick implementation of every royal whim seemed to place Henry VIII's prelate in the category Hume shaped to accommodate Henry VII's ecclesiastical councillors. Notwithstanding this, Hume thought Wolsey insufferably arrogant. He plainly preferred Warham who, stained only slightly by superstition, was apparently as obsequious as his monarch could have wished. Under Warham's leadership, from Hume's perspective, the church was a cipher in Tudor England, a system of rewards easily managed by the Crown. Under Wolsey's leadership, it was a monarchy within a monarchy. One suspects that the less-visible and more-pliant church better suited not only Hume the historian, but also Hume the philosopher, who rather facetiously enjoyed the reputation that he had acquired, in some circles, as an infidel.[32]

---

[32]Ibid., 2:203. Warham's superstitions are noted in connection with the subversive prophesies of the Maid of Kent (2:365-66). For Hume's Wolsey, 2:289-93. Also see Hume's remarks on his reputation for impiety, *New Letters of David Hume*, ed. Raymond Klibansky and Ernest C. Mossner (Oxford: Clarendon Press, 1954) 43.

Actually, Hume was not a vicious critic of clerics at court. He was much more amiable and matter-of-fact than Tudor polemicists. Bacon had predisposed him to expect a vigorous and creative political culture when he returned from the Stuarts to Henry VII. He found, however, that Henry was a rather awkward opportunist who intimidated his clerical councillors. Furthermore, Hume suspected that the king and his court were creatures of a people fatigued by faction. Ecclesiastical civil servants were reduced in stature in Hume's *History*, but so was their sovereign. Henry VII was essentially the subject of his subjects.

Reflecting on the Tudor narrative after he closed his account of Elizabeth's reign, Hume summarized the sense of historical causality that prompted him to minimize the part played by personality. He insisted that manners were often repatterned imperceptibly by subtle social and economic shifts. In turn, manners, rather than theories, parties, or personalities, shaped and reshaped political culture. Here was an anatomy of authority with a palpably modern taxonomy.[33] Hume could not have known of his prefiguration of *eco-démographie*, but he certainly and loudly proclaimed as its principal virtue its nonpartisan character. It was the very fulcrum of his history above party. If readers could not distinguish this position from partisan politics that had hitherto been superimposed on the early Tudor story, it proved to Hume only that they were "retainers to superstition," he confided to Adam Smith, and that they would always be opposed to true philosophies of history.[34]

Hume's realization followed quickly upon his "retrograde motion." The remarks annexed to his rehearsal of Elizabeth's reign only amplified those with which he concluded his narrative of her grandfather's. Together, they now sound like a charge against Bacon, who must have seemed to have labored in cramped and ill-equipped quarters. Hume was able to see farther and probe deeper into the socioeconomic setting. But it was not that Hume possessed data utterly inaccessible to Bacon. One other reason why Hume retreated from the Stuarts to the Tudors was that, had he moved forward, he would have had to migrate to London and petition hostile Whig archivists and antiquarians for their files. The Tudors could be consulted in the comfort of his Edinburgh library, which was stocked with many narratives that had been available for centuries. There also, he might enjoy the conversation of Robertson and Adam Smith, and it was probably from them that he learned to suspect revolutions in man-

---

[33]Hume, *History* 3:268-69. See also, in this connection, Ulrich Voigt, *Hume und das Problem der Geschichte* (Berlin: Duncker und Humblot, 1975) 99-106; Leo Braudy, *Narrative Form in History and Fiction* (Princeton: Princeton University Press, 1970) 48-50, 66-75; and Giarrizzo, *Politico e Storico*, 56, 216-17, 228-29.

[34]*New Letters*, 54.

ners, commerce, and popular expectations to have been behind the "secret revolution of government [that] subverted the power of the barons."[35]

The chance to remain in Edinburgh, the growing conviction that conditions in late-medieval England marked the commencement of modern history, Henry VII's reputation for suppressing factions, and possibly some confused desire either to pacify or pounce on Whig critics lured Hume to early Tudor political culture. Pocock rightly implies that the explanatory merit of the alleged anti-Whig strategy ought not be dismissed perfunctorily. After all, Hume's study of baronial chaos was a missile fired directly at idealistic Whig fables of ancient civil liberties orderly and progressively enshrined in the constitutions of medieval England.[36] Consigning personality to the back room, however, Hume cannot have been trying to court Tory friends. I prefer to take Hume at his word and to incorporate the *History*'s substance and its order of composition into an image of the historian's struggle for, and virtual obsession with, nonpartisan history. With what Hume learned from Bacon and Adam Smith, he easily would have seen that a reassessment of the sixteenth century would deflate the myths of Tories as well as those of Whigs and would also impress upon his discerning readers the superfluity and danger of factions, which were at all times chief obstacles to historical understanding, political "science," and the practice of political virtue.

The results were mixed. Hume was perhaps most effective in clouding the issue of clerical courtiers. As early as 1741, he conjectured that priestly government was a source of intolerance and violent party prejudice.[37] Nearly twenty years later, writing his early Tudor narrative, he all but congratulated Henry VII for taming his church as well as his barons, and he let Bacon's prelates and public servants slip from history. But Hume did not jolt scholars from their perches above the intrigue of Tudor court life and into the cities' streets to calculate shifts in manners and in class aspirations. That would take centuries. Subsequent historians remained caught between Hume's Henry VII and Rapin-Thoyras's Henry VII, trying to argue their way to an elusive consensus.

Composed in 1820, Henry Hallam's chapters on earliest Tudor affairs were printed decades later with his *Constitutional History of England* and seemed initially to endorse the dark picture painted by Rapin-Thoyras. Hallam remarked that Henry VII's greed and "sordid motives" were "drawback[s] from the wisdom ascribed to him," though his intemperate desire for personal profit "answered the end of invigorating his power." Yet Hallam seems also to concur with Hume, for he held that the population's weariness with incessant feudal wars, and not its "somewhat ov-

[35]Hume, *History* 2:257-58.

[36]Pocock, *Machiavellian Moment*, 482-83; Giarrizzo, *Politico e Storico*, 244-45.

[37]"Of Superstition and Enthusiasm," *Essays* 1:144-50.

errated" sovereigns, carried England from the Middle Ages into modern times.[38] He shared as well Hume's low opinion of the clergy. Parliament counseled and coaxed Henry to take measures necessary to secure the dynasty. Parliament pressed him to marry his way to peace with the Yorkists. And Parliament "bounded" the king's prerogative and restrained him when his greed might have alienated his people. Parliament, Hallam's great protagonist, accomplished all that Bacon had once attributed to Archbishop and Chancellor Morton. Hallam's salute to Parliament barely left room for royal absolutisms and crowded prelatical public servants from the stage.[39] The first Tudor monarch, Hallam insisted, left a trail of broken promises, arbitrary taxation, and unforgivable injustices, but in the last analysis, this deplorable record hardly punctuated the unhurried progress of parliamentary supremacy that Hallam made it his business to celebrate.[40]

John Lingard was attracted to the nineteenth century's sense of progress, but "progress" meant something quite different to Lingard, who had been monitoring the de-ecclesiasticization of English political culture. He reported, with some apology, how Innocent III, in the thirteenth century, absolved vassals of their oaths and allegiances to an English monarch.[41] But his relief is virtually audible when his *History* reaches the age in which neither native nor foreign prelate could topple a government. Fellow Catholics accused Lingard of catering too sedulously to Protestant tastes for the sake of reconciliation; yet he was compelled, nonetheless, to answer Protestant critics who complained that he distorted the true aims of the English Reformation. Lingard himself withheld his uncritical admiration from the likes of Becket and Cranmer.[42] He most respected Englishmen who could manage political affairs without religious pretensions, and he made this crystal-clear in his encomiastic account of Wolsey's career.

[38]Henry Hallam, *Constitutional History of England* (London: A. Murray & Sons, 1870) 22-25, 27, 34, 55.

[39]This was true, in Hallam's estimation, not only in the later Middle Ages but throughout English history, from Plantagenet to Hanover. See, e.g., *Constitutional History*, 19, 409, 494, 729-30.

[40]Unlike Henry VII and his councillors, Wolsey did browbeat Parliament. The contrast served only to underscore Hallam's point that earliest Tudor Parliaments were forceful, if not indomitable (*Constitutional History*, cf. 22 and 32).

[41]John Lingard, *A History of England from the First Invasion by the Romans*, 2d ed., 8 vols. (London: J. Mawman, 1823-1825) 3:35.

[42]See, e.g., Lingard, *A Vindication of Certain Passages in the Fourth and Fifth Volumes of the History of England* (London: Collins pamphlets, 1826) 71-72. Joseph Chinnici, *The English Catholic Enlightenment: John Lingard and the Cisalpine Movement, 1780-1850* (Shepherdstown: Patmos Press, 1980) 120-23, covers quite well Roman objections to Lingard's Becket; but also see Lingard's *History* 2:343.

In Lingard's estimation, Wolsey's amazing fortitude, "consummate address," "and commanding abilities" lifted him well above his immediate predecessors and above the self-obsessed and "cold-hearted" monarch who employed them. Henry VII seemed to Lingard the victim of an age of intrigue and imposture, too terrorized by real and imagined enemies to trust anyone. Hence the king was remote from his people and, on nearly every issue, at odds with "the hopes of the nation," as Lingard construed them. Polydore Vergil, Bacon, and Hume suspected that Henry had staged a mock invasion of France in 1492 to enrich himself, but they also allowed that the unreliability of England's allies proved an incentive to contract a hasty peace. To Lingard, the king was a counterfeit general and shameless dissembler from beginning to end.[43] When England yearned for peace, he rallied the people for war. When they had been reconciled to war and to the taxes necessary to wage it, he gave them peace and, amply rewarded by the French king, he returned to England to pocket both French tribute and English taxes. Lingard remorselessly scolded the first Tudor and his stooges for ruining the Crown's credibility. Wolsey, on the other hand, was acclaimed for mending England's reputation and for making his monarch the arbiter of European affairs.[44]

By the end of the nineteenth century, Henry VII and his courtiers had been all but forgotten. William Stubbs confided that "never in the course of a long historical experience [had he] met with anyone who wished to

---

[43]For the 1492 campaign, consult AH, 56-57; Bacon, History, 141; Hume, History 2:224-25; Lingard, History 5:414; and Yvonne Labande-Mailfert, Charles VIII et Son Milieu, 1470-1498 (Paris: Klincksieck, 1975) 119-20, 227. It is hard not to agree with Labande-Mailfert that a sincere preference for peace as well as a satisfactory financial settlement turned Henry VII homeward. A similar assumption was made by Vergil and his heirs, save for Rapin-Thoyras and Lingard. The latter was wholly convinced that Henry was heartless (History 5:404, 458-61). At times he carried his point to an extreme from which even Rapin-Thoyras would have recoiled. Suggesting that Henry trumped up charges to acquit him of Warwick's murder, Lingard characteristically added that "the whole nation" mourned the victim's passing, as if the helpless prisoner had been a national hero (History 5:438).

[44]Lingard, History 6:59-62. Lingard was especially concerned with the impeachment of Wolsey that, since Vergil, had widely circulated in historical literature. On each point he labored to overturn the verdict. If Wolsey grasped, he never hoarded but was "a constant and bountiful patron." If his fondness for pomp and his mob of retainers made him seem less of a clergyman, the display was nevertheless appropriate for a representative of his sovereign's majesty. If Wolsey's interference with judicial procedures served to enhance his power, the results demonstrated "the versatility and superiority of his talents." "The equity of his decrees was universally admitted and applauded." Lingard was absolutely sure that Wolsey's innovations were "improvements which were received with gratitude by the country." Henry VII, in Lingard's pages, invariably set himself against "the nation," but Wolsey was perceived by his countrymen as the realm's redeemer.

attend a second course of lectures on Henry VII, or indeed with anyone who expressed any interest in him at all." As Stubbs understood the problem, Henry was something of a bore. That did not deter Stubbs, however, from devoting the seventeenth of his statutory lectures to the dynasty's founder. "I chose the subject because I have to lecture," he said, possibly with a shrug and a grin, "and after sixteen successive ceremonies of humiliation, I thought I had a right to throw some part of the imputation of dullness off myself upon my subject. If men will not come, let it be as much Henry VII's fault as mine." It is not implausible that Stubbs started with every intention of rekindling interest in earliest Tudor political culture; he ended, however, by justifying indifference. He assessed Henry VII's conduct of foreign affairs as unimaginative, condemned his domestic legislation as "humdrum," and shelved his church and churchmen as unexciting. Stubbs wanted as little to do with Rapin-Thoyras's scheming, self-centered sovereign as with Bacon's inspired and crafty executive. Henry VII was simply too dull to have been duplicitous and too businesslike to have been original.[45]

The consensus about the vapidity of earliest Tudor political culture had become quite formidable. At the time Stubbs published his *Seventeen Lectures*, Wilhelm Busch, on the Continent, was planning a history of Tudor England. All preliminary signs encouraged him to believe that he could consign the story of the dynasty's first twenty-five years to an extended preface (*"nur einleitungsweise kurz zu behandeln"*). But Busch grew increasingly fond of Bacon's monarch.[46] His own examination of diplomatic sources convinced him that Bacon had been right and that England's cast-iron dependence upon the Crown for leadership in political, economic, and religious life was Henry VII's doing and not Wolsey's. Rapin-Thoyras, Lingard, and even Hume would not have recognized Busch's first Tudor, who was depicted as "prudent, clear-sighted, and far-seeing," presiding capably—indeed expertly—over his land's great experiment with "enlightened absolutism."[47]

As for the prelates, Busch believed them genuine collaborators in the formulation of earliest Tudor policy. Foreign ambassadors thought them so, and that was sufficient for the German historian. Stubbs's early Tudor prelates settled dispassionately into a comfortable subservience to royal whim, for religion as well as government awaited patiently the more vigorous authorities of Henry VIII and Wolsey. Busch had a different tale to

---

[45]William Stubbs, *Seventeen Lectures on the Study of Medieval and Modern History* (Oxford: Clarendon Press, 1886) 334-35, 342, 362-65, 369-70.

[46]See esp. Wilhelm Busch, *England under the Tudors: King Henry VII*, trans. Alice Todd (New York: Burt Franklin, 1895) 416-23; but also note the preface to the original edition, *England unter den Tudors: König Heinrich VII* (Stuttgart: J. G. Cotta, 1892).

[47]Busch, *England*, 240, 291-304.

tell. In his narrative the Crown reformed the church in an effort to rees-
tablish discipline lost during decades of political uncertainty and pervasive disorder. Ecclesiastical officials, fiercely loyal to their king, gave the
government quotidian direction and assured that court life would be relatively free of faction. The king was at the center of Busch's history, and
all advances in religion, administration, and law were *"durchaus monar-
chisch,"* yet Henry's closest clerical lieutenants formed a strong supporting cast.[48]

It was as if Francis Bacon lived again. Busch's lengthy historiographical appendix amounted to a blistering attack on the fictions crafted by
André, Vergil, and even Bacon. Notwithstanding his iconoclasm, Busch
essentially revived the "new monarchy" hypothesis that those fictions had
been arranged to substantiate and that his own immediate predecessors—Hallam, Lingard, and Stubbs—had variously tried to capsize. The
zone in which the earliest apologists operated seemed commodious to
Busch, once he had cleared it of obvious falsifications. When Vergil and
Bacon were untrustworthy, they were expelled, but their general sense
of Henry VII's character and achievements was retained and their arguments were supplemented with material from the diplomatic pouch of
Don Pedro de Ayala and from other state papers. In all this Busch had
allies, although he could not marshal quite enough evidence to give earliest Tudor political culture the notoriety necessary to weather the next
decades' developments in historical literature. Most Tudor scholars listened, not to Busch, but to James Anthony Froude, who had reassured
them that Henry VIII was the real founder of English liberties. The ob-
scurity of that king's father was nearly total after A. F. Pollard credited
the second Tudor with the great advances that Bacon and Busch had ascribed to the first.[49]

Unlike Lingard, Pollard conceded that Wolsey merely refined policies
first contemplated by Henry VII's episcopal advisers, yet the concession
was made only to show that Wolsey was little more than a medieval hold-
over. Pollard's Wolsey was the papacy's pitchman and was largely insen-

---

[48]Ibid., 269 (Stuttgart ed., 280).

[49]De Ayala was not an altogether sound source; see Garret Mattingly, "The
Reputation of Doctor De Puebla," *EHR* 55 (1940): 27-46. Still, it is not difficult to
see why the ambassador's vivid dispatches appealed to Busch. See, e.g., G. A.
Bergenroth, ed., *Calendar of Letters, Despatches, and State Papers Relating to the Negotiations between England and Spain*, vol. 1 (London: Longman & Co., 1862) 250-
51. Busch was critical of allies, like James Gairdner, for placing too much faith in
André's "superabundance of laudatory phrases," but it is doubtful that any concerted effort on behalf of the "new monarchy" could have seriously challenged
the authority of Froude and Pollard. See, in this connection, Busch, *England*, 394-
95; Froude, *History of England from the Fall of Wolsey to the Death of Elizabeth*, vol. 4
(New York: Charles Scribner's Sons, 1881) 490-92; and Pollard, *Henry VIII* (London: Cape, 1970) 86-108, 197-99 (first published in 1905).

sitive to the unique problems facing the English church. Only when Henry VIII "retrieved monarchy" from his overbearing chancellor and "weaved sovereignty" over church and state "in and out of parliament" did England slip from its medieval and Catholic moorings into the modern age.[50] If Wolsey were to be redeemed for this modern age, it was mainly because men who apprenticed in his household were catapulted to power by his fall and because they became the authentic founders of modern statecraft. Wolsey's wards and protégés, but not Wolsey, ultimately created "a veritable cult of authority in which the king [Henry VIII] was lauded as God's vicegerent on earth." On the face of it, this looks suspiciously like the line taken by earliest Tudor apologists, but despite Bacon and Busch, Pollard's disciples insisted that the Tudor theory of kingship leaped forward only after Henry VIII matured and drove Wolsey's heirs to develop Tudor absolutism.[51] Whether their particular fetishes were liberty, constitution, or absolutism, twentieth-century historians seemed bent on making Henry VIII their idol. Pollard, however, remained the first citizen of this community. He encouraged outsiders who might be tempted to pursue Busch's theme that "the careful student of Henry VII's reign soon finds himself less concerned with the things that began under Henry VII than with the things which did not end with Richard III."[52]

This provoked protest. Henry VII and not his successors, it was said, checked the disintegration of England's international reputation and reestablished the sovereign's privileged place in the realm's political culture.[53] Leading twentieth-century advocates of the "new monarchy"

---

[50]A. F. Pollard, *Wolsey* (London: Longmans, Green & Co., 1953) 73-76, 165-216, 330-39, 356-73 (first published in 1929).

[51]Franklin Le Van Baumer, *The Early Tudor Theory of Kingship* (New Haven: Yale University Press, 1940) 13-20. Also, for the importance of Wolsey's "nurseries," see Lacey Baldwin Smith, *Tudor Prelates and Politics* (Princeton: Princeton University Press, 1953) esp. 5, 35-38, 102, 222; and the early chapters of W. Gordon Zeeveld, *Foundations of Tudor Policy* (Cambridge: Harvard University Press, 1948).

[52]Pollard, *Wolsey*, 9.

[53]C. H. Williams, *The Making of Tudor Despotism* (New York: T. Nelson & Sons, 1935) 68-81, 156-57, 172-73; Kenneth Pickthorn, *Early Tudor Government: Henry VII* (Cambridge: Cambridge University Press, 1949) 28-31, 105-107, 128; W. C. Richardson, *Tudor Chamber Administration, 1485-1547* (Baton Rouge: Louisiana State University Press, 1952) 408-14, 442-47; Joel Hurstfield, "Was There a Tudor Despotism After All?" *TRHS*, 5th ser. 17 (1967): 83-108; J. D. Mackie, *The Earliest Tudors, 1485-1558* (Oxford: Clarendon Press, 1952) 81-111; W. G. Hoskins, *The Age of Plunder: King Henry's England, 1500-1547* (London: Longman, 1976) 183. There is general agreement that Henry's management of foreign affairs, though "unheroic" and "unspectacular," gave England peace and prestige, which his predecessors had been unable to acquire for the realm and which his son squandered

hypothesis disagreed with one another on the character of earliest Tudor despotism, but on one issue they reached a consensus: Henry VII had chained the church to his will. Though some care was taken to distinguish earliest Tudor ecclesiastical policy from Henrician legislation, on this side of the despotism debate, it was quite natural to think of Henry VII's rule as an "ominous prelude" to his son's reformation of the church.[54]

The installation of such "ominous preludes" into the religious history of the Tudors' first decades is hard to prevent. S. B. Chrimes made them especially unwelcome, but his solution was to reduce Henry VII's church to insignificance. Hardly five of his *Henry VII's* many hundreds of pages deal with the church, as if the author were casting only a furtive glance at a wholly unremarkable and nearly imperceptible phenomenon.[55] On this issue one is better advised to join Pollard and to relate religious developments between 1485 and 1516 to late-medieval rather than to later Henrician history.

Since the fourteenth century English authorities claimed the right to settle disputes and appointments without appeal to Rome. The bishops of Rome realized that they were losing hold of territorial churches and of-

---

away. J. R. Lander, however, insisted that Henry's irenicism rested less on conviction and competence than on "the parvenu's haunting sense of insecurity." Long before, Gairdner maintained that the king only feigned fear of his own nobility in order to escape involvement in wars and crusades abroad. Cf. Gairdner, *Henry the Seventh* (rpt., New York: AMS Press, 1970) 112-17; and Lander, *Government and Community: England, 1450-1509* (Cambridge: Harvard University Press, 1980) 347. In connection with the "new monarchy" hypothesis, and for the transmutation of the term *despotism* in English political thought subsequent to Henry VII yet before this century's historiographical debate, review Richard Koebner, "Despot and Despotism: Vicissitudes of a Political Term," *Journal of the Warburg and Courtauld Institutes* 14 (1951): 287-92. For Elton's reservations, chiefly about Pickthorn's and Richardson's versions of early Tudor absolutism, consult his *Studies* 1:40, 250, 290-93, 316-21; but also note Penry Williams, "The Tudor State," *Past and Present* 25 (1963): 47-48.

[54]Cf. Williams, *Tudor Despotism*, 66-68; and Pickthorn, *Tudor Government*, 144-48, 177-82. Williams made earliest Tudor despotism the rough equivalent of constitutional monarchy. Pickthorn replied that despotism was singularly undespotic unless the despot had complete mastery over his council. He surmised that early Tudor councillors were too independent of one another effectively to challenge complete conciliar dependence on the king. Members of Parliament, Pickthorn argued, were similarly incapable. The first Tudor's sovereignty, therefore, was unequivocal and, being so, it was "new." Williams, ironically, was more certain than Pickthorn of Henry VII's full mastery over the church. There, Pickthorn suggested that the king's control was exercised more indirectly and with the close collaboration of his bishops. Hence it was Pickthorn and not Williams who flinched at the notion that earliest Tudor ecclesiastical policy was a crude form of later royal supremacy.

[55]S. B. Chrimes, *Henry VII* (Berkeley: University of California Press, 1972) 240-44.

fered concessions during the fifteenth century, but politically the English church was the king's before it was the pope's. G. L. Harriss concluded that the English Crown's "stranglehold on papal provision" had been fixed long before Henry VII undertook to discipline his aristocracy.[56] All this can be recited in order to chip away one face of the "new monarchy" hypothesis, that is, to make Henry VII's church policies appear quite tame, to see them as the culmination of a long and gradual process, and possibly—though not self-evidently—to distinguish them from Henry VIII's initiatives. But when much of this is granted, as it must be, the choice of phrases, of which "stranglehold" is a perfect example, is still vexatious and misleading. It is symptomatic of a predisposition that, since Hume, has prohibited full appreciation of the nature of the church's contributions to the dynasty's early work. To historians on both sides of the despotism debate, the church was a slave rather than an ally, and its complicity in its own servitude is commonly equated with the subversion of religion and the proliferation of scandal. Whether or not the regime of Henry VII is construed as "new" or "despotic," its muscle always seems exercised, at least in historical literature, at considerable cost to the spiritual life, as well as to the independence, of the church. Questions of novelty divided political historians, yet they all featured, and some underscored, the church's susceptibilities to the Crown's bullying. For centuries the English court had been crowded with episcopal and abbatical civil servants, but earliest Tudor political culture is thought to have hastened, or precipitated, the collapse of English Catholicism. Perhaps scholars have listened too readily, not only to one another, but also to early Tudor grievances and complaints about the church's worldliness. Though the misgivings of humanists and the acid remarks of later Lollards and early English Protestants are not the stuff of which irrefutable findings are made, historians have been eager to believe that corruption necessarily followed from service (or servitude) to the Crown.

On the periphery of the despotism debate, church historians have been equally absorbed by the predicament and worldliness of Tudor Catholicism. It must seem to them that political historians set the casket before them and left them to sort through the probable causes of death, for it was generally accepted that the church had been chronically, if not fatally, ill before Henrician legislation pronounced the end of one order and the start of another. Some cited lethargy and apathy. Others blamed anticlerical agitation. Combining several diagnostic approaches, J. R. Lander appears closer to the cause than any of them taken separately. "Those in authority had drunk from the bitter cup of extremism [here, later Lollardy] and they would drink of it no more. Repressing speculation, they

---

[56]"Medieval Government and Statecraft," *Past and Present* 25 (1963): 15. Also see John W. Dahmus, "Henry IV of England: An Example of Royal Control of the Church in the Fifteenth Century," *Journal of Church and State* 23 (1981): 35-46.

held up as an example to their world a spirit of timid conservatism that, encouraging a conventional and unspeculative, though at its best a deep devotion, stifled whatever possibility there may have been of any Catholic reform of more than piecemeal scope."[57] But Lander's diagnosis is also something of a demurrer. He was not persuaded that the church was in such dreadful condition that it required much more than "piecemeal" reform. In part, this was because he had read and incorporated into his own study the work of Peter Heath and Margaret Bowker, which tunneled deeper into late-medieval religious life than gossip, Lollard acrimony, humanist aphorisms, and Protestant polemic tend to take one.[58] But most church historians and political historians have been stubbornly "verbocentric." Religion criticized has been, and perhaps always will be, more accessible and more valuable to historians than religion "performed." Hence overstatements and misrepresentations find their way from the satires of Thomas More and Erasmus, from the bitter denunciations of the practices of prelates authored by Tyndale and Simon Fish, and from the artless abjurations of Lollards into modern anthologies and textbook illustrations of decline and depravity. What G. R. Elton appropriately called "the political folklore of anticlericalism" has become a touchstone for determining the early Tudor church's weakness and worldliness—and the meaning of the second term is often contracted to fit received notions of the first—as well as the English Reformation's debts to late-medieval lay dissatisfaction.[59] This is especially so now that popular discontent has captivated students of the church's early Tudor history.

The shift from court to embittered nonconformists has indelibly marked the study of early Tudor religion and political culture. More must be made of this as we turn next from the historians to the critics, their idealism, and their various briefs against clerical worldliness. It is enough here to suggest that the anatomies of Tudor absolutisms commonly stripped the pre-Reformation church of whatever threads of respectabil-

---

[57]Lander, *Government*, 114.

[58]Heath and Bowker matched the many virtues against the few failings of the secular clergy and the parish priests' ingenuity and perseverance against the hardships of parish life. It occurred to them, and earlier to A. Hamilton Thompson, that scandals and improprieties had been overstated, the perversion of justice in ecclesiastical courts had been exaggerated, and the damaging consequences of absenteeism had been magnified in the literature of earliest Tudor discontent. A. Hamilton Thompson, *The English Clergy and Their Organization in the Later Middle Ages* (Oxford: Clarendon Press, 1947) 40-57; Margaret Bowker, *The Secular Clergy in the Diocese of Lincoln* (Cambridge: Cambridge University Press, 1968) 107-109; Peter Heath, *The English Parish Clergy on the Eve of the Reformation* (London: Routledge & Kegan Paul, 1969) 23-25, 187-93.

[59]G. R. Elton, *Reform and Reformation: England, 1509-1558* (Cambridge: Harvard University Press, 1977) 55-57.

ity Bacon and Busch managed to salvage, while some studies amplified late-medieval outrage against ecclesiastical abuses, corruption, and servitude.[60]

Historians will always have their great texts to ponder, their monarchs to measure and manhandle, and their masses to redeem. Unless the "polytyque churche's" contributions to political culture are regularly reasserted, however, there is a danger that we will forget something significant about early Tudor history or that we will readily believe the worst about that which is all but forgotten.

---

[60]A. G. Dickens, "Heresy and the Origins of English Protestantism," *Britain and the Netherlands,* vol. 2, ed. J. S. Bromley and E. H. Kossman (Groningen: J. B. Wolters, 1964) 61: "That the Reformation became possible in England was largely due to the formidable volume of anticlericalism which developed during the early decades of Henry VIII. Whether the Reformation be envisaged as an act of state or a movement of thought, it was based upon the grudges of laymen against priestly wealth and power, against the daily miracle of transubstantiation from which clerical privilege seemed to derive, against the tyranny of church courts." Claire Cross suggested that later Lollardy reflected "the longings, the uncertainties, [and] the discontents of the laity," and knowing more of this than of the chessboard, she declared that "by 1460 the church in England had been reduced to a checkmate." *Church and People, 1415-1660: The Triumph of the Laity in the English Church* (Atlantic Highlands: Humanities Press, 1976) 17, 30-31. Also consider Dickens, *Lollards and Protestants in the Diocese of York, 1509-1558* (London: Oxford University Press, 1959); John F. Davis, *Heresy and Reform in the Southeast of England, 1520-1559* (London: Royal Historical Society, 1983); and Margaret Aston, "Lollardy and Literacy," *History* 62 (1971): 347-71. For more cautious estimates, see John A. F. Thomson, *The Later Lollards, 1414-1520* (London: Oxford University Press, 1965); and for the associations between Lollardy and reform in the context of historiographical disputes, see Christopher Haigh, "Some Aspects of the Recent Historiography of the English Reformation," in *Stadtbürgertum und Adel in der Reformation,* ed. Wolfgang J. Mommsen (Stuttgart: Klett-Cotta, 1979) 91-97.

• Part II •

THE CRITICS

Nearly one hundred years ago, Francis Aidan Gasquet opened his vindication of pre-Reformation English Catholicism with some concessions to critics. Plagues, he said, had depleted the church's revenues as well as the stock of recruits for the clergy, and recovery was painfully slow. The higher clergy were often obsessed with "place-seeking," and this infectious "secularism"—this thirst for worldly honors and profits—passed to the parish priests. With the impartiality of influenza, greed diseased the laity as well. Gasquet's later Middle Ages was not a particularly pleasant epoch. Only monasticism held out against the advance of worldliness and corruption. Anxious to acquit England's religious orders of the charges of sloth and scandalous behavior that had circulated for centuries, Gasquet pioneered the publication of records that might salvage the cloisters' reputations for discipline and holiness. Yet even this achievement was stained by what one of his admirers sadly identified as "a capacity for carelessness [that] amounted almost to genius." On this count, Gasquet was an easy target. G. G. Coulton, for example, was unalterably persuaded that Gasquet had deliberately distorted the story of the late-medieval church, that errors and omissions were indications of a Catholic conspiracy to misrepresent the sorry state into which the church had fallen by the early sixteenth century.[1]

But Gasquet believed that late-medieval churchmen, despite clerical worldliness, were widely respected. He considered Thomas More's judgment unimpeachable, yet never more so than on this point. More had pronounced that confidence in English Catholi-

---

[1]See especially Gasquet's *Henry VIII and the English Monasteries*, 6th ed., vol. 1 (London: J. Hodges, 1895) 1-39; and *The Eve of the Reformation*, 3d ed. (London: George Bell & Sons, 1913). His "capacity for carelessness" is mentioned in David Knowles's tribute, "Cardinal Gasquet as an Historian," in *The Historian and Character* (Cambridge: Cambridge University Press, 1963) 240-63. For Coulton's relentless pursuit of Gasquet's errors and apparent frauds, see *Medieval Studies*, 2d ed. (London: Simpkin, Marshall, Hamilton, Kent & Co. Ltd., 1915) 79-132; *Five Centuries of Religion*, vol. 3 (Cambridge: Cambridge University Press, 1936) 551-55; and *Fourscore Years* (New York: The Macmillan Co., 1944) 329-36.

cism had not perceptibly eroded until William Tyndale and Simon Fish irresponsibly and malevolently sensationalized occasional clerical indiscretions. When the Reformation arrived, well on into the sixteenth century, it seemed to have come suddenly, as a result of royal arrogance and not of popular discontent. So it seemed to Gasquet. Did he and More suppress evidence when they wrote as if outrage against the *ecclesia carnalis* were a continental phenomenon?[2]

The fifteenth century has left less than a thorough scholar would want, but fragments of lay dissatisfaction and passages of cautious clerical criticism do turn up. The first challenge is to arrange them, to look from Wyclif to John Colet, in order to introduce the earliest Tudor critics and to place their idealisms in some historical perspective.[3] All this qualifies rather than belies the evaluation of lay respect relayed by More and Gasquet, to which I shall return as *The "Polytyque Churche"* draws to its conclusions.

---

[2]Gasquet, *Reformation*, 101-36. For continental dissent, see Gordon Leff, "The Apostolic Ideal in Later Medieval Ecclesiology," *Journal of Theological Studies* 18 (1967): 58-82; and Scott H. Hendrix, "In Quest of the *Vera Ecclesia*: The Crisis of Later Medieval Ecclesiology," *Viator* 7 (1976): 347-78.

[3]Once acknowledged as important, late-medieval anticlericalism raises a crop of questions. To classify all discontent as proto-Protestantism, which is, after all, another way of minimizing its significance, is to beg rather than to answer the questions. Yet scholars who are skeptical of generalizations and classifications and who sift through the various expressions of English anticlericalism, ranging from restorationist rhetoric to physical assaults on the clergy, will seem to have abandoned themselves to the ostensible randomness. Typologies help, but the tidiness that characterizes the best of them is only provisional and propaedeutic. I have borrowed from J. J. Scarisbrick, though he is unlikely to subscribe to what I have made of his brief discussion of earlier Tudor idealisms (*Henry VIII* [London: Eyre & Spottiswoode, 1976] 319-21).

Chapter 3

FROM WYCLIF
TO COLET

Conditions responsible for the fifteenth-century swells of anticlerical sentiment and criticism cannot be as easily catalogued as the symptoms of clerical "place-seeking" or the accumulation of clerical riches. But the aggressive pursuits of order and prosperity, which are ordinarily associated with the coming of the Tudors, probably occasioned greater envy of prelates' wealth and position and greater impatience with the church's efforts to discipline its own. What I have termed "idealistic criticism" thereafter yoked grievances to appealing visions of a more perfect spirituality, lay as well as clerical. A few visionaries gave dissent memorable expression in sermon, satire, and utopian fantasy, which still fascinate and inspire readers, most of whom fancy the idealists' devotion to peace and antipathy toward tyranny. The critics and their ideals seem so much more contemporary than the prelates and the practices they criticized that, without much reservation, they are trusted when they excoriate the worldliness of the "polytyque churche." After achieving some historical perspective, however, one should ask whether that trust, to some appreciable extent, has been misplaced, whether streaks of perfectionism have colored the idealists' imprecations. This inquiry is freighted with problems. Idealistic critics are elusive and their works are often allusive and multivalent. What has been said of poets' metaphors may be said as well of earliest Tudor idealism and its more perfect spirituality: the more thoughtfully one looks at them, the greater the distance from which they defiantly glare back. Nonetheless, since idealistic critics have been so influential in shaping current opinion, there is no choice but to proceed, mindful of these caveats but determined, in the end, to retrieve the "polytyque churche" as they perceived and misperceived it. John Wyclif's idealism is an excellent place to start.

Wyclif's polemics consolidated earlier protests against the church's worldliness.[4] He also pressed his campaign, more broadly and more recklessly, against "superstitions" attached to the sacraments. His ide-

---

[4]Gotthard Lechler, *Johann von Wiclif und die Vorgeschichte der Reformation*, vol. 1 (Leipzig: F. Fleischer, 1873) esp. 741.

alism was obscured and its force somewhat dissipated in the controversies that followed, whereupon more crudely anticlerical statements surfaced.[5] To fifteenth-century authorities, these were "dampnable opynyons" of brutish dissidents and malcontents, but they are the bricks from which great castles of medieval Lollardy are built by some of our industrious scholars.[6] For the moment, however, Wyclif himself shall detain us, for in some measure it was his cargo, his ecclesiology, that earliest Tudor critics uncrated and remodeled.

Wyclif persistently berated the church for allowing its preoccupations with wealth and power to screen its savior, for "nothing was more dangerous than to disguise the way in which we must follow Christ."[7] The papacy had wholly forfeited any claim to allegiance that it may have once possessed, insofar as its own way of following Christ was actually the way of the world.[8] Wyclif's point was that the church passed off its crooked paths toward riches as Christ's path toward righteousness, and consequently, Christians were led by their hypocritical shepherds, particularly pontiffs but also grasping mendicants, farther from a biblical piety. The management of church business bore no resemblance whatsoever to the conduct of disciples and apostles. As his touchstone Wyclif took St. Paul, *doctor universalis*, whose prudence and selflessness were fashioned as instruction for his heirs. When St. Paul spoke of himself as "least of the apostles," it was more than simply a reflection on that part of his career—his persecution of Christians—that made him unworthy of grace, popular esteem, and high office. *"Ego sum minimus apostolorum"* was an indictment against prelates of any age who assumed their peculiar worthiness and talent for church leadership, who took pride in their promotions, and who transferred the great glory of their offices to their per-

---

[5]E.g., Margaret Aston, "William White's Lollard Followers," *The Catholic Historical Review* 68 (1982): 469-97.

[6]See above, ch. 2, n. 60. Although lists of Lollard offenses and "dampnable opynyons" appear standardized, John A. F. Thomson believed that authorities made genuine efforts to ascertain the truth and that the lists reliably reflect Lollard attitudes. Thomson conceded, however, that the formal abjurations give those attitudes theological integration and polish that they probably did not possess. See Thomson's *Later Lollards*, 75, 229, 239; and John Fines, "Heresy Trials in the Diocese of Coventry and Litchfield, 1511-1512," *JEH* 14 (1963): 171-73.

[7]Wyclif, *Tractatus de potestate papae*, ed. Johann Loserth (London: Wyclif Society, 1909) 65; "Nihil enim periculosius in ecclesia quam obumbrare viam sequendi Christi vestigia."

[8]Wyclif, *De Christo et suo adversario antichristo*, in *Polemical Works*, ed. Rudolf Buddensieg, vol. 2 (London: Wyclif Society, 1883) 692. Also note Wyclif's *De apostasia*, ed. Michael Henry Dziewicki (London: Wyclif Society, 1889) 12; and *Joannis Wyclif Sermones*, ed. Johann Loserth, 4 vols. (London: Wyclif Society, 1887-1890) esp. 2:44-49.

sons.[9] Wyclif told St. Paul's story so often and so enthusiastically that barriers between the apostle's time and his own seemed to dissolve, and primitive Christianity became something of a manifesto for the late-medieval church.[10]

Wyclif's broadsides stirred several churchmen to reply, and often with invective equal to that hurled at them.[11] Thomas Walsingham compressed some stinging countercharges in his epitaph for "that diabolical agent, enemy of the church, corrupter of the masses, specter of the ancient heretics, image of hypocrits, instigator of schism, originator of hatred, and fabricator of lies."[12] Yet it was possible both to object that Lollard condemnations were too fierce and too categorical and to protest that certain censurable clerical practices were an embarrassment to the church. John Bromyard, for example, warned that incontinent priests gave the church's critics greater occasion to preach schism. Bromyard's own reprimands, by the early fifteenth century, were lodged in his popular and impeccably "orthodox" *Summa praedicantium*.[13] Priests and mendicants who read the *Summa* to pieces, pillaging the text for sermon topics, anecdotes, and apt phrasing, found that Bromyard was as impatient with clerical worldliness as he was with immorality. He insisted that the clergy's addictions to ornate churches and gilded plate offended both wisdom and piety. He reminded readers that neither Socrates nor Christ thought that they could simultaneously achieve wealth and virtue.[14] Yet Bromyard knew that the very sinews of the ecclesiastical system were fortified by preoccupations and practices that he deplored. Advancement and influence most often fell to those who, like their princely patrons, single-

---

[9]See, *inter alia*, Wyclif's *De veritate sacrae scripturae*, ed. Rudolf Buddensieg, 3 vols. (London: Wyclif Society, 1905-1907) 2:87-92.

[10]E.g., see Gustav Adolf Benrath, *Wyclifs Bibelkommentar* (Berlin: Walter de Gruyter, 1966) 242-51.

[11]Much of interest, with respect to Wyclif's enemies, especially Adam Wodeford and Thomas Netter, comes out when Paul De Vought questions their reliability, "Wiclif et la scriptura sola," *Ephemerides theologicae Lovanienses* 39 (1963): 50-86, which is a reply to Michael Hurley's "*Scriptura Sola*: Wyclif and His Critics," *Traditio* 16 (1960): 275-353.

[12]Thomas Walsingham, *Chronica Monasterii S. Albani*, ed. Henry Thomas Riley, vol. 2 (London: Longman, Green, Longman, Roberts, & Green, 1864) 119-20: "Organum diabolicum, hostis ecclesiae, confusio vulgi, haereticorum idolum, hypocritarum speculum, schismatis incentor, odii seminator, mendacii fabricator."

[13]John Bromyard, *Summa Praedicantium*, 2 vols. (Basel: Johann Amerbach, 1480). See under "Homicidium," article 1.

[14]Ibid., see under "Paupertas," article 6: "Nos suffarcinati auro, Christum pauperem sequimur." Also note "Humilitas," article 5.

mindedly cared for material gain and who became adept in its pursuit. Their influence and power, in turn, protected the church.

We will never know whether and to what extent Bromyard was secretly attracted to Wyclif's idealism and ecclesiastical primitivism. Though repelled by clerical worldliness, he ventured criticisms that were relatively limited in scope. He scolded incontinent clerics, but he denounced lay intervention in church life. By providing and promoting worldly priests, lay patrons cheated themselves and their people of the prayers of good candidates, who were left without livings.[15] Lay patronage, according to Bromyard, was responsible for the spiritual lassitude in England, for the *"refrigeratio spiritualis caloris."*[16] Lollards, however, looked to lay intervention as part of the solution to clerical immorality and dereliction. "In defawte of prelatys," temporal lords were advised, barons and kings might manage church business and even preach God's law as well as promulgate their own.[17] Wyclif was not innocent of this, but his "heresy" was essentially academic. Yet as protest filtered from Oxford through song and satire (and perhaps also through Bromyard's *Summa*), through angry mendicant preaching, to England's tenants and tradesmen, solutions became simple and radical. The church's difficulties in enforcing standards for discipline were overdrawn.

Bishop Reginald Pecock would have none of this. Prelates, he answered, should be not "overmuch" blamed for "badde passiouns" that moved all men. From the time he was promoted to the episcopacy in 1444 to his disgrace and dismissal a dozen years later, Pecock tackled Lollard extremism and particularly objected to the way Lollardy turned its bible against the clergy. "Doom of natural resoun . . . and not Holi Scripture is the ground of all the seid governauncis, deedis, virtues, and trouthis." Pecock's "rationalism" irritated his colleagues and eventually led to his humiliation, but his argument is more moderate than it at first appears. Set free in scripture, sincere yet simpleminded persons without reason's guidance could come to the most absurd conclusions, which inflamed re-

---

[15]Ibid., see under "Electio," article 6, and "Missa," article 1: "Si nullus namque malos sacerdotes conduceret, vel promoveret, de facto saltem ad bene vivendum attraherentur et artarentur et fames eos ad deum reduceret, sicut reduxit filium prodigum. Sed quia vident quod ita bene conducuntur et promoventur mali sicuti boni minus bene vivere curant. Illi ergo qui eos tenent, vel conducunt non solum seipsos bono defraudant spirituali . . . sed etiam peccant, dum occasionem eis probent delinquendi."

[16]Ibid., see under "Judicium divinum," article 4.

[17]*The Lay Folks' Catechism*, ed. Thomas Frederick Simmons and Henry Edward Nolloth (London: Early English Text Society, 1901) 15.

sentment against those very men ordained to train and guide them.[18] Like Bromyard, Pecock acknowledged the church's difficulties, but he settled for small remedies. Cautious optimism inclined him to expect some return to reason, which, in his terms, meant reliance on the church and its authorities to right the apparent wrongs in ecclesiastical government and to reject outlandish demands voiced by querulous and irresponsible critics.

But what of the Lollards themselves? If not Wyclif's idealism in its purest form, what possessed fifteenth-century critics who clutched at the prospect of baronial interference, who waved the Bible as a weapon against the medieval church, and who spoke openly and with disdain of the clergy's secret sins? Possibly some fear of divine retribution moved them to expose scandalous behavior and to complain of Christians' attachments to silly and profitless exercises such as pilgrimages. Sermons and ballads, even before Wyclif's death, conjectured that drought and earthquakes were signs of impending judgment, "warnyng[s] to be ware."[19] Yet the promise of divine punishment ordinarily prompted penitential devotion—quite incompatible with arrogance and anticlericalism—undertaken to appease an angry deity. William Christian wisely placed this intention at the center of the "lay theology" of local religion; and it indeed does appear to have absorbed the efforts of late-medieval laymen until chance rather than personal sin and clerical corruption was widely used to explain natural disaster and collective misfortune. Still, it is not inconceivable that clerical malpractice caused considerable alarm among an already fearful people. All might be required to suffer for the inconstancy of their prelates. Elizabeth Sampson may have been terrorized by something more global than personal pollution when she proclaimed that she would not permit her mongrel dog to nibble at the sacrament blessed by an incontinent priest.[20] Notwithstanding the cosmic importance of each priest's foul thoughts and misdeeds, smaller grievances were surely the catch on which much resentment and anticlericalism fed; and the "here," more than the hereafter, was likely to concern most critics most of the time.

---

[18]See Pecock's *Repressor of Over Much Blaming of the Clergy*, ed. Churchill Babington, 2 vols. (London: Longman, Green, Longman, & Roberts, 1860) 1:87-88, 127-28; 2:449-51. For the spread of protest, G. R. Owst's two searching studies are quite useful: *Preaching in Medieval England* (Cambridge: Cambridge University Press, 1926); and *Literature and Pulpit in Medieval England* (New York: Barnes & Noble, 1961).

[19]*The Minor Poems of the Vernon Manuscript*, ed. F. J. Furnivall, pt. 2 (London: Early English Text Society, 1901) 718-19.

[20]Quoted from the London episcopal registers of Richard Fitzjames, in *The Reign of Henry VII from Contemporary Sources*, ed. A. F. Pollard, vol. 3 (London: University of London, 1914) 244. For Christian's analysis of divine chastisement and "lay theology," see *Local Religion in Sixteenth-Century Spain* (Princeton: Princeton University Press, 1981) 206-207.

"Local" grievances can be divided into two related classes. The church was frequently charged with administering justice ineffectively and unfairly and with snatching greedily at commoners' purses. The failures of ecclesiastical courts were worrisome to all who had occasion to bring litigation there. The church's penalties and prohibitions appeared to have lost their compelling power over consciences that they once instructed and corrected. London's mercers left tokens of their piety in benefactions and in their ledgers, which were punctuated with prayers and marked by signs of the cross; yet when those same businessmen, as creditors, found cause to go to court, they appealed to the court of aldermen, not to the church's institutions and arbitration. By 1500 London's commissary court was less crowded with neighborhood nuisances, whose victims sought reparations and justice elsewhere, and suits for petty debt had virtually disappeared from the docket of the bishop's consistory court.[21] Rumors of bribery and extortion, though they may have referred chiefly to the waiver of assigned penances, possibly kept other lay plaintiffs away. It was possible, then, to escape the church's courts. It was harder, however, to avoid the church's tithes, rental rates, and compulsory offerings.

Occasionally, tithe collectors encountered open defiance. Some church officials feared that priests, as collectors, were compromised by deteriorating discipline. Visitors asked to monitor one London parish's accounts were encouraged to inquire whether the clergy "dare not ask their tythes

---

[21]Consult Brian Woodcock, *Medieval Ecclesiastical Courts in the Diocese of Canterbury* (Oxford: Oxford University Press, 1952) esp. 43-45, 88-92: Ralph Houlbrooke, "The Decline of Ecclesiastical Jurisdiction under the Tudors," in *Continuity and Change: Personnel and Administration of the Church in England, 1500-1642*, ed. Rosemary O'Day and Felicity Heal (Leicester: Leicester University Press, 1976); and Richard M. Wunderli, *London Church Courts and Society on the Eve of the Reformation* (Cambridge: Medieval Academy of America, 1981). Houlbrooke suggests that writs of praemunire were sued by Henry's VII's officials in order to accelerate passage of litigation from ecclesiastical to royal courts, but evidence for this is rather sketchy. The letter of Richard Nix, bishop of Norwich, to Archbishop Warham, with which Houlbrooke illustrates his point, does complain about a single writ of praemunire, but in the context of an angry account of general discontent with ecclesiastical procedures, which Nix takes quite personally (PRO, SC 1:44, 7.83). In connection with ecclesiastical proceedings against clerics and with clerical immunities in secular courts, see Leona Gabel, *Benefit of Clergy in the Late Middle Ages*, Smith College Studies in History 14 (1928-1929); but also note R. H. Helmholz, "Crime, Compurgation, and the Courts of the Medieval Church," *Law and History Review* 1 (1983): 1-26. Helmholz places in fresh perspective the use of compurgation and the low conviction rate in ecclesiastical courts. For the Mercers' piety, review Sylvia L. Thrupp, *The Merchant Class of Medieval London* (Ann Arbor: University of Michigan Press, 1968) esp. 174, 180; and for a corresponding decline in cases brought before the courts of common pleas and king's bench, see Marjorie Blatcher, *The Court of King's Bench, 1450-1550* (London: Athlone Press, 1978) 10-32.

for fere of any slaundyr of their own gylte." The Carmelites' constant carping against clerical avarice echoed in the guildhalls where prelates' "gylte" was probably a favorite topic of gossip.[22] Reports of corruption and mismanagement presumably alienated donors. Contributions to monasteries declined. Thomas Gascoigne had stipulated that subsidies given for pious purposes, when diverted by ecclesiastical administrators, endangered benefactors' spiritual well-being.[23] If W. K. Jordan's survey of revenues can be trusted, this prospect must have been taken seriously, for the discernible downward trend is otherwise inexplicable. Much is known about lay resistance to funeral taxes or mortuaries, which had once been given as compensation for the deceased's delinquency in tithing, but which were seen increasingly as the most repulsively inconsiderate intrusion by the church into the lives of its faithful.[24]

In 1511 a well-to-do merchant named Richard Hunne refused to surrender the item demanded as a mortuary payment by the priest who presided at his infant son's funeral. The priest sued and obtained a favorable verdict from the archbishop's auditor of causes. Hunne wanted nothing more of the church's justice and countersued a writ of praemunire to remove proceedings from the church's jurisdiction.[25] Unpopular and controversial, mortuaries were frequently contested: more than a century before Hunne's challenge, thugs in Cornwall intimidated mourners into withholding burial fees.[26] Hunne, however, took the issue to a new level. He could have objected more narrowly to the church's power to determine the rector's right, for, properly speaking, the article asked for belonged to him and not to his son's estate. Instead, he named as defendants

---

[22]For the visitation article, see Richard Arnold, *The Customs of London* (London: F. C. & J. Rivington, 1811) 274. Also note F. R. H. Du Boulay, "The Quarrel between the Carmelite Friars and the Secular Clergy of London, 1454-1458," *JEH* 6 (1955): 156-74; and John A. F. Thomson, "Tithe Disputes in Later Medieval London," *EHR* 78 (1963): 1-17.

[23]*Loci e libro veritatum*, ed. James E. Therold Rogers (Oxford: Clarendon Press, 1881) 112.

[24]Michael M. Sheehan, *The Will in Medieval England* (Toronto: Pontifical Institute of Mediæval Studies, 1963) 298-99; and W. K. Jordan, *Philanthropy in England, 1480-1660* (London: George Allen & Unwin, 1959) 146-47.

[25]For the precedents, see W. H. Waugh, "The Great Statute of Praemunire," *EHR* 37 (1922): 173-205; and E. B. Graves, "The Legal Significance of the First Statute of Praemunire," in *Anniversary Essays in Medieval History by the Students of Charles Homer Haskins*, ed. C. H. Taylor (Boston: Houghton Mifflin Co., 1929) 57-80.

[26]*Select Cases in Chancery, 1364-1471*, ed. William Paley Baildon (London: Selden Society, 1896) 23-25.

all who participated in the priest's suit in ecclesiastical court: summoner, witnesses, and advocates. The whole system was on trial.[27]

Hunne's action, then, fixes attention on the two immediate causes of lay resentment: mistrust of the church's courts and displeasure with compulsory offerings. His fate demonstrates that the church was unprepared to tolerate such a challenge. Hunne was imprisoned for heresy and, late in 1514, he was found dead in his cell. Church officials pronounced the death a suicide, but a coroner's jury suspected murder. Despite Thomas More's willingness to accept the sugared account, evidence now all but corroborates the jury's suspicions.[28] A plan to eliminate the troublesome merchant may have been laid in advance or, as has been suggested, Hunne may have been killed accidentally in a scuffle. Whatever the circumstances, the dismissal of William Horsey, the serpentine chancellor of the bishop of London, was a virtual *cognovit* of the church's complicity.[29]

Bishop Richard Fitzjames was not implicated at the time, but subsequently John Foxe described him as an indefatigable and cruel persecutor of dissidents. The bishop is more properly understood, however, in the tradition of Bromyard and Pecock, but also as a prelate whose single and rather unimaginative response to anticlericalism was likely to intensify resentment. Before he was promoted to the episcopacy, Fitzjames had preached against "euuil prestys" who displayed greater diligence in the acquisition of worldly gain than in their adherence to God's laws. Moreover, "by byenge and sellynge and dyvers and many other corrupte meanes [they] causid in this manere wyse the people to erre from almyghty God theyr maker." Like Bromyard, Fitzjames blamed noblemen and politicians for appointing worldly and corrupt clerics to positions of influence, yet, also like Bromyard, he refused to counsel or countenance disobedience. He shared the laity's indignation and vexation, though he insisted that rancorous litigation only compounded the problem. Christ's example, his "nighying" to humankind, was reduced in Fitzjames's ser-

---

[27]Hunne's praemunire was heard before the King's Bench in 1513 (PRO, KB 27:1006, membrane 37) and was adjourned without verdict from term to term until Hunne's death. Consult Arthur Ogle, *The Tragedy of the Lollards' Tower* (Oxford: Pen-in-Hand, 1949); S. F. C. Milsom, "Richard Hunne's Praemunire," *EHR* 76 (1961): 80-81; Richard J. Schoeck, "Common Law and Canon Law in Their Relation to Thomas More," in *St. Thomas More: Action and Contemplation*, ed. Richard S. Sylvester (New Haven: Yale University Press, 1972) 32, 41; and J. Duncan M. Derrett, "The Affairs of Richard Hunne and Friar Standish," in *CWTM* 9:215-46.

[28]For More's postmortem, *CWTM* 6:1:326-27; for the jury's, *Acts and Monuments*, 196-97.

[29]Richard Wunderli has published a penetrating examination of the case against Horsey and his apparent accomplice, Charles Joseph, "Pre-Reformation London Summoners and the Murder of Richard Hunne," *JEH* 33 (1982): 218-23.

mon to a lesson in submission. To rush the revisions that God would make in due time was a self-assertion tantamount to idolatry. Genuine and lasting reformation could come only from God. Fitzjames, then, was predisposed to see the impetuosity of dissent and criticism as a far more serious violation of divine order than the church's deplorable yet temporary substitution of unworthy, worldly pursuits for God's laws. He might have agreed with the Lollards that the clergy's "byenge and sellynge" profoundly jeopardized lay piety, but he hunted heretics (though perhaps less relentlessly and ruthlessly than Foxe alleged) because they rejected Christianity's cardinal rule, which remained unchanged by any grievance. The laity owed obedience to its clergy.[30]

The unflinching demand for obedience must have annoyed John Colet, dean of St. Paul's Cathedral and thus one of the bishop's most influential colleagues. Colet had a different approach: willingness to amend conduct and eliminate abuses would earn the clergy respect and obedience, which could not be expected as long as indiscretions were overlooked. On this question of priority, and on more important matters as well, Colet and earlier Tudor idealists were to part company with many moderate Catholic officials. Fitzjames, however, was not about to abide disagreement. He and Colet were harnessed to the same church, and they would pull together or the dean would have to be disciplined. Colet's friend Erasmus wrote tendentiously about the controversy.

> Take note of Colet's misfortunes. He had never been at peace with his bishop, about whose manner I shall say nothing, save that the bishop was an insuperably superstitious Scotist and thought himself almost divine. . . . Moreover Colet failed to please many members of his collegiate church, for he was too strict a disciplinarian. . . . The bishop was at least eighty years old and his hatred became unmanageable. He associated two other bishops, as virulent as himself, with his campaign and he followed the procedure common among those who plot another's destruction. Parading excerpts from the dean's sermons, he accused Colet before the Archbishop of Canterbury.[31]

---

[30]*Acts and Monuments*, 174, 179; Richard Fitzjames, *Sermo die lune in ebdomada pasche* (London: Wynkyn de Worde, 1495). Also see *Reg. Fitzjames*, 77. 25(r)-26(v).

[31]Allen, *OE* 4:523-24: "Iam ne quid defuisse putetur absolutae Coleti pietati, tempestates quibus agitatus est accipe. Nunquam illi bene convenerat cum suo Episcopo; de cujus moribus ne quid dicam, superstitiosus atque invictus erat Scotista, et hoc nomine sibi semideus videbatur. . . . Nec admodum gratus erat plerisque sui collegii, quod tenacior esset disciplinae regularis. . . . Sed cum iam odium senis Epsicopi—iam enim erat non minor annis octoginta—atrocius esset quam ut premi posset, ascitis duobus episcopis aeque cordatis nec minus virulentis, incipit Coleto negotium facessere, non alio telo quam quo solent isti, siquando cuiquam exitium moliuntur. Defert eum apud Archiepiscopum Cantuariensem, articulis aliquot notatis quos ex illius concionibus decerpserat."

Hugh Latimer later recalled that Colet's daring brought him within inches
of the stake, but now there is really nothing to suggest that Colet's dissent was so sinister or Fitzjames's reaction so extreme.[32] It is difficult,
however, to say more. Colet's preaching *ad populum*, from which the
bishop drew his evidence, is lost. The only sermon that survives was delivered *ad clerum* and then quickly printed in 1512, more than six years
after Fitzjames was translated and Colet transferred to London. It is there
that one must begin if one wishes to discern some definite cause for
Fitzjames's "plot" against the dean and to comprehend the differences
between the older critics and the new.[33]

By convoking in 1512 the clergy may have had every intention of reforming the church as well as of eradicating heresy and resisting secular
interference in religious affairs; yet Colet, chosen by the archbishop to
preach before the assembly of leading prelates from the southern province, emphasized the need for reform rather than the promise of reform.
He seems to have mistrusted his colleagues, and with his parting shot,
he goaded them:

> Consyder the miserable fourme and state of the churche, and endevour your
> selfes with all your myndes to reform it. Suffre nat, fathers, this your so
> greatte a getherynge to depart in vayne. Suffre nat this your congregation
> to slyppe for naughte. Truly ye are gethered often tymes to gether; but, by
> your favour to speke the trouth, yet I se nat what frute cometh of you as-
> semblyng, namely to the churche.

The sermon thus concludes with the memory of failure, but the whole
homily attributes this poor record to previous convocations that distracted attention from the real source of the problems to the symptoms.
On the one hand, fear of royal and parliamentary abrogation of ecclesiastical liberties and immunities and, on the other, intense concern about
the spread of heterodox opinion blinded authorities to the debilitating
worldliness that made the church susceptible to both. Colet was convinced that the improvement of personal habits would remove the threat
from the government.

> Ye wyll have the churches liberte, and nat to be drawen afore secular juges:
> and that also is ryght. . . . But if ye desire this liberte, first unlouse your
> self frome the worldlye bondage, and from the services of men; and lyfte
> up your selfe in to the trewe lybertie, the spirituall lybertye of Christe, into

---

[32]*The Sermons and Remains of Hugh Latimer*, ed. George Elwes Corrie, vol. 27
(Cambridge: Parker Society, 1845) 440.

[33]*Conv.*, 293-304. Arguing for an earlier date (1510), Michael J. Kelly concludes
that Colet's lament that reforming councils had been wanting suggests that the
sermon could not have been preached a mere two years after the last convocation. But Colet was most distressed with the inability of councils to take decisive
action and not with the infrequency of such assemblies. See *Conv.*, 294, but cf.
Kelly's *Canterbury Jurisdiction*, 112.

grace frome synnes; and serve you God, and raygne in him. And than, beleve me, the people wyll nat touche the anoynted of theyr Lorde God.[34]

As for heresy, "the invasion of heretykes, the churche beynge shaken was made wyser and more cunnyng in holy writte." The real peril to religion, the toxin that destroyed the church's spiritual life from within, was "the secular maner of lyvynge" that captivated churchmen and extinguished charity. For Colet, the "heresy" of "our evyll lyfe" was more devastating than Lollardy.[35] Indeed, it has been argued that Colet had connections with London's "Lollard literary underground," and John Foxe published Lollard depositions, which indicate that several of the dreaded malcontents attended and approved of the dean's sermons.[36] It would have been uncharacteristic for Colet to have made direct overtures, but it is possible that his criticisms and ideals, in some measure, resembled Wyclif's and that the similarities struck certain dissidents as well as the authorities dedicated to hunting them down. To elaborate on this, I shall need more than the single surviving sermon can give.

John Colet's Oxford lectures, treatises, and conversations are more familiar than his London works. His capital has increased in value with the proliferation of Erasmus studies that proposed Colet as a pivotal figure in Erasmus's early intellectual development. The two met in Oxford in 1499 and thereafter continued to correspond until Colet's death in 1519. After piecing together the extant letters with Colet's lectures, nineteenth-century scholars awarded the lecturer his own "Oxford Reformation." Erasmus was named its most compelling representative, but Colet retained his place as the pioneer of theologically conservative, but morally demanding, Catholic reform. With a generous tolerance for ambiguity, generations of admirers have more or less accepted the story.[37]

---

[34]*Conv.*, 303-304.

[35]Ibid., 298.

[36]*Acts and Monuments*, 229-30; Aston, "Lollardy and Literacy," 367-68.

[37]With the exception noted below, I subscribe to Sears Jayne's dating of Colet's commentaries, *John Colet and Marsilio Ficino* (London: Oxford University Press, 1963) 29-34. For the virtually indestructible tale of Colet's leadership, see Frederic Seebohm, *The Oxford Reformers*, 3d ed. (London: Longmans & Co., 1887); Karl Bauer, "John Colet und Erasmus von Rotterdam," *Archiv für Reformationsgeschichte*, Ergänzungsband 5 (1929): 155-87; Piero Rebora, "Aspetti dell' Umanesimo in Inghilterra," *La Rinascita* 2 (1939): 383-86; and E. Harris Harbison, *The Christian Scholar in the Age of the Reformation* (New York: Scribner's, 1956) 70-78. Eugene F. Rice, Jr. has made the best effort to overturn the Seebohm verdict, "John Colet and the Annihilation of the Natural," *Harvard Theological Review* 45 (1952): 147-48. For a different analysis of recent interest in Colet, consult Leland Miles, "Platonism and Christian Doctrine: The Revival of Interest in John Colet," *Philosophical Forum* 21 (1963-1964): 87-103.

The problem with this, from the perspective of this undertaking, is that the few remains of Colet's London career have too often been swept into the "Oxford Reformation," as if one could collapse Colet's final fifteen years into the myth created to dramatize the preceding ten. Relationships between these two parts of Colet's professional life, familiar Oxford and foggy London, have to be renegotiated. At Oxford, Colet tentatively launched his protests against the deterioration of church discipline and reiterated apostolic ideals. The case for apostolic Christianity was then intensified in Colet's little and little-known treatise, *De sacramentis ecclesiae*. From that manual his rather startling ambitions for the church probably seeped into his preaching *ad populum*, whence subversives might have drawn their own inferences. The *De sacramentis* is central, yet it is commonly thought to have been composed at Oxford, to be bookish and stuffy, and therefore to have no bearing on Colet's career in England's busiest urban cathedral.[38] All this is humbug, and parallels between *De sacramentis* and Colet's verifiable Oxford work are only prima facie convincing.

The best reason to separate this small-but-important treatise from the Oxford lectures and paraphrases is, fortunately, the one that most clearly illumines our picture of earliest Tudor idealism, that is, Colet's dedication, in *De sacramentis*, to detailing the sanctification of the Christian life

---

[38]See *Sac*, Joseph H. Lupton's introduction, 16. Jayne (n. 34) is unsure of what to do with the *Opus de sacramentis ecclesiae*, but the argument for Oxford origin survives, perhaps because circumstantial evidence begets more circumstantial evidence. For instance, it is presumed that Colet would never have patterned a treatise on the pseudo-Dionysius's *Hierarchies* after 1501, when his colleague William Grocyn shattered the apostolicity of *Divus Dionysius* in a set of lectures delivered in London. The hidden premises here, which should be disallowed, or at the very least seriously questioned, are (1) that Erasmus had not earlier discussed with Colet other "proofs" of pseudonymity (e.g., see Allen, *OE* 1:249), (2) that Colet, though he traveled in Italy, returned to Oxford with no sense that Lorenzo Valla had already badly bruised the pseudo-Dionysius's apostolic authority, and (3) that Grocyn had succeeded where others had failed. It is more likely, however, that Colet received Grocyn's disclosures in the same way that he would have greeted Erasmus's intelligence. Accepting both as plausible, he continued to honor the pseudo-Dionysius's contribution to ecclesiology and sacramental theology. John Jewel may have known of some utterance, lost to us, when he explained that Colet eventually repudiated his close pairing of "Paulus et ejus discipulus Dionisius Ariopagita." *The Works of John Jewel*, ed. John Ayre, vol. 1 (Cambridge: Parker Society, 1845) 113-14. Yet there is every indication that, to the end of his life, Colet trusted in the authority and usefulness of the *Hierarchies*. See J. B. Trapp, "John Colet, His Manuscripts and the Pseudo-Dionysius," in *Classical Influences in European Culture, A.D. 1500-1700*, ed. R. R. Bolgar (Cambridge: Cambridge University Press, 1976) 219-20.

as an extension or expansion of the priesthood.[39] In London, as at Oxford, Colet complained that clerical greed had contaminated the church. "In the name of Christianity, the greater part of humankind became pagans," inasmuch as "lay people have great occasion of evils and cause to fall when those men whose dutie is to drawe men from the affection of this world, by their continual conversation in this world, teche men to love this world, and of the love of this world cast them heedlyng in to hell."[40] But in London, and only in *De sacramentis*, Colet formulated what it must be like to be drawn from the world in terms that minimized differences between clerics and laymen.

Priests were a special, yet not a privileged, breed. Colet insisted that they were servants, not masters, of their church, and he was alarmed that they had become virtually indistinguishable from worldly persons whom they had been ordained to summon from irresponsibility to righteousness. At Oxford he seems to have experimented with several ways to shock listeners into an awareness of both the immense obligations and the tragic defilement of the priesthood. In most instances he challenged proud and greedy prelates with the example of St. Paul. Like Wyclif, Colet was not merely persuaded by Paul, he was charmed, even mesmerized by him. If the apostle's humility and unaffected piety were not the cornerstones of every priest's decorum, Christians, bereft of examples, would not be led or "drawn" to God. For every reprobate priest who remains unreformed, one avenue "from the affection of the world" closes.[41] The argument here was fashioned in Oxford and repeated in London where, assuming the voice of a deprived layman, Colet preached to his colleagues: "Unto you we loke as unto markes of our direction. In you and in your life we desyre to rede, as in lyvely bokes, howe . . . we may lyve . . . you spirituall phisitians, fyrste taste you the medicine of purgation of maners, and then after offre us the same to taste." This imperative, which sounds faintly like an ultimatum, betokens a slight, though perceptible, development from the earlier remarks. Colet had stipulated that St. Paul's effectiveness depended on his unpretentious posture, his willingness to be reckoned the equal of others, "though he was bringing them Christ." Yet Colet otherwise confirmed that clerical spirituality was superior to that of *"perfecti et consummati Christiani."* By the time he had preached his sermon *ad clerum* in London, "offre us the same to taste," he appears to have decided that righteousness, *"sacerdotificans,"* might

[39]See my "John Colet's *Opus de sacramentis* and Clerical Anticlericalism," *The Journal of British Studies* 22 (1982): 1-22, which makes a more complete case for the later dating and for the discussion of Colet's position, from which the next paragraphs have been condensed.

[40]*Sac*, 75; and *Conv.*, 297.

[41]*EEr-b*, 187-88; *EEC*, 117-78, 183, 250; and *PSD*, 175-76, 206-207, 220-22, 241, 248.

make the laity a spiritual priesthood. At Oxford laymen could be distinguished, *"sub nomine sanctae plebis,"* from their priests, *"spiritales homines."* In *De sacramentis,* perhaps echoing 1 Peter 2:9, Colet ventured that the communion of truly humble, pious, and therefore spiritual Christians made priests of all participants.[42]

The propagation of righteousness makes spiritual priests of upright laymen and "truer" priests of those in holy orders who instruct others as St. Paul instructed them, by example as well as by precept. This is the gist of Colet's position in *De sacramentis.* Barriers between commoners and their clergy began to topple in his Oxford lectures and treatises. He warned colleagues against the conceit that derived, he said, from a faulty interpretation of the "keys passage" in Matthew 16. Priests cannot declare others righteous with a set of inflated pronouncements, for that implied that the church could compel divine compliance with its infallible decisions. Priests must lead or draw believers to righteousness by encouraging emulation of their own blameless conduct.[43] *De sacramentis* also argued that the extension of righteousness (*"amplificatio justitiae"*) required perfect priestly morality as well as the scrupulous administration of the sacraments. By example and by miraculous transformation respectively, morality and sacraments mediated God's generative, purgative, and redemptive activity to the world. The whole hierarchy, priests and sacraments (*"comprehensam sacrorum dispositionem"*), was an instrument in the church's reform and return to God, now understood as the divine reclamation of humankind. Each prelate, performing as a *"medius inter deum et hominem,"* must shun interests and habits that bind him to earth.[44] Persons easily seduced by worldly pleasures were chased from Colet's spiritual priesthood. It was no place for men unnerved by the enormity of their obligation to cleanse creation and return it to divine favor. Colet either said or implied this at Oxford, but *De sacramentis* directly insisted that everyone enter or reenter the church as a full citizen, or not at all.[45]

Citizenship now involved nothing less than full participation in the propagation of righteousness and thus in the ministry of the church. St. Paul's humility and industry were yardsticks—exacting but, for Colet, appropriate standards for the measurement of each Christian's commitment. He usually exercised superb control over his exposition—which skillfully and often traverses the distance between the restoration of the single sinner to God's favor through the sacraments and the general reform of all creation through the spread of righteousness—so it is difficult to think of this perfectionism as accidental. After reiterating the Chris-

---

[42]Compare *Sac,* 35 and *Conv.,* 299 with *PSD,* 250-52.

[43]*PSD,* 264-65. Also note *Sac,* 90-91.

[44]*Sac,* 35-41, 81-82. "Medius" had a slightly different meaning in *PSD,* 200, 207.

[45]*Sac,* 84-86.

tian's solemn duty to disavow worldliness, *De sacramentis* presumes that "it was predetermined that a power would proceed from heaven, and seizing man, it would creep into the flesh of those fallen and (*spiritificans*) make them spiritual." This was but the start of a large-scale "*restauratio mundi*," which Colet also called "repair" ("*reparatus*") and "rebuilding" ("*reaedificatus*"). With this impressive task in mind, he ordained, so to speak, the entire church.[46] After all, had not St. Paul urged Roman Christians

> to become a holy and priestly race, for it is the priestly office to extend the priesthood. In fact, nothing is the duty and the office of the priesthood unless self-expansion whereby it offers itself to God to bring it to pass that others offer themselves with it. Thus the whole church may be a priesthood altogether offering righteousness [as] a living sacrifice to God.[47]

For Colet, then, there could never be too many "priests." Later, in 1532, his friend Thomas More turned his considerable talents to the church's defense. When clerical crimes were recited with relish by public officials who wished to reduce the church's privileges and immunities, More brooded that it would be impossible to find and recruit, among those enraged by their priests' misconduct, a sufficient number of scrupulous replacements. There were, perhaps, few good priests, but there were also few good men and fewer still who were willing to take on the hardships and deprivations of the priesthood. Of course, More and Colet were thinking of two different clergies. Colet, in this instance, was the idealist that More had been during the first fifteen years of the sixteenth century, and Colet's "priesthood of all believers" was better suited to More's *Utopia* than to the London they shared. A dozen years after Colet's death, More was a seasoned and shrewd administrator. He reflected realistically on the difficulty of staffing the church with virtuous as well as capable men, a problem that may have accounted for the church's reluctance to deprive clerical offenders and its decision to require only public penances for transgressions that seem to have called for unsparing condemnation.[48] Colet might have been a sterner judge, far less inclined toward

---

[46]Ibid., 62-64.

[47]Ibid., 71; "Et ad eosdem Romanos, quos velit gentem esse sanctam et sacerdotalem (nam est sacerdotis sacerdotium propagare: nihil enim est munus et officium cujusque, nisi propagatio ejusdem et qui se sacrificavit Deo efficere ut secum alii consacrificans justitiam, id est, quisque in ea se justum, vivam hostiam, offerat Deo) scribit." The position here was foreshadowed in two Oxford lectures, *ERR-a*, 228 and *EEC*, 243.

[48]See More's *Apology*, CWTM 9:79-82. Reporting on visitations undertaken from 1487 to 1527, Bishop Fox mentioned, as a matter of pride as well as of necessity, that he "never pryved person in noo dyoces that I have been in." *The Letters of Richard Fox*, ed. P. S. Allen and H. M. Allen (Oxford: Clarendon Press, 1929) 151. Also in this connection, consult Bowker, *Secular Clergy*, 118-19.

clemency, for his whole career was a protest against clerical worldliness. But in *De sacramentis*, his dream of a more perfect spirituality got the best of him. There he had little sense that Christians might persistently have trouble shaking the clay from their feet. His church had become a utopia, ruled by the Holy Spirit's "quiet authority" (*"latens imperium"*), which worked ubiquitously to tame human nature's self-seeking and to produce common aspirations. Christians would be empowered to obey the most demanding of St. Paul's precepts, even the prohibition *"neminem cognovimus secundum carnem."* The spiritual priesthood places the layperson in an altogether different life. This new life is dominated by consuming passions for the propagation of righteousness and for the perfection of Christian spirituality, which in turn extend the rule of righteousness and the *imperium* of the Holy Spirit.[49]

Colet's idealism, particularly the notion of "priest-making" (*sacerdotificans*), is too prominent in *De sacramentis* to permit one to assume its effective suppression elsewhere. By 1513 Bishop Fitzjames was searching through the dean's sermons for sedition, and it would have been remarkable only had he not found what he was seeking.

This is not to suggest that John Colet was a Lollard. When he spoke of the Lollards' "marveylous folysshenes," doubtlessly he emphasized the second word.[50] He was, however, a subversive critic. His protests in London were shaped by a vision of a new "priestly people" and of a more apportionable perfection than the church could imagine. To explore this most profitably and to say more of early Tudor idealism and criticism in general, I shall borrow several of Colet's charges that refer to the church's worldliness, and in so doing take a closer look at the criticisms, at the critics, and at the "crimes."

---

[49]*Sac*, 44-45, 55-59, 93-94. For earlier remarks on the power and authority of the Holy Spirit, see *EER-a*, 263-64; *EER-b*, 184-87; *EEC*, 221-22, 230, 234, 246-49; and Colet's *De corpore Christi mystico*, in *Opuscula quaedam theologica*, ed. Joseph H. Lupton (London: G. Bell & Sons, 1876) 187-94. For discussions of these and related ideas, consult Catherine A. L. Jarrott's two papers, "John Colet on Justification," *Sixteenth Century Journal* 7 (1976): 59-72, and "Erasmus's Annotations and Colet's Commentaries on Paul: A Comparison of Some Theological Themes," in *Essays on the Works of Erasmus*, ed. Richard L. De Molen (New Haven: Yale University Press, 1978) 125-44; my "John Colet and Erasmus' *Enchiridion*," *Church History* 46 (1977): 304-305; and my *Augustinian Piety and Catholic Reform*, 68-81, 105-10.

[50]*Conv.*, 298.

Chapter 4

CRITICS
AND THE COURTS

S*tories of clerical misconduct* sometimes found their way into England's secular courts. Church officials occasionally registered their complaints against lay malefactors and delinquent debtors with local magistrates. Critics increasingly associated prelates' involvements with the courts— as accused or as accusers—with decadence. Thomas Gascoigne's protest that legal expenses drained too much of the church's revenue was probably inspired by cases like the one brought by the mayor of Leicester in 1433. The mayor objected that the cathedral chapter had been charging citizens for the use of common pasture. To uphold its rights to the land and to the fees, the church was compelled to go to court and to bear the burdens of a costly defense.[1] It is likely that many differences between churchmen and their neighbors were resolved before disputants resorted to court action and enforced arbitration, yet other disagreements proved otherwise unmanageable.

William Sever's decision to enclose land claimed by the city released a flood of ill will in York in 1500. Sever, abbot of St. Mary's while also bishop of Carlisle, refused municipal authorities' offers to have the rival titles "indeferently examyned," for they also requested him to stop building on the site. Sever dared them to sue, but the city was hopeful that a compromise could be arranged. When the matter dragged on, however, agitated citizens contemplated ransacking the prelate's property (April, 1501). Finally, nearly two years after the controversy started and a year after troublemakers were restrained, a justice at assize ruled in favor of the abbot, but also stipulated that some portions of the contested land be leased from the city. Apparently this was not the compromise that the city council had expected, and it immediately declared that York "wold not be agreable to take any rent." Town officials then threatened to bring a case of trespass before the king's council.[2] Other contests, of course, were more expeditiously and more amicably settled. During the same period, the prior of Barnwell and the town of Cambridge battled for

---

[1]Thompson, *Newarke*, 102-103.

[2]*YCR* 2:148-51, 157-58, 162-63, 173.

the rights to a ditch along Midsummer Common. After arbitration, a mutually satisfactory compromise was found, yet costs for "examining evidences" were still assessed against the church.[3] At the other extreme, some disputes raged almost beyond control. Eight years later the prior of Tynemouth renewed efforts to build wharves and mills several miles downriver from Newcastle and thus to compete for business that would otherwise have sailed for the city. The mayor assembled troops, as did the prior, yet just when it seemed as if both sides preferred armed combat to the courts—that is, after several violent scuffles—grievances were forwarded to the king's council.[4] Owning land and engaged in commerce, the church could hardly escape litigation.

From what has been said so far, one might assume that batteries of barristers were fired only when the church clashed with municipalities that can be expected to have hired influential counsel of their own. A glance at the *Year Books* and *coram rege* plea rolls shows that such an assumption will not hold. In the equity courts of the king's council, to which Newcastle petitioned against Tynemouth and where York threatened to take its trespass against Sever, common lawyers could be little more than technical advisers. But relatively few cases ended up there; most were heard in the courts of common law. In that arena church officials, like the prior of Dunstable, were occasionally hounded by their creditors. Much more often, prelates, as landlords or as dissatisfied consumers, were the plaintiffs. The Augustinian canons of St. Paul, Newnham, employed a carpenter to complete some new construction on their properties within a set time. When the time elapsed and the contract collapsed, the problem was handed to the chapter's lawyers and transferred to the courts. The abbot of Bordesley publicly denounced and apparently excommunicated John Middlemore, who had stolen some fuel from the order, yet he also brought the matter before the King's Bench. For allegedly stealing their priest, Thomas Bodefield was summoned to court by the churchwardens of St. Mary's, Bridgestreet, in London. (Bodefield argued that he was merely trying to induce the priest to honor obligations to another parish that had paid a retainer for his services.) Lawyers for the abbot of Hyde relentlessly pursued an obdurate tenant who, with equal tenacity, refused to acknowledge his debts. In most of the plea rolls for the King's Bench, one finds an abbot, prior, or other ecclesiastical official on every fourth or fifth membrane, and behind each there were one or more law-

---

[3] *Annals of Cambridge*, ed. Charles Henry Cooper, vol. 1 (Cambridge: Warwick & Co., 1842) 249, 255.

[4] *SC* Bayne 2:68-74.

yers dogging defendants on behalf of their clients. Peterborough Abbey kept seven lawyers on its payroll.[5]

Lawyers and courts were unpopular and often ridiculed. Most difficulties in bringing offenders to justice were due to the labyrinthine procedures of common-law courts. Blame rained down upon all officials, who were captives of an intricate decorum that criticism made them all the more eager to preserve, but lawyers seem to have been inculpated more than justices and sheriffs.[6] Thomas Gascoigne did not analyze the problem at length, but he alleged that he had overheard a rather callous confession of self-interest: "If only there were more lawbreakers," one wistful member of the profession reportedly had said, "we *legistae* would make larger profits."[7] Alexander Barclay agreed that lawyers were wholly motivated by greed and too frequently unconcerned with the welfare of those who could not afford inflated fees.

> *Honest maners nowe ar reputed of no more,*
> *Lawyers ar lordes: but justice is rent and tore*
> *Or closed lyke a Monster within dores thre*
> *For without mede or money no man can hye se.*
> *Al is disordered: Vertue hathe no rewarde.*[8]

John Skelton, seven years later, in 1516, added a slap at shady solicitors and disreputable justices to the speech he composed for Counterfeit Countenance in "Magnyfycence." Skelton's antihero presided over "counterfeit matters in the law of the land" and he was richly rewarded for his improbity.

> *With gold and groats they grease my hand,*
> *Instead of right that wrong may stand.*[9]

Richard Pace gave a slight twist to the common complaints of bribery and greed when he charged lawyers with manufacturing disagreements to create business and with conspiring in the proliferation of abstruse interpretations of simple legislation and familiar custom to prove their own

---

[5]*YB* Michaelmas, 13 Henry VII, pl. 2, pp. 2-3 (Dunstable); PRO, *KB* 27:940, m. 1(v) (Newnham); *KB* 27:1009, m. 28 (Bordesley); *KB* 27:1012, m. 39 (St. Mary's, Bridgestreet); *YB* Trinity, 13 Henry VII, pl. 6, pp. 27-28 and Michaelmas, 16 Henry VII, pl. 2, pp. 1-2 (Hyde); and Ives, *Common Lawyers*, 131 (Peterborough).

[6]Blatcher, *King's Bench*, 97, 101-103, 167-71; Ives, *Common Lawyers*, 194-207; and *The Reports of Sir John Spelman*, ed. J. H. Baker, 2 vols. (London: Selden Society, 1978) 2:90-91.

[7]Gascoigne, *Loci*, 128: "Utinam essent plures malefactores quam sunt, quia tunc nos legistae habemus magnum lucrum."

[8]Barclay, *Fools*, 12.

[9]Skelton, *Poems*, "Magnyfycence," ll. 431-33.

erudition.[10] Faultfinders were under no illusion that the insults they hurled would bring down bribery or redeem purportedly contemptible characters. As critics, they may have accepted their duty to discover the unvarnished truth, but then, as literati and entertainers, they gilded it.

Thomas More's earliest satire is a fine example. His "Mery Jest" makes a buffoon of an earnest-but-vain sergeant-at-law who disguises himself as a friar to catch his prey, an improvident merchant. The masquerade ended with a comic brawl, during which both actors were thrashed, but the "freered" sergeant was the more bruised by the satire of the young barrister, who could not resist taking his literary pleasure at some expense to his professional colleagues.[11]

Turning from slapstick, More struck again at lawyers in the pages of his *Utopia*. In the first book Cardinal Morton silenced a dinner guest, "learned in law,"[12] and More hushed the whole profession in the second. There, as most know, More's protagonist, Raphael Hythloday, gives a detailed account of civilization on the island of Utopia, which had institutionalized values quite different from those of late-medieval England.[13] He found no lawyers there, for the worthy inhabitants wished neither to exacerbate nor to perpetuate the few controversies that surfaced. Utopians had learned from other cultures that massive volumes of laws studied by hives of lawyers made society ungovernable. It was better to have few laws and no lawyers. Hythloday explained that Utopian jurispru-

---

[10]Pace, *De fructa qui ex doctrina percipitur*, ed. Frank Manley and Richard S. Sylvester (New York: Renaissance Society of America, 1967) 63, 83, 105. Erasmus anticipated Pace, though he had scant knowledge of English secular courts and was applying the same measure to canon lawyers who interminably added glosses to glosses ("glossematis glossemata, opiniones opinionibus cumulantes") to complicate the law, to bewilder the uninitiated, and oftentimes to obstruct justice. See his *Moriae Encomium*, in *Opera Erasmi* 4:3:142-44.

[11]*EWTM* 1:327-32. Also see Mary Edith Willow, *An Analysis of the English Poems of St. Thomas More* (Nieuwkoop: De Graff, 1974) 21-72; and Alastair Fox, *Thomas More: History and Providence* (New Haven: Yale University Press, 1982) 23-27. For "the estate and degree of the sergeant-at-law," consult John Fortescue, *De laudibus legum Anglie*, ed. S. B. Chrimes (Cambridge: Cambridge University Press, 1942) 120-26; and Margaret Hastings, *The Court of Common Pleas in Fifteenth-Century England* (Ithaca: Cornell University Press, 1947) 72-74.

[12]*CWTM* 4:70-71.

[13]It is hazardous to identify Hythloday's enthusiasms for things Utopian with More's own interests in 1516. But, for now, we shall assume that *Utopia*'s second book may nonetheless be mined for the idealists' prepossessions. For justification of this, see chs. 5 and 6.

dence was unambiguous and, without interference from sly and crafty professionals, he had every expectation that it would remain so.[14]

John Colet was most distressed by the church's apparent dependence on lawyers and its fondness for litigation. He responded with a comprehensive condemnation of the world's courts. Humanity's first sin, he argued, left an indelible mark on all society's laws, which consequently were "foul and filthy." Jurisprudence, as a science, merely coordinated fallible opinions about the character of the society's altercations and commended absurdly complex solutions to simple moral problems.[15] Colet urged that, if laymen cheat their church and withhold rents and promised services, the best and sinless strategy is to make the church so pure that such swindlers would find their dishonesty unbearably disconcerting. He assured colleagues that by despising the things of this world, by seeking only charity and righteousness, they would receive material support in unprecedented abundance from grateful laymen. In other words, what might be gained from court-awarded reparations could not compensate for what was lost in reputation.[16] But practical consequences of the church's involvement in or avoidance of litigation were of secondary importance. Colet's was a theological rejection of the world's laws and lawyers, and his argument was antinomy in the very strictest sense. He maintained that canon law enshrined "the law of faith and charity"; indeed, it is fair to say that he bragged that pontifical decrees and canonical statutes, uncontaminated by the world's courts, generated the only standards by which the Christian life could be measured and the church and clergy reformed.[17]

As a party to certain property actions and civil suits, the church was virtually obliged to enter common-law courts and hire lawyers. In special circumstances, cases reached the equity courts of the king's council and dragged ecclesiastical litigants with them. But criminal prosecution was another matter. The clergy had long enjoyed certain immunities. Until the fifteenth century they could refuse to answer charges. Pleading their

---

[14]*CWTM* 4:194-95; but also note Erasmus's *Institutio principis Christiani*, in *Opera Erasmi* 4:1:194-204. Similarities are not startling, for Erasmus had ample opportunities to discuss the issue with More in the year preceding the publications of *Utopia* and the *Institutio*. For a plausible account of their "Collaboration," see J. H. Hexter, *More's* Utopia (Princeton: Princeton University Press, 1952) 99-102; and also note *CWTM* 4:489-90.

[15]*EER-a*, 261-63; *EEC*, 189-90; and *PSD*, 220.

[16]*EER-b*, 219-20: "Nec Deus noster istis munusculis delectatur, nec hujusmodi rebus, quae a mundo habentur in pretio, ecclesia Dei constat, sed maxime in hiis despiciendis elucet. Sed virtus, fides, charitas, justitia est, quae grata est oblatio in conspectu Dei. Quae si ante omnia in tua plebe quaeritas, illa alia etiam te non quaerente et largius quam petas sequentur."

[17]*EER-a*, 226; *EEC*, 254; and *Conv.*, 299-300.

"clergy," they were thereupon remanded to the custody of their bishops. During the later Middle Ages, however, such pleas were increasingly postponed until the inquest's end, and even then the privilege was apparently a last resort, reserved until other means of defeating the action had been exhausted.[18] The immunity, whenever invoked, was the principal form of protection from "foul and filthy" laws that Colet condemned. England, it was supposed, could be shielded from foul and filthy clerics by the detention of criminous clergy in bishops' prisons and by strict regulation of canonical purgation, the process by which oath-swearers could testify to culprits' good character and plausible innocence and thus obtain their release. Precautions were taken: thirteen "witnesses" were required in Ely to clear John Sewell of manslaughter in 1492, and the purgation was announced one week in advance to allow others who possessed damaging information to come forward and present a contrary case.[19] John Colet must have thought the safeguards sufficient and perjury rare, for he gave unqualified support to colleagues pressing for the preservation of the immunities.[20] Thomas More printed a more equivocal endorsement in the second book of his *Utopia*.

> To no other office in Utopia is more honor given, so much so that, even if [priests] have committed any crime, they are subjected to no tribunal but left only to God and to themselves. [Citizens] judge it wrong to lay human hands upon one, however guilty [*"quantumvis scelestum"*], who has been consecrated to God in a singular manner as a holy offering. It is easier for them to observe this custom because their priests are very few and very carefully chosen.[21]

"Easier" suggests a halfhearted confirmation of English practice. In an imperfect world scoundrels passed as priests, and More certainly seems reluctant to extend immunities to those other than an elite, consecrated *"singulari modo."* Like Colet, however, he apparently thought the immunities worth retaining. Earliest Tudor officials had no wish to eliminate them altogether and thereby to enrage immunists. To have challenged the privilege would have gained the government no notable advantage and would have left the king's courts with a fresh flock of felons to dispatch. Still, parliament claimed in 1488 that immunities had been too promiscuously distributed. Literacy had come to be taken as a token of one's intentions to serve the church, so a successful encounter with a passage from the psalms resulted in one's transfer into a bishop's custody. All this was ended by statute, and measures were passed to make it difficult for recidivists in inferior orders, *in minoribus*, to enjoy the im-

---

[18]Gabel, *Benefit of Clergy*, 31-47; but also Blatcher, *King's Bench*, 57.

[19]*Reg. Alcock*, 79-80.

[20]*Conv.*, 303.

[21]*CWTM* 4:229 (Surtz translation).

munities a second time. Yet Henry VII, his council, his courts, and his parliaments never interfered with canonical purgation and, on only one other occasion, restricted the privilege by striking petty treason from the list of "clergyable" crimes. Nothing here seems particularly infelicitous or offensive. Colet's protest and More's reflections were presumably prompted by the provisional parliamentary legislation of 1512, three years after Henry VII's death, that limited the privilege to clerics in holy orders, but the experiment was abandoned two years later. I suspect that More approved of the initial change, but that Colet approved of its repeal.[22]

It is more difficult to gauge, or even to guess, the idealists' attitudes toward ecclesiastical courts. Since both Colet and More maintained that litigation was inimical to virtue, it is mildly surprising that so little was said of the church's apparatus. Procedures themselves were no secret. Bishops or their officers regularly convened hearings on matters ranging from nonpayment of tithes and petty debts to defamation of character and heresy. Medieval critics were frequently scornful of ecclesiastical tribunals but particularly of their field investigators, the summoners who acquired a reputation for greed and extortion in ecclesiastical proceedings similar to that acquired by lawyers in the secular courts. At first, summoners only summoned defendants to answer for slander, tithes, fraud, and sorcery, yet in some dioceses their responsibilities gradually increased. To the extent that they became the commissary courts' detectives, they could easily part laymen from their purses by threatening to disclose misdemeanors or to fabricate charges. Whether or not such opprobrious behavior was commonplace, and even when they merely delivered their subpoenas, summoners appeared at just the point where clerical pressure was applied, so it is quite understandable that they were much maligned. Hinting at something only slightly less than a reign of terror, one ballad declaimed that they "polketh in pyne" every parish.[23]

Chaucer's *Canterbury Tales* arguably came closest to heresy when it intimated that court decisions, be they purchased absolutions or pious excommunications, were equally trifling, but most memorable is the stifling,

---

[22]"Colet's protest" refers to his "Convocation sermon" (*Conv.*). The Oxford lectures with their vituperation of secular law were composed nearly two decades earlier. See, e.g., H. C. Porter, "The Gloomy Dean and the Law: John Colet, 1466-1519," in *Essays in Modern English Church History in Memory of Norman Sykes*, ed. G. V. Bennett and J. D. Walsh (New York: Oxford University Press, 1966) 18-43. Also consult C. B. Firth, "Benefit of Clergy in the Time of Edward IV," *EHR* 32 (1917): 175-91; Gabriel le Bras, "Le privilège de clergé en France dans les derniers siècles du Moyen Age," *Journal des savants*, n.s. 20 (1922): 163-70; Gabel, *Benefit of Clergy*, 87, 122-24; and Schoeck, "Canon Law and Common Law," 25-26. For the 1512 legislation, *SR* 4 Henry VIII, c.2; and for restrictions enacted by Henry VII's parliaments, *SR* 4 Henry VII, c.13; 7 Henry VII, c.1; and 12 Henry VII, c.7.

[23]"A Satyre on the Consistory Courts," in *The Political Songs of England*, ed. Thomas Wright (London: Camden Society, 1839) 156-57.

sulfurous odor of the leprous summoner that spreads over the pro-
logue.[24] But there is nothing of this in Colet and More. The church's courts
and their summoners found no place in the worlds that they abstracted
from reality, yet early Tudor critics appear to have recognized that those
courts provided "legal space" for the reform of lay and clerical discipline,
space that the church's immunities screened from the corruption that
plagued secular courts.[25]

The idealists, then, were prepared to make some concessions when
confronted with certain palpable problems of administration. But there is
something quixotic, even about the concession, and especially about
Colet's sense that discipline and budgets could be maintained without
strife and secular interference. When litigants were apt and able to throw
considerable political weight behind their briefs, cases were bound to spill
from clerical courts into the king's council. The battle between the archbishops of Canterbury and their suffragans for the rights to probate certain wills and thus to collect fees from the realm's wealthier testators is
an excellent example. Ecclesiastical commissions and courts could not
contain, much less compose, the disagreements. Each party waited for
the other to founder, and the quarrel so intensified that ancillary appointments and promotions were transformed into battlegrounds. The problem passed to the pope and from him to the king, whose intervention,
though unpopular, finally proved decisive.[26]

In another, quite different affair, royal initiative was divisive. When
Henry VII announced his intentions to have his Lancastrian predecessor
canonized, a bitter dispute flared between Windsor, which possessed
Henry VI's sepulchre and Westminster, which wanted it. Conciliar courts
ordinarily took cognizance of cases brought for or against interests whose
power was thought likely to prejudice the outcome in courts of common
law, and perhaps the same principle applied to ecclesiastical titans and
their courts. Be that as it may, the dean of Windsor and the abbot of Westminster carried the battle for Henry's bones to the king's council, which
thought the problem sufficiently grave and ambiguous to require written
arguments. Westminster industriously collected depositions that told of
the former king's desire to be buried there, while Windsor, to prevent the

---

[24]*Canterbury Tales*, ed. A. C. Cawley (London: J. M. Dent & Sons, 1958) pro-
logue, ll. 623-28 (pp. 19-20). Also note *Piers Plowman: An Edition of the C-Text*, ed.
Derek Pearsall (London: York Medieval Texts, 1978) passus 3, line 170 (p. 72).

[25]Late in his career More vigorously defended the integrity of ecclesiastical
courts, chiefly the proceedings against heretics but also the reliability of ecclesiastical justices—e.g., *The Debellacyon of Salem and Bizance* (London: W. Rastell, 1533)
pt. 1, c.14, f. 94(r).

[26]*Concilia* 3:653-57; *Literae Cantuariensis*, ed. J. Brigstroke Sheppard, vol. 3
(London: Eyre & Spottiswoode, 1889) 416-40; and Kelly, *Canterbury Jurisdiction*,
42-94. Also note *EER-a*, 243.

abduction, spent liberally *"pro prandio," "pro dietis," "pro materia testificanda,"* subsidizing its own witnesses.[27] The feud featured just those elements of late-medieval religion that repelled the Tudor idealists who were intransigently opposed to superstition and to the profiteering that it inspired. Had Henry VII been successful, the place that acquired the rights to Henry VI's remains would have become a prosperous pilgrimage site to rival Canterbury. But what most horrified critics, one suspects, was the spectacle of such internecine conflicts in other than Christian courts.

Was referral to conciliar courts a descent into the hell to which Colet, for one, consigned society's laws? Most panels adjudicating issues in the star chamber were likely to number prominent clerics among the judges. Nearly one-third of Henry VII's councillors were churchmen. Bishops Leybourne (Carlisle) and Sherbourne (St. David's) regularly sat with other justices between 1500 and 1509 on the king's "council learned in the law." Other conciliar courts were like committees of the council, convened, subdivided, and adjourned as the flow of business dictated. They worked without the tangle of writs, precedents, and local juries that retarded resolutions of cases in common law. It would seem that judgments were formulated much as they were in Utopia, that is, according to the most obvious interpretation of law and after a painstaking pursuit of the facts. When, as in the case against the abbot of Malmesbury, who was accused of suppressing documents, evidence was not immediately accessible, councillors relied upon other churchmen *in remotis* to gather depositions and inspect charters.[28] The expanse of early Tudor equity or prerogative jurisdiction—that is, the increased activity of conciliar courts—gave churchmen greater opportunities, as suitors and as court officials, to obtain and render prompt, impartial judgment and arbitration. Of course, tradition and pressures of property management forced them into other chambers as well. Contests over patrons' rights to present candidates to vacant livings, for instance, were customarily settled in courts of common law. When challenged, cathedral chapters or convents to which livings had been appropriated had no choice but to answer, even when the challenger was an influential member of the royal family.[29] Moreover, it should not be forgotten that in certain liberties and lordships, abbots or bishops were responsible for the maintenance of order and hence for the selection of justices of the peace, justices of oyer and terminer, and some-

[27]The documents have been collected in *Henrici VI, Angliae Regis miracula postuma,* ed. Paul Grosjean (Brussels: Société des Bollandistes, 1935) 179-200.

[28]*SC* Leadam, 1:118-29. For conciliar courts, *SC* Bayne, lx-lxxxii; R. Somerville, "Henry VII's 'Council Learned in the Law,' " *EHR* 54 (1939): 427-42; *Select Cases in the Court of Requests,* ed. I. S. Leadam (London: Selden Society, 1898) xxi-xxvii, cii-cix; esp. G. R. Elton, "Why the History of the Early Tudor Council Remains Unwritten," *Studies* 1:308-38.

[29]*YB* Paschal, 16 Henry VII, pl. 11, pp. 7-8.

times justices of jail delivery.[30] In the face of the church's multiform involvement in the courts, of which all this has been but a sketch, Colet's unequivocal differentiation between society's laws and ecclesiastical justice was extremist, neither illuminating now nor apposite then.

Colet insisted that it was patently unspiritual to engage in litigation. Thomas More dreamed of a world from which ambition and faction had been all but purged. More's earthbound prelates who troubled the courts with their wrangling may often have been a disgrace and embarrassment, but others who expedited the administration of early Tudor justice were not. Idealistic critics were aware of the distinction, befriended many of the latter, and countenanced *a silentio* the proceedings in ecclesiastical courts.[31] But when they imagined uncompromising, incontrovertible "laws" of faith and charity or lawyerless commonwealths, they rocketed beyond the realities of late-medieval political culture and their criticisms must be read accordingly.

---

[30]E.g., *Reg. Alcock*, 7, 57; and W. T. Mellows, *The Last Days of Peterborough Monastery* (Kettering: Northamptonshire Record Society, 1947) liii-liv.

[31]See, e.g., G. D. Squibb, *Doctors' Commons* (Oxford: Clarendon Press, 1977) 5-7, 19-20, 57-58.

Chapter 5

CRITICS AND
CLERICAL MISCONDUCT

In 1497 Henry Medwall staged his *Fulgens and Lucres* to entertain the guests of John Morton, archbishop of Canterbury and lord chancellor of the realm. *Fulgens* dramatized a principle that had become somewhat axiomatic during the Renaissance, "virtue humbles fate."

Medwall's protagonist, Gaius Flaminius, competed with Cornelius, a rather stuffy patrician, to win the love of Lucres. Cornelius dragged a kennel of ancestors into the contest, inasmuch as Lucres was determined to marry the more noble of the two rivals. And the nobleman's pedigree was impressive!

> *Amonge all thistoryes of Romaynes that ye rede*
> *Where fynde ye ony blode of so gret noblenes*
> *As hath ben the Cornelys whereof I am brede?*
> *And if so be that I wolde therein hold my pease*
> *Yet all your cornecles beryth gode witness*
> *That my progenytours and ancetours have be*
> *The chef ayde and diffence of this noble cyte.*[1]

Onlookers had been dazzled: "He that hathe most nobles in store / Hym call I the most noble ever more." They calculated that Cornelius had inherited enough money "to bye a rable of suche as Gaius is."[2] Lucres, however, was not about to purchase a fancy label.

Flaminius, for his part, summarized his rival's case with a contemptuous couplet implying that one was foolish to deduce from a family's "noble gests" the sterling character of the heir to its bequests. He followed this with a recital of his own virtues, which of course convinced Lucres.

> *I have been borne unto God all my daies*
> *His laude and prayse with my due devocion*
> *And next that I berre allwayes*

---

[1] *Fulgens and Lucres,* in *The Plays of Henry Medwall,* ed. Alan H. Nelson (Cambridge: D. S. Brewer, 1980) pt. 2, ll. 458-64.

[2] Ibid., pt. 1, ll. 1376-85.

To all my neyghbours charitable affeccyon.
Incontynency and onclennes I have had in abhominacion,
Lovyng to my frende and faythfull with all,
And ever I have withstonde my lustis sensuall.[3]

Nobility, then, might be defined by personal piety, industry, and un-impeachable conduct. Breeding, however, usually induced arrogance and indolence. This was precisely what Henry VII's "new" administrators, men of common origins, wished to hear. One of their more formidable challenges was to guarantee the tractability and cooperation of the old aristocracy, whose squabbles had perpetuated previous dynastic disputes and the recent civil war.[4] Variations of the theme were welcome in other circles as well. The triumph of character over class was but one indication of virtue's power to surmount obstacles that privilege and position might raise against institutional reform. Idealistic critics were especially suscep-tible to such optimism.

Before noting the idealists' hopes and impatience, perhaps I should turn to the official attempts to detect and to deter clerical "onclennes." "For the more sure and likely reformacion of preestis, clerkys, and reli-gious men," Henry VII's first parliament encouraged bishops and their deputies to imprison prelates whose misconduct seemed otherwise ir-repressible. Officials were told that they need fear no reprisals. Should they choose to battle incontinence with confinement, the king's courts would back them.[5] Archbishop Morton quickly got word to his suffra-gans that unlawful behavior and outrageous apparel were to be prohib-ited, and other authorities continued to issue reform statutes and to formulate codes for dress and decorum. There is really nothing, how-ever, that sets early Tudor regulations apart from those that mark the his-tory of the medieval church.[6] Possibly momentum was lost soon after the

---

[3]Ibid., pt. 2, ll. 672-78.

[4]For the political context, J. R. Lander, "Attainder and Forfeiture, 1453-1509," *HJ* 4 (1961): 119-51; but for important qualifications, M. M. Condon, "Ruling Elites in the Reign of Henry VII," in *Patronage, Pedigree, and Power in Later Medieval England,* ed. Charles Ross (Gloucester: A. Sutton, 1979) 109-42. Also see David Bevington, *Tudor Drama and Politics* (Cambridge: Harvard University Press, 1968) 45-46; F. P. Wilson, *The English Drama, 1485-1585* (London: Oxford University Press, 1969) 1-11; and for Henry's "new" men, Bacon, *History,* 242-44.

[5]*SR* 1 Henry VII, c.2.

[6]For Morton's appeal, *Concilia* 3:619-20: ". . . sic sint [sacerdotes] dissoluti, et adeo insolescant, quod inter eos et alios laicos et seculares viros nulla vel modica comae, vel habituum, sive vestimentorum distinctio esse videatur; quo fiet in brevi, ut a multis verisimiliter formidatur, quod sicut populus ita et sacerdos erit, et nisi celeriori remedio tantae lasciviae ecclesiasticarum personarum quantocius obvie-mus, et clericorum mores corruptos hujusmodi digna acrimonia maturius com-pescamus." Also note Thompson, *Newarke,* 121-35; and *Reg. Mayew,* 106-109.

first parliament adjourned. Maybe Morton and others gradually realized the magnitude of the problem, abjectly resigned themselves to the impossibility of perfecting discipline and obedience, and perfunctorily publicized restrictions, as had their predecessors, to minimize ineradicable abuses. Is it unreasonable to suggest that Morton had given up hope by the time he "met" Flaminius?

Ah, but this is truly a dark view of reform legislation. With equal plausibility one could argue that the statutes demonstrate a sustained interest in clerical discipline and, if visitation records are factored, an earnest effort to police and improve clerical behavior. Yearly, the archdeacons were to call and inquire about each parish's maintenance and fiscal well-being. Every third year, bishops or their agents were to visit parishes and convents to hunt for a variety of improprieties. Visitations have been construed as meager and crudely mercenary gestures, as excuses to extort fines and procurations. The charges are often spiced with hyperbole, presumably dictated by disenchantment, about which more must be said. But surviving evidence indicates that our cynicism would be dispelled had examiners been scrupulous diarists. For example, a compendious list of "fawtes to be presented when the Bysshop visiteth" in London instructed officials to check whether vicars "intend to rybawdes or mynstrelles," play at dice, frequent taverns, and "exercize hawkynges or huntinges" as well as to note whether they keep their churches in repair and themselves in residence.[7] Such protocols were thorough, and the findings or *detecta* often come as a disappointment to persons who assume the scandals retailed in early Protestant polemic were but amplifications of clerical shortcomings with which nearly every parish was well acquainted.

John Vaughan inspected numerous certificates of ordination and collected lay depositions for more than forty parishes when he visited the rural deanery of Bosmere and Cleydon for Archbishop Morton in 1499. Most informants reported that all was in order. Several priests were accused of nonresidence, but only one was branded grossly incompetent and apparently incontinent.[8] That same year, during the *sede vacante* visitation of the Norwich diocese, Morton's examiners heard close to one hundred reports of sexual offenses, but most offenders were laymen. Very few complaints about the morality of the parochial clergy were lodged.[9] This does not necessarily reflect widespread clerical continence, and the few disclosures and penances do not represent great gains. Yet it must be

---

[7]*The Accounts of the Churchwardens of the Parish of St. Michael, Cornhill*, ed. William Henry Overall (London, 1871) 208-11.

[8]*Reg. Morton*, ff. 106-108.

[9]Christopher Harper-Bill, "A Late Medieval Visitation—The Diocese of Norwich in 1499," *Proceedings of the Suffolk Institute of Archaeology and History* 34 (1977): 34-47.

admitted that ecclesiastical administrators were obliged regularly to face some of their failures and that the experience doubtlessly imparted a valuable lesson, denied to those critics who were concerned with, yet somewhat detached from, the shabbier aspects of church life. Reform was not most profitably understood as a question of feast or famine.

It was certainly not "feast," and some suspected that ecclesiastical administrators were to blame. The *Sermo de informatione episcoporum*, then ascribed to St. Ambrose, circulated through the network of clerical critics.[10] It starts by declaring bishops the senior and "most sublime" partners in the world's noblest enterprise, but the treatise quickly adds that the more sublime the office, the greater the misfortune and the scandal of venality.[11] He is but a bogus bishop who has not lived up to the standards set by St. Paul and other apostles. Moreover, unless bishops preside over their own passions, they can hardly be expected to correct others and to meet their managerial obligations. The pseudo-Ambrose advanced from these concerns to a blistering attack on simony, which he and presumably his early Tudor admirers acknowledged as the mainspring of church business; and then he concluded with a warning that the appointment, consecration, and toleration of bogus bishops virtually license parish priests and laymen to favor their own "forbidden desires" (*"voluptates illiciti"*). The church thereby becomes little more than a cesspool of incontinence and crime.[12]

This was common fare or, to be more precise, a common approach to the challenge of improving clerical discipline. The medieval church's ministry was contrasted with a uniformly perfect primitive church. The latter set the standards that critics rehearsed in order to shame their clerical colleagues. The point was to censure "the covetize of men of holychurche" and to inspire prelates to behave more nobly.[13] Some criticisms of clerical misconduct also doubled as declarations of the critics' personal piety and superior righteousness. Lollards frequently staged their protests—and perhaps their defiant abjurations as well—not only to pillory their priests but also to underscore their own virtue. Others passed sentence to entertain. John Skelton, for example, histrionically likened a priest's hawking in church to ancient tyrants' most ruthless atrocities.[14]

---

[10]E.g., see Trapp, "Notes on Manuscripts," 95.

[11]*PL* 139:170-72.

[12]Ibid., 175-76.

[13]See, e.g., John Mirkus, *Instructions for Parish Priests*, ed. Edward Peacock (London: Early English Text Society, 1902); and Melton, *Sermo*, which concludes with the same Pauline passage over which the pseudo-Ambrose draped his prescriptions. For "the covetize of men . . . ," *Middle English Sermons*, ed. Woodburn O. Ross (Oxford: Early English Text Society, 1940) 311; and *Conv.*, 295-96.

[14]Skelton, *Poems*, "Ware the Hauke," ll. 190-221.

Mockery and burlesque would be manipulated by the most adroit critics, who could gore the church with the shards of its own shattered discipline in a way that amused rather than pained their clerical friends. Criticism was polymorphous, yet critics generally agreed that "worldly affecyon" had all but prohibited the restoration of that unassuming piety that purportedly distinguished apostolic models for ministry.[15]

What separates idealistic criticism from other types are the dreams of a far better world that lay behind many of the idealists' ironies and overstatements. This is not to suggest that every critical comment uttered by Colet, Erasmus, or More was laden with special, secret importance. They often wrote as occasion or frustration prompted. In his *Epigrams* More let it be known that he had brushed up against ecclesiastical officials, proprietors of vast estates, and employers of innumerable attendants, yet he found them startlingly closefisted and simpleminded.[16] Erasmus harbored some contempt for the *"episcoporum vulgus,"* and even in his glowing tribute to Archbishop Warham, he included a few oily remarks about political chores that squandered his patron's intelligence.[17] John Colet also enjoyed Warham's confidence and support, yet he was understood to have had reservations about Warham's motives and to have inferred that, *"in causis peccati correctionum,"* his metropolitan was more jealous of his suffragans' authority than zealous for reform.[18] For all this, however, the idealists' remarks commonly overreached the circumstances surrounding one class of clerical misconduct. Had they been given to making promises, they would have pledged not only to restrict incontinence and tame extravagance, but also to reform the world of compromises from which clerical indiscretion derived.

John Colet's more visionary remedies have already been discussed. His convocation sermon advocated only tougher enforcement of existing laws and sanctions, but his *De sacramentis* conjured up a radically reordered Christian community that did not readily translate into statutes and pro-

---

[15]E.g., Medwall's *Nature*, in *Plays*, pt. 1, ll. 1272-91; and *Stephen Hawes, The Minor Poems*, ed. Florence W. Gluck and Alice B. Morgan (London: Oxford University Press, 1974) 80-84 ("The Covercyon of Swerers," ll. 227-336). Toward the end of the period under consideration, Christopher Urswick was convinced that critics were everywhere, BL. Add. MSS.15.673, f.113(v): "Qui sane, quod dolendum est, ubique sunt plurimi." Thirty years earlier the same sentiment was voiced by a highly placed preacher, who urged colleagues to reproach and discipline subordinates circumspectly, for there were many ill-disposed persons, "goats among the sheep" ("cornuti haedi admixti cum ovibus"), avidly collecting evidence of clerical misbehavior. *Oratiuncula*, 75-76.

[16]*Epigrams*, 159, 195-96.

[17]*Ecclesiastae sive de ratione concionandi* (Basel, 1535) bk. 1, 54-56; and *[Adnotationes] in Epistolam Petri I*, in *LB* 6:1055. Cf. Allen *OE* 1:420, ll. 71-86.

[18]*Concilia* 3:655.

hibitions.[19] Perhaps for this reason, hardly a glimmer of Colet's idealism flickers from the accounts of recent admirers. His close friends, I suspect, knew him better. It was left to them, to Erasmus and young Thomas More, to give idealistic criticisms livelier and more enduring expressions.

Erasmus came to England for the first time in 1499. Colet swiftly grew fond of him and the two took undiminished pleasure in each other's company and in the correspondence that passed between them through the next two decades. Colet's Oxford lectures probably inspired Erasmus to try his own hand at biblical commentary, but miscellaneous tasks and travel made serious study so difficult that he abandoned his initial attempt. In 1501, however, his reflections on the Pauline epistles found their way into an impromptu essay (*"extemporalis scriptiuncula"*) on the Christian life, the *Enchiridion militis Christiani*.[20]

The *Enchiridion*'s orientation bears a remarkable resemblance to that of Flaminius's "creed." Whereas Medwall's paladin of the "new" nobility made "nobility" accessible to persons nominated, so to speak, by their virtue, Erasmus insisted that holiness was within the layman's reach. Flaminius challenged the assumption that nobility was a matter of bloodline, a possession of a few families lifted by their ancestors' good fortune above the commonfolk. Erasmus argued that perfect piety need not incubate within cloisters and sealed off from commonplace events. The *Enchiridion* equates virtue with piety. Christians need only bridle their disreputable desires as had Flaminius ("Incontynency and onclennes I have had in abhominacion"). Moral choices thereafter were transformed into *occasiones pietatis*, through which every "Christian soldier," monarch or peasant, might alter and redeem the human condition. In Erasmus's scheme, personal integrity was accompanied by a readiness to acknowledge religion as something of an "open system," that is, as instruction that incorporates the wisdom of classical antiquity and that directly relates doctrine to life. Alfons Auer judged all this a memorable token of Erasmus's "sober realism." To me, however, it seems a thoroughgoing optimism.[21]

England made Erasmus optimistic. He had been nearly as enthusiastic about the Augustinian monastery at Steyn when he entered, but he tired of apologizing for his studies.[22] He craved friendships seasoned with

---

[19]Cf. *Conv.*, 299-302, and ch. 3.

[20]See my "John Colet and Erasmus' *Enchiridion*," *Church History* 46 (1977): 296-312.

[21]Cf. Alfons Auer, *Die vollkommene Frömmigkeit des Christen nach dem* Enchiridion militis Christiani *des Erasmus von Rotterdam* (Düsseldorf: Patmos-Verlag, 1954) 183-84.

[22]See Erasmus's *Liber apologeticus*, in *Opera Erasmi* 1:1:72, l. 21-74, l. 16; and 1:1:84, l. 32-85, l. 1. Also note Allen, *OE* 1:129-30.

learned conversations, yet his Dutch acquaintances and correspondents were somewhat disappointing. William Herman was irresolute; Cornelius Gerard was skeptical about Lorenzo Valla, whom Erasmus idolized; Servatius Rogers evinced little sympathy. When Rogers, as prior, urged him to return to Steyn, Erasmus respectfully explained that his pet projects were likelier to prosper in England and among his new admirers and friends.[23] By 1505 Erasmus was back in London, entertained by Colet, More, Thomas Linacre, and William Grocyn. What he craved at Steyn, he found across the Channel.

Nonetheless, Erasmus was quick to depart again in 1506, when an opportunity to travel in Italy presented itself. Early in their careers, most of his English companions had been to Italy, a Mecca for Northern European belletrists; but Erasmus, at forty, had not. Before leaving he wrote to Colet of his regrets, yet he averred that it was simply impossible to forfeit the chance he had been waiting for ever since he escaped Steyn. He promised to return and, while away, to hunt for rare editions and to send them to his English friends.[24]

Erasmus's return was probably hastened by Piedmont and Tuscan warfare that greatly inconvenienced his travels and considerably diminished his enjoyment of the Italian adventure. He sadly informed Rogers that learning languished while everyone was wholly devoted to combat (*"verum hic jam frigent studia, fervent bella"*).[25] He only later revealed that he thought the pope's involvement in the turmoil unforgivable. Erasmus fled Italy in 1509 and rejoined his English friends. He stayed in London, first with Thomas More and then for an extended time with Grocyn, until John Fisher lured him to Cambridge to teach Greek.[26] Though he often grumbled about his decision, about the weather, and about the wine, Erasmus remained there for two and a half years.[27] The plague claimed his physician in October 1513, and by January's end he returned to London. This time, however, his friends were otherwise preoccupied, so within several months he again left for the Continent.

Notwithstanding his displeasure with the climate and cuisine, and his sense that he maintained a pathetically precarious existence in Cambridge, Erasmus remained rhapsodic about England. When John Reuch-

---

[23]Allen, *OE* 1:414-15. Also see Yvonne Charlier, *Érasme et l'amitié* (Paris: Société d'Edition "Les Belles Lettres," 1977) 65-94.

[24]Allen, *OE* 1:428, 439.

[25]Ibid., 433 ("quo maturius revolare studebimus").

[26]Ibid., 473.

[27]Ibid., 482 (to Andrea Ammonio), ll. 8-12: "Plane cum hoc hominum genere nobis hic res est, mi Andrei, qui cum summa rusticitate summam malitiam conjunxere; nec est omnino quicquam quod mihi hujus secessus nomine gratuleris, verum solus pudor querimoniis finem imponit: sed haec coram in sinu."

lin prepared to send his nephew abroad for study, Erasmus counseled that "England contains Italy," that England's splendor "exceeds that of Italy."[28] Erasmus, of course, is notorious for hyperbole. Nonetheless, it is plain here that genuine admiration for English scholars and disenchantment with Italy prejudiced his advice as it prejudiced much of what he wrote from 1501 to 1514. This is especially true of his writing about piety and clerical impropriety.

Learning most impressed Erasmus's English friends when it was brought to bear on religious renewal. This helps to explain why the distinction between the alleged secularism of Italian humanisms (*"rein innerweltliche Humanitas"*) and the Christianity of Northern European humanisms, though tremendously exaggerated, has been so popular among scholars. It also helps to explain Erasmus's inclinations after 1500. The *Enchiridion* eschews scholastic controversy. "I want rather to instruct you *ad bonam mentem*," Erasmus announced and referred thereby to psychological attitudes similar to those of Gaius Flaminius.[29] Every person could approach *ad bonam mentem*. Proper instruction could lead virtually anyone to perfect piety. If only they were not addicted to the pursuit of wealth and worldly honor, Christians could be taught to weigh the fine-grained satisfactions of an untroubled conscience against momentary pleasures. Discerning companions should assist. Classical literature on moral philosophy was a mine of encouragement. The counsels and "laws" of St. Paul were trustworthy guides. If all else should fail, recollection of Christ's life and sacrifices should incite the regeneration of the most reprobate character. The *Enchiridion* was composed as a compendium of strategies, which were packaged, according to Erasmus, more conveniently than the ethical principles in the *secunda secundae* of Thomas Aquinas's *Summa*.[30]

What was missing from all this—and apparently expendable—was the teaching authority of the church. True, direct criticism of the church was also rare. The *Enchiridion* only once scolds monks and prelates for preferring wealth to virtue.[31] Thereafter, however, criticism came in a steadier

---

[28]Ibid., 2:331, ll. 58-59: "Fortassis ille sitit Italiam. At his temporibus Italiam habet Anglia et, ni plane fallor, quiddam Italia praestantius."

[29]*Ench.*, 72, ll. 9-10. Also note Michael Seidlmayer's "Wandlungen des humanistischen Lebensgefühls und Lebensstils," in *Wege und Wandlungen des Humanismus*, ed. Hans Barion (Göttingen: Vandenhoeck & Ruprecht, 1965) 118.

[30]*Ench.*, 4, ll. 5-15; 52, ll. 10-11; 78, ll. 13-14; 113, ll. 8-12; 122, l. 10-123, l. 11; and 128, ll. 14-27. The *Enchiridion* was a work of exhortation and not of analysis, but I have argued elsewhere that Erasmus's "program" for the reform of Christian life was not recycled pelagianism. See *Augustinian Piety and Catholic Reform*, 121-33; but also review Ernst-Wilhelm Kohls, *Die Theologie des Erasmus*, 2 vols. (Basel: Friedrich Reinhardt Verlag, 1966) 1:91-93.

[31]*Ench.*, 92, ll. 31-36.

stream, as if Erasmus were trying to uphold the *Enchiridion*'s line of argument and to brace its equation of piety and spirituality against the clerical excesses that he had witnessed in Italy.

Few letters survive from the period that immediately followed Erasmus's return to London in 1509. Perhaps, as J. K. Sowards conjectured, other correspondence was so peppered with protest that Erasmus subsequently suppressed its publication.[32] He was cautious, yet he was certainly not silent. His *Julius Exclusus* was a clever fable anonymously circulated as something of a cruel epitaph for Pope Julius II. In the story the pope recounted for St. Peter, then guarding heaven's gates, his military adventures and he boasted of his aptitude for duplicitous diplomacy as if it were the mark of a "genius superior to that of the apostles." Peter failed to recognize Julius as pontifical and refused to admit him.[33] But the *Julius* was not Erasmus's first printed assault on the papacy. He parodied Rome's pretensions in his *Praise of Folly* where the entire church comes under indictment. Incontinence and covetousness were said to have infected popes and priests, even mendicant friars whose sermons were horridly embellished to attract merchants' money and ladies' favors.[34] Erasmus complained that piety was all but extinguished. Popes assumed that bishops taught it, bishops that priests preached it, and priests that friars impressed upon the laity the importance of charity and humility. Nobody, however, was willing to forgo the mad dash for profit and pleasure.[35] Against this madness, incontinence, greed, and extravagance, *Folly* sets the spiritual life, which it associates with a madness that overpowers persons and that distinguishes those "possessed," much as the heterodox and puritanical Montanists once privileged their prophets.[36]

Perhaps this comparison was another thrust at the church. *Folly*'s first critics, however, were not interested in recommencing ancient arguments against Montanism. Erasmus was first reprimanded by scholastic theologians who thought that *Folly* had maligned their own work and had ridiculed their reputations.[37] Thomas More took Erasmus's side without hesitation. He admitted that what were vexing questions for others were, for Erasmus and for himself, mere trifles. Yet he noted that refusal to en-

---

[32]"The Two Lost Years of Erasmus," *Studies in the Renaissance* 9 (1967): 161-86.

[33]*Dialogus, Julius exclusus e coelis*, in *Erasmi opuscula*, ed. Wallace K. Ferguson (The Hague: Martinus Nijhoff, 1933) 108, ll. 860-64: "Petrus: 'Si tales sunt, nondum intelligo quo pacto potueris summos reges ad gravissima bella concitare, praesertim ruptis tot foederibus.' Julius: 'Atque si nunc assequi possis ea quae dicam, intelliges ingenium plus quam apostolicum.' "

[34]*Opera Erasmi* 4:3:168.

[35]Ibid., 170-76.

[36]Ibid., 192-95; and cf. *Ench.*, 92, l. 31-93, l. 5.

[37]Allen, *OE* 2:11-16, 125-36.

ter or to defer to endless debates about impractical points of doctrine did not reflect heterodoxy. It proved common sense. More explained that by getting straight to the moral meaning of Christianity, Erasmus had simply followed venerable exegetes who were concerned with the measure of piety and noble behavior and who had revealed to the first Christians the practical implications of their confession of faith. Subsequent scholastic theoreticians, More hinted, served their communities less well.[38]

A decade earlier, in 1504, More had begun to ponder practical or behavioral implications. He then translated into English several letters and devotional works composed by Giovanni Pico della Mirandola, a noted Florentine scholar. More was so taken with Pico that he also Englished a biography published by Pico's nephew. Before all this, More had suggested in verse that to serve fortune and eagerly to await her rewards was to court anxiety and misery. Only poverty, he claimed, imparted a sabbatic tranquility to life.[39] More, therefore, was well disposed to Pico's more concentrated arguments against ambitious and hypocritical Christians who pretended that their possessions and prestige had been acquired for the sake of their God and their churches ("God is he whiche hathe no need of our good").[40] Pico's logic could lead to the monastery, and More's own previous verses were redolent of *contemptus mundi*. But in 1504 Pico doubly appealed to More because the Florentine remained "within the world." One passage that More devised and slipped into his translations indicates that his admiration for Pico and his own decision to enter public life were loosely connected with the theme that Medwall's Flaminius introduced some pages back. More's interpolation begins with the familiar disclaimer: our ancestors' nobility and honor "maketh us not honorable." But More gave the subject fresh life.

> Never the more noble be we for their nobleness if ourselves lack those things for which they were noble. But rather the more worshipful that our ancestors were, the more vile and shameful be we, if we decline from the steps of their worshipful living, the clear beauty of whose virtue maketh the dark spot of our vice the more evidently to appear and to be the more marked. But Picus . . . was himself so honorable, for the great plenteous abundance of all such virtues the possession whereof every honor followeth (as a shadow followeth a body) that he was to all them that aspire to honor a

---

[38]*The Correspondence of Sir Thomas More*, ed. Elizabeth Frances Rogers (Princeton: Princeton University Press, 1947) 41-43, 52-56, and esp. 66-72.

[39]Willow, *English Poems*, 200-203.

[40]*EWTM* 1:375-76.

very spectacle, in whose conditions as in a clear polished mirror, they might behold in what points very honor standeth.[41]

Erasmus had threaded this theme through his *Enchiridion*. When he visited England a second time in 1506, More readily renewed the friendship, and the two collaborated on several translations of Lucian into Latin. More either chose or was assigned *The Cynic*, a short dialogue wherein Lucian had set rival definitions of virtue edge to edge.[42] One interlocutor, the cynic, for whom extreme ascetic self-denial was the sure route to perfection, had his way through much of the text. The other, Lycinus, however, is manifestly less abrasive and more companionable. Lycinus's concept of virtue does not preclude enjoyment of the world's bounty, from soft beds to sweet wine.[43] Erasmus could not have asked for a better advocate. Pico might have taken him as a model. While the cynic forcefully rebuked those who lie indolently in the lap of luxury, Lycinus merely intimated that one need not take flight to the margins of society in order to attain virtue. The Christian life, notably "simplicity, moderation, and thrift," did not require isolation.[44]

Lycinus, like Flaminius, is a guide whom we would be wise to hire if we wish to understand Tudor idealism. But Lycinus's creator is also important inasmuch as idealistic critics appear to have emulated Lucian to

---

[41]Ibid., 349. One must agree with Professor McConica that monastic spirituality is never too deeply submerged in More's exhortations to virtue. Still, it is curious that McConica should insist that More's religion was therefore quite unlike that of the *Enchiridion*. Cf. James K. McConica, "The Patrimony of Thomas More," in *History and Imagination,* ed. Hugh Lloyd-Jones, Valerie Pearl, and Blair Worden (London: Duckworth, 1981) 56-71; and for More's other revisions, chiefly omissions, with respect to Pico's biography, consult Stanford E. Lehmberg, "St. Thomas More's Life of Pico della Mirandola," *Studies in the Renaissance* 3 (1956): 61-74.

[42]My analysis here follows that of Alastair Fox, *Thomas More, History and Providence* (New Haven: Yale University Press, 1983) 35-44. But it is also important to note that neither More nor Erasmus selected Lucian's more defamatory dialogues. For instance, in "The Dead Come to Life," Lucian lunged at philosophers who knew to despise wealth and reputation yet who squared and sold their "wisdom" for pay and popular esteem. *Lucian,* ed. A. M. Harmon, vol. 3 (London: Loeb Classical Library, 1921) 51-57. At the time, I suppose, "The Dead" may have seemed too censorious and subversive. *Folly*'s criticisms, three years later, would be just as sly, but that was after Erasmus had traveled in Italy.

[43]*Translations of Lucian,* ed. Craig R. Thompson, *CWTM* 3:13: "Quanquam si tu his contentus recte sapis, tum Deus profecto neutiquam recte fecit, primum quod oves effecit pingues, deinde vites dulces vini feraces, ac reliquum deinde apparatum varietate mirabilem, et oleum, et mel, et reliqua, omnia ut nos haberemus, edulia quidem omnigena haberemus, potum dulcem haberemus pecunias haberemus, mollem lectum haberemus."

[44]Ibid., 3:4 (letter to Thomas Ruthall).

some extent. Indeed, after 1506 they increasingly censured with wit, aph-
orism, and anecdote.[45]

Folly follows this course, as does the *Julius Exclusus*. Thomas More's
Utopia might be added to the list. Erasmus seemed inclined to make
something of a monument of More's small, complex book. In 1519, when
he touted the *opera Morum* as comparable to Alexander's illustrious
achievements, his friend's "works" included little more than *Utopia*.[46]
Possibly Erasmus sensed that More's fiction was, as J. K. McConica has
claimed, "a fuller exposition of the Erasmian programme" than Erasmus
himself had ever set forth in a single work.[47] But it is unlikely that any
audit will settle to everyone's satisfaction precisely how much *Utopia* owed
to Erasmus or how much to Pico and to Lucian. Nonetheless, since 1952,
when J. H. Hexter published his penetrating analysis of *Utopia*'s second
book, it has been difficult to shake the conviction that More tried, for
whatever purposes, to sketch the lineaments of an alternative, ideal commonwealth that would reflect idealistic critics' principles.[48] Raphael
Hythloday, More's narrator, could not help but "become thrall to the
phantasmal possibility of the temporal perfecting of the world." More, as
I shall argue, did not share his narrator's enthusiasms, but it is worth re-
viewing, in part, Hythloday's story.[49]

The second book whisks the tourist-reader around an island where all
forms of outrageous self-indulgence had been suppressed, private own-

---

[45]Ibid., 3:2.

[46]Allen, *OE* 4:13. Cf. Erasmus's more qualified assessment of John Colet's
writing, ibid., 4:523, esp. ll. 519-27.

[47]McConica, *English Humanists*, 41-43.

[48]Hexter, *More's* Utopia, esp. 81-96; but cf. Brendan Bradshaw, "More on Utopia," *HJ* 24 (1981): 6-18.

[49]For Hythloday's thralldom, see Fox, *More*, 52. Professor Fox's solution to the
problems of More's use of, and relation to, Hythloday is as involved as Hexter's
was simple. For Hexter, Hythloday was More's spokesman in book two. Fox slices
both in half and each of the two Hythlodays has a somewhat complicated connection with each of the two Mores. D. B. Fenlon was first, I believe, to suggest
that More turned *Utopia* against his fellow humanists and that Utopian social theory and Hythloday's endorsement were not More's final answers. More recently,
George M. Logan approached Fenlon's conclusion, though from a different direction. The second book, according to Logan, was a "best-commonwealth exercise" designed to document the compatibility of expedience and morality in
political planning. This seems to return More to Hythloday's camp. But Logan
also contends that *Utopia* was intended as "a corrective to the naive idealism" of
Christian humanists, which was echoed, at least in part, by Hythloday's "exercise." See D. B. Fenlon, "England and Europe: *Utopia* and Its Aftermath," *TRHS*,
5th ser. 25 (1975): 121-27; and Logan's *The Meaning of More's* Utopia (Princeton,
1983) 59-60, 217-18, 235, 255-59.

ership of property had been disallowed, and large-hearted inhabitants seemed sublimely happy with arrangements made by provident rulers. Clerical conduct was, of course, unexceptionable. Each priest's conscience was an effective deterrent to discreditable behavior, but that was true as well for most other citizens. Utopia was blessed by More with a natural religion, a submissive medium through which the benevolent aims of island society reached, and became the aims of, each of its members. Odd and esoteric religious confessions, with their befuddling divinations (*"auguria, caeterasque superstitionis vanae divinationes"*), were considered ephemeral. Utopians tolerated them, but only as long as evangelists' urgings conformed to the generally accepted, rational decorum of religious discourse. Irrationality, like extravagance and incontinence, was taboo. The few priests in this wholly imaginary little world presided over worship directed without elaborate ritual to the God who had endowed every individual with the will and wherewithal to work in concert for the realization of society's purposes.[50] Michel Despland was quite right: Utopian religion bears *"tout les marques d'une religion idéale,"* and it boasts few traces of contemporaneous Christianity.[51]

This is predictable because, after all, Utopia was literally "nowhere," a fictional refuge from reality, remote from late-medieval political culture. "Operative political thought," as it has been called, presupposed rank and hierarchy; Utopians wished them away.[52] Hythloday, who reported their successes, charged that most English noblemen were shamelessly idle and that they fleeced their hard-working tenants in order to finance their own wasteful extravagances.[53] The clergy were similarly excoriated. Hythloday assures us that there was nothing comparable in Utopia to the gang of good-for-nothing priests and monks that lived parasitically off England's strained economy.[54] Utopians were as eager as Medwall's Lucres to take the measure of noble character and equally oblivious to social position and "gentil condicyons." Anemolian ambassadors to the realm learned this the hard way. Noblemen in their own land, according to Hythloday, they thought it would be strategic to parade through their hosts' streets in their most ornate attire, the better to display their own authority and influence. But Utopians associated their gold necklaces, plaited garments, and assorted finery with fetters. They mistook the "noble" ambassadors for the slaves of their retainers who were dressed as simply and humbly as the Utopians themselves.[55]

---

[50]*CWTM* 4:216-37.

[51]*La religion en Occident* (Montreal: Fides, 1979) 167-70, 333-35.

[52]*CWTM* 4:104. Also note Logan, *Meaning,* 260-61.

[53]*CWTM* 4:62-66.

[54]Ibid., 130.

[55]Ibid., 154-56. Cf. Allen, *OE* 2:414, esp. ll. 40-48.

Utopia's second book is something less than a sustained attack on aristocracy. Like *Fulgens and Lucres,* it is ultimately more concerned with the new nobility than with the old. Utopians were devoutly committed to "nobility," as Flaminius defined it, and their devotion inspired them to achieve a degree of personal piety, social harmony and, one might say, "spiritual" solidarity of which Colet and Erasmus would have been envious.[56] The ecclesiastical hierarchy, however, was part of the cost.

Idealistic critics might have been tempted to migrate to a lawyerless land. When not altogether wrapped in their romances or in their rhetoric, however, the prospect of a bishopless commonwealth and the triumph of the plain over the plaited probably seemed unattractive. Yet idealists' scathing criticisms of clerical misconduct and covetousness, coupled with a nearly exclusivist emphasis on personal piety, left little of the church. More's Utopians simply dragged the implications beyond the point of no return to answer some significant questions that his friends had not raised. What might happen to the sacraments if, as Colet dreamed, a righteous life were universally considered chief among them? What would religion look like in a realm populated by Erasmus's Christian soldiers? If More's and Hythloday's sympathies in the second book are identical, then by developing the logic of early Tudor idealism, More may have planned, as Quentin Skinner suggests, only to wean colleagues from their residual faith in the aristocracy's virtue and political virtuosity.[57] But it is also possible that he wished to lever idealistic critics from their cherished illusions, from their optimism that sweeping reform and social salvation might be accomplished *sola virtute.* A huge step separates this modest skepticism from an outright defense of the ecclesiastical courts and hierarchy, but it was a step Thomas More was soon prepared to take.

---

[56]For the equivocal character of More's use of *"nobilitas,"* consult Ward S. Allen, "The Tone of More's Farewell to *Utopia:* A Reply to J. H. Hexter," *Moreana* 13 (1976): 108-18.

[57]*The Foundations of Modern Political Thought,* 2 vols. (Cambridge: Cambridge University Press, 1978) 1:257-62.

Chapter 6

CRITICS AND
COURT LIFE

Ten years before More completed his *Utopia,* Baldassare Castiglione visited England and, as a proxy for the duke of Urbino, he was inducted into Henry VII's Order of the Garter. Castiglione was lavishly entertained and he returned to Italy with favorable impressions of the royal family and of the English court, which he subsequently incorporated into his *Cortegiano.*[1] He composed those four books of polished conversation to alert fellow courtiers to the challenges facing their profession. Local dynasties were disappearing, and employment was most often found at the courts of great kings whose good judgment could not safely be presumed.[2] *Cortegiano* briefly ponders the merits of monarchy, but the fear of tyranny is put to rest when Ottaviano, speaking for the author, explains that courtiers may be trusted to rescue court politics from a prince whose breeding had somehow failed to produce the instincts, virtues, and intelligence necessary for government.[3] The courtier was to instruct and

---

[1]Castiglione, *Il libro del Cortegiano,* ed. Giulio Preti (Turin: G. Einaudi, 1960) bk. 4, ch. 38, 395-96: ". . . ed a quella d'Inghilterra il signor don Enrico [VIII], che or cresce sotto il magno padre [Henry VII] in ogni sorte di virtù, come tenero rampollo sotto l'ombra d'arbore eccellente e carico di frutti . . . la natura in questo signore abbia voluto far prova di se stessa, collocando in un corpo solo tante eccellenzie quante basteriano per adornarne infiniti."

[2]Erich Loos, *Baldassare Castigliones* Libro del Cortegiano: *Studien zur Tugendauffassung des Cinquecento* (Frankfurt: V. Klostermann, 1955) 183-93, 201-207; Lawrence V. Ryan, "Book Four of Castiglione's *Courtier:* Climax or Afterthought," *Studies in the Renaissance* 19 (1972): 156-79; and J. R. Woodhouse, *Castiglione* (Edinburgh: Edinburgh University Press, 1978) 189-96.

[3]*Cortegiano,* bk. 4, ch. 22, 375-76: "E perchè avete detto che più facil cosa è che la mente d'un solo si corrompa che quella di molti, dico che è ancora più facil cosa trovar un bono e savio che molti; e bono e savio si deve estimare che possa esser un re di nobil stirpe, inclinato alle virtù dal suo natural instinto e dalla famosa memoria dei suoi antecessori ed instituito di boni constumi; e se non sarà d'un'altra specie più che umana . . . essendo aiutato dagli ammaestramenti e dalla educazione ed arte del cortegiano, formato da questi signori tanto prudente e bono, sarà giustissimo, continentissimo, temperatissimo, fortissimo e sapientissimo, pien di liberalità, magnificenzia, religione e clemenzia; in somma sarà gloriosissimo e carissimo agli omini ed a Dio."

serve the wise king, to transform the fool and, of course, to distinguish between the two. Though susceptible to quick summation, this was the warrant for Castiglione's faith in court life and, in the idiom of a later generation, a very tall order indeed. But Castiglione seems to have counted on courtiers who were somewhat larger than life. Their discretion and discernment would be impeccable. They would be able to charm and amuse their sovereigns while informing them of astringencies and while recommending unpopular but necessary restraints. They would know how to exploit their positions without exciting envy. In short, Castiglione's courtiers, without affectation and arrogance, would make the court a school for prudence, virtue, and courage.[4]

English critics agreed that a king's companions were as important for sound rule as a king's character.

> Lyberte to a lorde belongyth of ryght
> But wyfull waywardnesse muste walke out of the way;
> Measure of your lustys must have the oversyght[5]

"Measure," in this utterance, which draws John Skelton's "Magnyfycence" to its close, was a noble and faithful courtier ostracized through much of Skelton's story. In "Measure's" place, Counterfeit Countenance, Crafty Conveyance, Clokyd Colusion, and their cronies held the court hostage to their mischief. Deceit and mutual suspicion poisoned political culture. The picture was far different from the one Castiglione painted, yet Skelton was disposed to believe that his farces and allegories captured the spirit of early Tudor court life.[6] Clokyd Colusion, for example, personifies the hypocrisy and obsequiousness that Skelton mapped as the customary route to power. "I sowe sedycyous sedes of dyscorde and debates," he brags, in what the author wishes us to think a rare moment of candor. The entire court seems to conspire to sustain

---

[4]Ibid., bk. 4, ch. 10, 360-61. Also note bk. 2, chs. 6-7, 117-21; and review Alfredo Bonadeo, "The Function and Purpose of the Courtier in *The Book of the Courtier* by Castiglione," *Philological Quarterly* 50 (1971): 41-46. Bonadeo suggests that the courtier's "ascendancy" thinly masks Castiglione's contempt for kings, and there is considerable justification for his reading, e.g., *Cortegiano*, bk. 4, ch. 44, 402-403. But Castiglione does make careful distinctions between ideal monarchs and tyrants: see Ryan, "Book Four," 164-68; and Loos, *Studien*, 190-92.

[5]Skelton, *Poems*, "Magnyfycence," ll. 2489-91.

[6]Ibid., e.g., ll. 401-93. Also see Skelton's "The Bowge of Court," in *Poems*, 46-61; and "Why Come Ye Nat to Courte?" 278-311. David Bevington (*Tudor Drama*, 60-61) was convinced that Skelton took to the field in behalf of the aristocracy and against the Tudors' "new men" who had seized offices and opportunities for gain at court. Arthur Heiserman, however, argues that "Magnyfycence" was a more general assault on conventional vices and abuses. A. R. Heiserman, *Skelton and Satire* (Chicago: University of Chicago Press, 1961) 117-24.

intrigue and dissimulation, yet Clokyd Colusion ("I brewe moche bale") is truly a master craftsman.[7]

Several years before Skelton composed "Magnyfycence," Erasmus scattered similar assessments of court life through his *Folly*. Friends worried that other intemperate remarks might fall into the wrong hands and that their disclosure would jeopardize his standing; yet satirists were addicted to ridiculing courtiers, and they could no more keep from caricaturing their extravagant ambitions than courtiers, according to critics, could keep from brewing bale.[8] Castiglione's school for virtue was, for Skelton, Erasmus, and also for Alexander Barclay, a veritable school for scandal.

Barclay's approach inclines one to make a rather tantalizing conjecture with reference to the clerical presence at the early Tudor court. The point of his first three *Eclogues*, which recapitulated Aenea Silvio Piccolomini's *Miseriae Curialum*, was familiar enough: courts and councils had become hatcheries for courtiers' worst habits. Court was no place for a civil servant with a conscience; "Favour and coyne . . . worketh all."[9] Godly men like Moses and the prophets found it necessary at times to attend court, but they hastened to leave, Barclay insisted, as soon as their business was done. Only Joseph stayed, but his "marvelous wisedome" saved him from corruption when he ventured into those halls where "envy possesseth the place of charitie [and] onely ambition hath there aucthoritie."[10] Could leading churchmen at court have shared the critics' perspective and nonetheless have thought themselves heirs to Joseph's "marvelous wisedome"? We shall never know, for critics of the "polytyque churche," and not the criticized, believed it important to vindicate their positions by harvesting an assortment of biblical allusions.

The earliest English Protestants were especially expert in underscoring the contrasts between late-medieval prelates and the early church's apostles and martyrs. Though in 1549 many offenders had been dead for decades, Hugh Latimer stridently objected to the public employment of unpreaching prelates. "St. Paul was no sitting bishop, but a walking and preaching bishop." If mid-Tudor churchmen would not emulate St. Paul, Latimer, for one, would make no secret of their reasons.

Methinks I could guess what might be said for excusing of them. They are

---

[7]Skelton, *Poems*, "Magnyfycence," ll. 735-44.

[8]*Opera Erasmi* 4:3:168-70; and Allen, *OE* 1:491. Also note A. R. Heiserman, "Satire in the *Utopia*," *PMLA* 78:3 (1963): 163-74; Heiserman, *Skelton*, 66; and J. H. Hexter, *The Vision of Politics on the Eve of the Reformation; More, Machiavelli, and Seyssel* (London: Allen Lane, 1973) 114.

[9]*The Eclogues of Alexander Barclay*, ed. John Cawood (London: Early English Text Society, 1928) 85.

[10]Ibid., 99-100.

so troubled with lordly living, they are so placed in palaces, couched in courts, ruffling in their rents, dancing in their dominions, burdened with ambassages, pampering themselves. . . . They are otherwise occupied, some in the king's matters, some are ambassadors, some of the privy council, some to furnish the court, some are lords of parliament. . . . Well, well, is this their duty . . . their calling?[11]

Such sentiments sprawl across the history of English Christian traditions. They had been harnessed to reformanda presented to a clerical convocation just before Henry VII's accession and to Colet's own convocation address, which was delivered several years after Henry's death. The former complained that ambition made mercenaries of the Catholic clergy, who galloped shamelessly from their pastoral responsibilities as soon as opportunities for gain and worldly glory materialized elsewhere. The very groundwork of evangelical religion, the intimacy between prelates and laymen in the parishes, thereby collapsed. St. John's Jesus ordered disciples to feed his sheep, and this required dedicated and resident clerics to provide pious orations and examples of upright character.[12] A faint echo of this pastoral idealism can be heard in Colet's convocation sermon ("unto you we loke as unto markes of our direction"), yet the indictment of court life, of the "secular business" that seduced prelates from their duties, mattered more than the parishes left behind.[13] Political culture seemed to pervert every talent that crowded too close to its center. This, and not the margins of biblical history or outlying English parishes, worried idealistic critics, who were preoccupied with court life's corrupting influence on human nature and who particularly feared for their friends.[14]

Idealistic critics were compelled to count their losses. A companion's appointment to court was an occasion for mourning.[15] A resignation that restored another to the twin pursuits of virtue and learning was cause for rejoicing. Archbishop Warham's retirement as chancellor in 1516 was apparently a special triumph; Erasmus referred to it as a release from

---

[11]"The Sermon of the Plough," *Select Sermons and Letters of Dr. Hugh Latimer,* Religious Tract Society: The British Reformers (London: Religious Tract Society, 1830 [?]) 41.

[12]*Oratiuncula,* 69-72.

[13]*Conv.,* 300. Also see *Epigrams,* 190; and Margaret Bowker, *The Henrician Reformation* (Cambridge: Cambridge University Press, 1981) 45.

[14]It was easy, then, for Erasmus to credit Ammonius's analysis of Bishop Ruthall, whom business at court had not merely distracted but had transformed into a suspicious, almost paranoiac, and thoroughly disagreeable character. Allen, *OE* 1:539, ll. 36-37.

[15]Ibid., 543, ll. 2-4.

prison.[16] Thomas More's letter of congratulation is an excellent and, under the circumstances, an extraordinary example of the idealists' response. "I cannot decide whether to admire most your modesty, that is, your willingness to give up so much dignity and power, or your detachment, which enables you to despise them, or your integrity. . . . [T]ogether with many others, I endorse the appropriateness and the wisdom of your decision."[17] Some of those "many others," however, had good reason to suspect that More's remarks were disingenuous. He himself admitted to Warham that he was increasingly being drawn into the kind of life that the archbishop was leaving, and Erasmus was soon to identify him as another casualty (*"Nobis certe et litteris ademptus es"*).[18] We may be thankful, nonetheless, that More did not leave the critics' camp for the royal court unobtrusively, for the first book of his *Utopia* is a stunning statement of the idealists' brief against court life.

The first book was composed soon after More returned from lengthy trade negotiations on the Continent, the expenses for which were met from his own purse. When his reward came in the form of a councillor's handsome annuity, he accepted it.[19] Hence *Utopia's* dialogue on counsel aired both sides of the public-service issue. Raphael Hythloday, that adventurer of exceptional insight, pulled one way; More, as himself, pulled the other. The fiction's maker entrusted to his character, More, the conviction that every citizen owes some service to the commonwealth. Philosophers, he volunteered, are especially obliged to counsel their sovereigns.[20] In 1504, when More was under Pico's spell, it seemed sufficient for virtuous persons to disburden themselves, distribute their

---

[16]Ibid., 2:246, ll. 1-5; P. S. Allen, "Dean Colet and Archbishop Warham," *EHR* 17 (1902): 304; and Kelly, *Canterbury Jurisdiction*, 145-53. It is likely that Warham's place at court was made increasingly uncomfortable, partly because of Thomas Wolsey's meteoric rise. Moreover, after the Hunne affair, disputes over ecclesiastical immunities and privileges took a course contrary to the one Warham would have wished.

[17]Rogers, *Correspondence*, 86: "Quamobrem hujus animi tui nescio modestiorisne qui munus tam amplum ac magnificum voluisti relinquere, an sublimioris qui potuisti contemnere, an innocentioris qui non metuisti deponere, certe optimi ac prudentissimi, multos quidem sed imprimis me suffragatorem et admirationem habes, qui dici non potest huic tam rarae faelicitate tuae quam impense gratuler, mihique tuo nomine gaudeam."

[18]Allen, *OE* 3:295.

[19]Elton, *Studies*, 1:129-54; and J. A. Guy, *The Public Career of Sir Thomas More* (New Haven: Yale University Press, 1980) 4-11. I tend to agree with Elton and Guy that More was preparing for his promotion for some time, if not from 1505, when his marriage silenced speculation that he might join the Carthusians, at least from 1510, when he was appointed undersheriff of London.

[20]*CWTM* 4:86.

property, pursue their studies, guard their freedom, and avoid political involvements. Hythloday followed precisely this pattern, but More had changed his mind.[21] In *Utopia* he prized Hythloday's unconventional disdain for wealth and power no less than he had esteemed Pico's, yet he emphasized that the noble, generous, and philosophical spirit was no recluse. It was more honorable to place oneself in harm's way, to enter public service, despite the necessary compromises. More's confidence in the courtier's importance was not quite equivalent to that of Castiglione, but the critic's calling, as he and friends once shaped it, no longer suited him. It was not enough simply to carp at official corruption. One must import virtue into court life and endeavor to influence the formulation of policy. "You [Hythloday] would be a truly remarkable councillor."[22]

Hythloday, however, was unmoved. He thought that his interlocutor had overestimated the impact that one man's wisdom and experience might make. Wisdom, he stressed, could not be balanced on top of the pile of lies, fraud, and flattery stacked at every monarch's court. If he were to give advice, it would be simple yet wholly subversive. Kings must adjust their expenses to their revenues, and mischievous methods of obtaining subsidies must be forsaken: "crooked craftiness" must cease.[23] Yet "crooked craftiness," according to Hythloday, was so pervasive at court that the wise and candid councillor would be pilloried by his peers. More's noble, generous, philosophical spirit was a *morceau de musée,* too rare to be risked at court.

Hythloday's position was a caricature of the idealists' outlook. More must be made of this because his aversion to court life is considered atypical.[24] To be sure, More and not Hythloday would have been at home in Castiglione's company. To Colet, Fisher, and certainly Erasmus, however, Hythloday's resolution to the problem of counsel was more congenial. Better to devise literary strategies or to conjure up an ideal commonwealth than to take one's chances with a real and imperfect one. The humanists' responsibilities to criticize and to instruct, Erasmus once averred, might best be fulfilled in texts and through carefully crafted overstatement and adulation—all from a safe distance.[25] This is not exactly Hythloday's argument, but he and Erasmus share the opinion that active public service steals one's freedom and court life steals one's virtue.

More had come to a different conclusion. He offered it in *Utopia,* yet he somewhat concealed it and occasionally misrepresented it to his

---

[21]Cf. ibid., 54 and *EWTM* 1:353-56, 370, 374.

[22]*CWTM* 4:56.

[23]Ibid., 96-97.

[24]Bradshaw, "More on Utopia," 21-25.

[25]Allen, *OE* 1:402-403.

friends. He wrote to Fisher that he had been disinclined to come to court.[26] He apparently permitted Erasmus to entertain and spread the idea that the king had coerced him (*"pertrahere"*).[27] The tale tells nothing of the inducement. It speaks falsely of More's reluctance to enter more fully into government work. Nonetheless, the excuse, for such it was, volunteered by More and repeated by Erasmus, speaks volumes about the idealists' expectations: one who knew what they knew about courtiers' corruption would only accept an appointment at court under extreme duress. By 1516 More voiced doubts and acknowledged that a dexterous councillor might make a difference and still protect himself from the scoundrels in politics. His friends *and* his Hythloday thought otherwise.

Perhaps it was possible and anticipated in some circles that persons of integrity, should they enter public service, could restore or buttress trust in government. Writing of Florence, Richard Trexler suggested that "trust among laymen was possible only if certain key governmental posts were manned by men of God," that is, by "representatives of the principle of ethical objectivity."[28] Earliest Tudor idealists would have been skeptical about the arrangement, to say the very least. According to Hythloday, when an exceptional integrity collided with the consensus at court, the former and not the latter invariably gave ground. "The very worst counsels must be endorsed and the most pestilential decrees approved unless one wishes to be branded a spy and traitor for having praised those propositions insufficiently." Principled persons' sole hope for survival was to surrender their principles.[29] And if survival of this sort was an art, then in Hythloday's estimation clerical courtiers were its foremost virtuosi. Preachers, he noted, were practiced chameleons and were able to accommodate Christian doctrine to court morality—or rather immorality—to console unscrupulous colleagues and thus to earn approval and promotion for themselves.[30]

Hythloday's arguments and examples illustrate the theme set at the very beginning of his speeches. At court the only difference between *ser-*

---

[26]Rogers, *Correspondence*, 111: "In Aulam (quod nemo nescit et Princeps ipse mihi ludens interdum libenter exprobrat) invitissimus veni." For Fisher's general attitude, see Allen, *OE* 2:90, ll. 7-9: "Utinam juvenis praeceptorem illum [Rudolph Agricola] fuissem nactus! Mallem id profecto, neque sane mentior, quam archiepiscopatum aliquem."

[27]Allen, *OE* 4:20, ll. 218-20; and 4:294, ll. 99-100.

[28]*Public Life in Renaissance Florence* (New York: The Academic Press, 1980) 30-33.

[29]*CWTM* 4:102: "Quippe non est ibi dissimulandi locus, nec licet connivere; approbanda sunt aperte pessima consilia, et decretis pestilentissimis subscribendum est. Speculatoris vice fuerit, ac pene proditoris, etiam qui improbe consulta maligne laudaverit."

[30]Ibid., 100, 376.

vias and *inservias* (between service and servitude) is a syllable; beyond that, no substantial distinction can be drawn.[31] Or, to transfer the idealists' conviction into a more inelegant idiom, it is absurd to imagine that one can venture out in the rain and remain dry.

More stubbornly insisted in *Utopia*'s first book that conscientious councillors could make pragmatic choices, that they could choose the better of two courses without jeopardizing their honor. More, as noted, had already resolved to take a larger part in public service. Hythloday, nevertheless, dominates the dialogue. This puzzling literary tactic makes greater sense if we assume that More was disposed to dispatch his idealism with elaborate last rites. The second book also serves this purpose. Designed before the dialogue was conceived, *Utopia*'s Utopia, a society for which the best course had been authoritatively charted, gives Hythloday's remarks a deeper resonance. But it seems as well to trade on an idea that More smuggled into his own section of the dialogue: "Unless all persons are made virtuous, society cannot be set right." He added, however, that such concomitant improvements could not be expected in the forseeable future.[32]

His friends closed the interval between the now and then by filling their texts with advice. Shunning court, they pressed for small increments to the world's store of virtue by educating princes and prelates from afar and often obliquely. Simultaneously, they dreamed of a far better world, conjured up literate peasants reciting psalms at their ploughs, and tried to wish away late-medieval political culture and ecclesiastical bureaucracy and to replace them with idealizations of the Christian and classical cultures of antiquity. In *Utopia* Thomas More enlightens and dreams so well, but for the last time. (Erasmus was right: he was for some years thereafter lost to literature.) Yet More also attaches two significant "qualifications." In the first book he argues that small increments or small gains cannot be achieved at great distances. Despite the apparent impenetrability of political culture, the humanist must personally bring virtue, sound judgment, and sage counsel to court. In the second, he reminded his friends that their dreams were illusions. Only a fresh start, with an unleavened people on a fictional island, could produce the perfections for which idealistic critics yearned. In short, More deposited their printable but impracticable ideals in the only place, apart from dinner conversations and garden colloquies, in which they might survive, a "no place" (*ou topos*) created by learned and literate "nonsense" (*Ethlos deios*).

---

[31]Ibid., 54-55.

[32]Ibid., 100: "Nam ut omnia bene sint, fieri non potest, nisi omnes boni sint, quod ad aliquot abhinc annos abhuc non expecto."

Part III

THE
"POLYTYQUE
CHURCHE"

Chapter 7

THE KING'S PAGEANTS

If one were to judge solely by public ceremonies, religion and late-medieval political culture would seem inseparable. Nearly a dozen centuries—during which pontiffs ceremonially wore purple and princes solemnly donned *"sanctus"* and *"sacer"* and claimed their inflated titles *Dei gratia*—assured religion, if not always Rome, a role in the making and unmaking of territorial monarchs. Ceremonies were packed with religious imagery, which imparted dignity and legitimacy to the office, to the office-bearers, and to their subjects, and which sanctioned patterns of belief and behavior associated with the stability of political culture. It is generally known that Machiavelli shrewdly and dispassionately analyzed religion's political utility, yet it would be nonsense to assume that such a resource otherwise and earlier had gone unrecognized and unexploited. The suggestiveness and power of religious language, reset in political celebrations, demonstrably impressed rulers or, at least, their publicists, who seldom bothered to ask the church for its theories of state but who nonetheless invoked religion to guarantee statesmen their subjects' goodwill and obedience.[1]

The new Tudor regime in 1495 understood that ritual, perhaps more effectively than decree, generated civic pride and shaped civic responsibility. Citizens must not only be told of their new dynasty's legitimacy, they must also be shown. Pulpits were ready-made for the telling: Richard Fitzjames's homily on obedience fo temporal as well as ecclesiastical authorities was not atypical. The showing, however, required the participation of a greater number of citizens and the church's involvement was not always immediately apparent. Dialogues had to be invented, pageants orchestrated, and the legendary blended with the commonplace in order to persuade citizens that the most recent dynastic change was not simply necessary but monumental and divinely ordained.

---

[1]Percy Ernest Schramm, "Sacerdotium und Regnum im Austausch ihrer Vorrechte," *Studi Gregoriani* 2 (1947): 403-57. For Machiavelli's analysis, see Michel Despland, *La Religion en Occident* (Montreal: Fides, 1979) 351-53; and J. Samuel Preus, "Machiavelli's Analysis of Religion," *Journal of the History of Ideas* 40 (1979): 171-90.

In 1486, at the first sign ⌐f spring, Henry VII embarked on a journey or "progress" to the north. No sketch of his tour would be complete without conjuring up awed and curious spectators who must have lined the route and competed with one another for the best summits from which to watch their king and his court. Yet the reports that survive describe only the elaborate welcomes staged by larger towns to entertain, flatter, and reassure Henry, who had good reason to doubt and to test northerners' allegiance. Municipal leaders, guild officials, and their neighbors—many of them masquerading as biblical patriarchs and medieval saints—conspired to make the first of the Tudors feel at home and at ease in those parts of his realm that had been conspicuously hospitable to his predecessor and adversary, Richard III.[2]

This was precisely what the king had planned. He chose not to visit several cities that had given adequate indication of their loyalties. For instance, he bypassed Leicester, which opportunely had demonstrated its prompt switch from York to Tudor the previous year by tending Henry's wounded soldiers.[3] To the south and west, however, Worcester had proven intractable and had supported Yorkist partisans even after Richard III's defeat. To atone, Worcester staged elaborate ceremonies filled with effusive inventories of Henry's virtues, chief among them forbearance and mercy.[4] Farther north, the city of York had provoked Henry's "grete displeaser." No alibi was acceptable to the Tudors, who thought that part of their territory crowded with conspirators. It was no secret that the north would have been happier had Richard defeated the invaders, but Henry nonetheless rummaged for reasons to extend his general amnesty to those disappointed citizens. He accepted as some token of good faith and as a promise of acquiescence to his rule the north's previous allegiance to Henry VI. In the final analysis, however, one may conclude that pardons were issued pragmatically and principally because the new

---

[2]John Leland copied, from BL Cotton MSS Julius B XII, detailed accounts of several urban pageants, which one of Henry's heralds kept as "A Shorte and Briefe Memory . . . of the First Progresse of Our Souveraigne Lord Henry the VII." Sydney Anglo's work on this document has not been surpassed—*Spectacle, Pageantry, and Early Tudor Policy* (Oxford: Clarendon Press, 1969)—but the following draws extensively on studies of pageantry and politics elsewhere. See especially Richard Trexler's impressive *Public Life in Renaissance Florence* (New York: The Academic Press, 1980) esp. 43-46, 280-81, 336-47; but also Edward Muir, "Images of Power: Art and Pageantry in Renaissance Venice," *AHR* 84 (1979): 16-52; and editorial remarks in the introduction to *Les entrées royales Françaises de 1328-1515*, ed. Bernard Guenée and François Lehoux (Paris: Éditions du Centre National de la Recherche Scientifique, 1968).

[3]William Kelly, *Royal Progresses and Visits to Leicester* (Leicester: S. Clarke, 1884) 262-63.

[4]Leland, 192-96.

regime needed Yorkshiremen: "They of thoos parties be necessarye and according to ther dutie most defend this land ayenst the Scotts."[5] Yet it was not hard then to see the grimace as well as the grace behind official clemency. Soon after the pardon arrived in York, municipal authorities were ordered to round up and imprison all vagabonds and other suspicious persons in the city's streets and taverns.[6] York's reception and pageants would have to be particularly persuasive to appease its skeptical sovereign. Customarily, two sheriffs and twenty horsemen rode to meet royal parties. For Henry, York doubled the numbers. Mayors and aldermen usually lingered at the franchise's boundary, two miles from the city's center. On this occasion they ventured from three to five miles to greet the king, while richly costumed characters waited to pay their tribute to their guest.[7]

To be sure, royal entries were grand entertainment, punctuated by encomiastic flourishes and by moments of special pleading. Yet submerged just beneath the ceremonies' literal levels, there were meanings for which one would be wise to look and listen. The pageants simultaneously generated and expressed collective sentiment and civic identity. They demonstrated each city's unimpaired ability to transcend tensions that divided its inhabitants. Municipalities represented themselves as harmonious, trustworthy, and even venerable. Founders and patrons appeared, *redivivi*—Ethelbert at Hereford, Bremmius at Bristol, Ebrauk at York—and their appearances transformed legend into vivid proof of their cities' antiquity and endurance. Monarchs come and go, yet their time-honored cities remain as indelible testimonies to royal wisdom and generosity. Local guilds assumed responsibilities for *tableaux vivants* that cumulatively dramatized the city's coherence insofar as an orderly, unified ceremony developed from its distinct parts. To the king, this was probably a welcome sign that the town was at peace with itself and that the town's authorities therefore had diplomatic credibility. But the ritual was not simply a costly charade staged cosmetically to conceal stubborn difficulties. The pageant's preparations and the celebration's formal behavior actually suspended rivalries and inspired collaboration. Householders beautified their properties. Drapers and other craftsmen dressed the town's passages and pageant cars. Shared work vivified the sense of shared community, and performances that marked the king's entry and trumpeted the city's antiquity and honor could only have intensified pressures to place individual feelings in harmony with the situation. Without joining Durkheim's hunt for laws governing the ritual formula-

---

[5]*YCR* 1:125-26.

[6]Ibid., 139-40.

[7]Ibid., 155 (five miles); Leland, 187 (three miles). Also note Trexler, *Public Life*, 308.

tions of *l'esprit collectif* and without pausing to pronounce on Victor Turner's evocations of feudal structure, "antistructure," and urban polity, one may nonetheless presume that the preparation for and reception of monarchs crafted as well as reported municipal solidarity.[8] Such public ceremonies bound citizens and obligated the king to the life and history of the region—a life that transcended inhabitants' quotidian experiences and a history thought honorable and even worshipful, despite the north's recent political miscalculations. And, of course, the rituals bound the cities to their king.

For all this binding, traditional hierarchical relationships held firm. English citizens were somewhat more subdued than the Rouen prelates who welcomed Charles VIII in 1485 with nearly idolatrous good cheer (*"longuement vive le chef mistique"*), yet municipal pageants unmistakably privileged the king's spiritual place in the political order. In a sense, the pageants were local coronations. They confirmed the divine empowerment of the sovereign whose election had been irrefutably proven by his victory over Richard III. From the king's perspective, it may have seemed prudent ritually to reclaim the region for the Crown and claim it for his dynasty. Clifford Geertz, in unforgettable fashion, says that "when kings journey around the countryside, making appearances, attending fetes, conferring honors, exchanging gifts, or defying rivals, they mark it, like some wolf or tiger spreading his scent through his territory, as almost physically part of them." Be that as it may, local celebrations were replete with fetes, honors, and exchanges. The cities' mythological founders and caretakers solemnly handed Henry symbols of their authority and placed their subjects and municipalities in his safekeeping. At York "Oure Lady" confessed that her son, "in whome is eleccion," had "callid victoriously" the Tudor champion as "his knyght" to rule all England. The Worcester gatekeeper was made to confuse Henry with King David, for they both were "chosen of God." Eulogies abounded and, along with the gifts of

---

[8]The works of Durkheim and Turner nonetheless figure in this discussion of municipal pageants. See Durkheim's "De la définition des phénomènes religieux," *L'Année sociologique* 2 (1898): 23-28; translated in *Durkheim on Religion*, ed. W. S. F. Pickering (London: Routledge & Kegan Paul, 1975) 93-98; and *Les Formes élémentaires de la vie religieuse* (Paris: F. Alcan, 1912) esp. 465-592 (available in several translations). Also consult Turner's *The Ritual Process: Structure and Anti-Structure* (London: Routledge & Kegan Paul, 1969) 94-203; and his "The Center Out There: Pilgrim's Goal," *History of Religions* 12 (1973): 191-230.

scepters and swords, constituted a late-medieval expression of "liturgical kinship."[9]

A pageant's spiritualization of royal power was commonly yoked to a recital of the municipality's current economic difficulties, which were symptoms of widespread urban decline. The Tudors apparently were expected to sweep hardship away as expeditiously as they swept away their Yorkist predecessors. The Bristol personifications of prudence and justice agreed that Henry VII, "preserved by dyvyne power certeygn," was the answer to the town's problems, which King Bremmius had discreetly divulged in the preceding pageant address. After all, Henry had been "seint hider by the holsome purviaunce of Almighty God moost mercifull and gracious to reforme thyngs that be contrarious unto the comen wele."[10] York officials had similar expectations. Their pageant also featured a litany of urban problems, yet distress was ritually overmastered when Solomon prophesied a renewal of the entire realm. Then David related the promise of renewal to divine judgment and election on Bosworth field and surrendered to Henry his own "swerd of victorie."[11] Providence had given England a new dynasty, and the north was prepared to submit. These public ceremonies were rituals of submission. From pathos and special pleading, they quickly passed to optimism and, when reparations for previous misgivings about the Tudors had been paid with encomium and eulogy, the pageants became rituals of rededication as well.

Formal behavior and flamboyant rhetoric enshrined ideals of social order that were consecrated, one might say, by the enthusiasms generated and articulated by the pageants. To orchestrate submission and rededication, to chronicle ills and prophesy cures, to glorify the new king's gifts and *gesta* and simultaneously to toast the honor and trustworthiness of cities filled with his former enemies; all this required considerable imagination, sophistication, and delicacy. Ritually to redeem municipal

---

[9]See Ernst Kantorowicz, *The King's Two Bodies* (Princeton: Princeton University Press, 1957) 42-61, 318-28; Glynne Wickham, *Early English Stages, 1300-1660,* 3 vols. (London: Routledge & Kegan Paul, 1980-1981) 1:53-63; and *Entrées royales,* 22-29. For the Rouen celebration, "Premiere entrée du roi Charles VIII a Rouen," in *Entrées royales,* 247; for "Oure Lady," YCR 1:158-59 and Leland, 189; and for the gatekeeper's confusion, see Leland, 195-96. Geertz's remark introduces his paper on "Centers, Kings, and Charisma: Reflections on the Symbolics of Power," in *Culture and Its Creators,* ed. Joseph Ben-David and Terry Nichols Clark (Chicago: University of Chicago Press, 1977) 153.

[10]Leland, 199-202. Also note R. B. Dobson, "Urban Decline in Late Medieval England," *TRHS,* 5th ser. 27 (1977): 1-22; Charles Phythian-Adams, *Desolation of a City: Coventry and the Urban Crisis of the Late Middle Ages* (Cambridge: Cambridge University Press, 1979) 283-84.

[11]YCR 1:157-58; Leland, 189-90.

society—to present it as a complex yet invincibly harmonious whole—was
a miracle by any measure. Officials realized the magnitude of the assignment and they turned directly to their clergy.

One catches a glimpse of this in York, where surviving evidence shows
how citizens found and financed their agents. When the king's itinerary
was first announced, municipal leaders promptly petitioned their archbishop for advice and assistance. He agreed to help, and the city sent a
representative to him "to be sufficiently instructed." Officials subsequently engaged Henry Hudson, a local priest, and commissioned him
to compose and to stage "the show." Remuneration was set at five marks,
and the mayor was instructed to find some way to compensate Hudson's
parish for the time that the priest was to lavish on city business. Ultimately, more than sixty shillings were paid to Hudson and to unnamed
clerics for their cooperation.[12]

Some churchmen, like Hudson, worked behind the scenes, as it were.
For other prelates, visibility was highly desirable. Several accompanied
Henry to York. Others joined an impressive delegation of canons and friars
from the city that had assembled to escort the king to the cathedral, where
the procession and pageants culminated with a solemn mass. The church
was very much a part of York's "civic" celebration, yet is it reasonable to
assume that the clergy elsewhere instigated, shaped, and supervised such
ceremonies? The assumption may hold, for it is compatible, not just with
the evidence from York and with intimations of clerical participation in
Henry's tour, but also with late-medieval society's conviction that hospitality was largely an ecclesiastical obligation. The royal family and other
dignitaries, along with foreign ambassadors, were regularly given the run
of episcopal palaces. Lambeth's chambers were bustling with countrymen who had journeyed to London for business, and the archbishop of
Canterbury rarely dined alone. York's metropolitan not only boarded
Henry's daughter Margaret in 1503, as she moved north to meet her new
husband in Scotland; he also "held open hows" for the royal party and
for the city's flock of officials.[13]

Prelates were expected to be amiable hosts, but especially to be able
masters of ceremonies. Insofar as moral instruction and the mass itself
regularly transformed the church into a theater, aptitude was easily acquired. The clergy's counsel and cooperation were indispensable when
processions and amusements were played for political profit. The church,
as noted, had long offered its promotional services to temporal powers,
and hospitality and promotion, in both senses of the word, were often
closely connected. By the late fifteenth century, it was the church's sa-

----

[12]Ibid., 1:150, 153, 159.

[13]Leland, 274-75; *YCR* 2:186-89. Also review Felicity Heal, "The Archbishops
of Canterbury and the Practice of Hospitality," *JEH* 33 (1982): 544-63.

cred duty (as well as good politics) to sanctify the center of neofeudal political culture.

Emphasis upon clerical participation and management does not seriously qualify my claim that urban society composed and animated the royal entries. Citizens seized upon them as opportunities to efface civic tensions and to elicit common sentiments, but virtuosity was needed to make social forces speak effectively. Perhaps, to be concise, one might say that the church "scripted" the pageants. This would be no less true when the performances' primary language was visual. Glynn Wickham was quite right to apply Volumnia's observation to the late-medieval impresarios' apparent prejudices: "The eyes of the ignorant [were] more learned than [their] ears."[14] Impressions of what had been said publicly to Henry VII's wife as she was ferried to her coronation were probably lost or confused, but "the barges fresheley furnyshed with baners and stremers" and the dragon "spowting flamys of fyer" into the Thames must have been memorable.[15]

For many pageants, the repetition of "sumptuosus" in chronicles or ledgers is all that remains. Probably the best place to look for a glimpse of the Tudor ideology of extravagance is the extensive account of the betrothal of princess Mary to Charles of Castile (1508).[16] The groom's representatives were met and initially entertained by Thomas Goldstone, prior of Christ Church, Canterbury. From there, the party proceeded to Richmond where English nobles and courtiers had gathered at the king's palace. The commentary, which was printed immediately after the event, stressed that each guest had private and commodious quarters, and it made a special point of the incomparable opulence of the carpeting, furnishings, and tapestries. The meaning of it all was not left to the imagination. The commemorative account drew the intended conclusions in Latin and English. Richmond's glitter signified that Tudor England had been so lifted above Europe's other realms that shrewd diplomats were eager to contract marriage alliances and to consolidate friendships. The palace's amplitude and amusements placed England at the world's center. From there, the new dynasty aspired to spread its sublime sentiments and to plant "florisshyng redde roses . . . in the highest imperiall gardeyns and houses of power and honoure." Such ambitions for Tudor "buddes and braunches" are virtually unbounded. By marriage, "all

---

[14]Wickham, *Early English Stages*, 2:81-111.

[15]Leland, 218.

[16]E.g., see "Emptions and Provisions of Stuff for the Coronation of Henry VII," in *English Coronation Records*, ed. Leopold G. Wickham Legg (Westminster: Archibald Constable & Co., 1901) esp. 213-14; note Mervyn James, "Ritual, Drama, and Social Body in the Late Medieval English Town," *Past and Present* 98 (1983): 13.

Christen regions shall hereafter be unite and alied" to one another and to England.[17]

Sydney Anglo has captioned pageants "instruments of prestige propaganda," and Richmond's affluence and ambitions seem to provide an excellent example. But Anglo's understanding of instrumentality is rather narrow. He reduces the celebrations to their scripts, costumes, and winches that can be taken apart analytically and then recomposed as if they were sets of gears, which were shifted to whip up and control emotions and to inflate influential egos.[18] On this score, Thomas More was similarly skeptical.

In one of his early Aesopian tales, More conjured up a rural peasant and transported him to London. There, the peasant stumbled into a royal procession, but the crowd's excitement puzzled him even as it thrilled him. He was unable to identify the cause of the grand commotion until another bystander assisted him and pointed out the king. The rustic was immediately disillusioned: how could that be the king, the object of all this adulation, when he was only an ordinary man in an embroidered garment? With his peasant's ingenuous remark, More ridiculed both royal vanity and popular fatuity and fawning.[19] Had he not been so preoccupied with sham and pretense, however, More might have noticed that his truth-teller's disappointment was a double disenchantment. Common sense unlaced the king's majesty and mystery. It also sabotaged the peasant's own expectations. The crowd's rapture persuaded him, if only momentarily, that their monarch was something more than a man—until Thomas More enlightened him. In the contest between More and the crowd, the lawyer was the winner. But he and his peasant were quite wrong, because the king was just then something more than an ordinary

---

[17]*The Spousells of the Princess Mary, Daughter of Henry VII, to Charles, Prince of Castille*, printed in two editions and collated by James Gairdner, in *The Camden Miscellany*, vol. 9 (London: Camden Society, 1893) 32-33. Tudor horticulture, as described here, was a failure in this instance. Charles renounced the arrangement and it fell to Henry VIII to find his sister a husband. Comparisons between the Latin text and the shabbier, imperfect English edition may shed some light on popular attitudes toward extravagance. Pages with descriptions of Richmond's splendor are missing in the English version. The Latin contains allusions that only cultivated readers would grasp: " . . . quod neque Cresi Lidorum regis gaza, neque Midi Phrygum opes, aut Tagi Pactolive seu Padi auree arene hujus tanti Regis opibus conferri queant." Is it possible that the English edition abridged the Latin's cloying depictions of canopies, tapestries, and paneled ceilings, if it rendered them at all? By 1508 Englishmen had wearied of Henry's excessive taxation and of Empson's and Dudley's extortions. It would have been imprudent to broadcast in detail how money had been spent. Gairdner does not suspect extensive alterations, yet the loss may have been a matter both of default and of design.

[18]Anglo, *Spectacle*, 106.

[19]*Epigrams*, 205-206.

man in an embroidered garment. The sovereign himself had become a symbol of the pageant's integrative function.

To some extent, all public appearances of royalty, painstakingly prearranged or unscheduled, must have kindled collective sentiments. Nevertheless, history is left with only a few fragments of earliest Tudor political ritual and so one can never reconstruct with confidence the public life of Henry VII and his family. Yet certain fragments, examined here, are revealing, and to them one should add the reports of Catherine of Aragon's arrival in London to marry Prince Arthur (1501). I mentioned earlier that these celebrations featured "the most intemperate formulation of the early pageants' theme," and thus repeating this now may seem misguided. Nonetheless, the intemperance has gained in meaning and importance, and it must now be evaluated from a different angle.[20]

The first of several scenes was staged on London Bridge where St. Catherine and St. Ursula, surrounded by virgins, urged the princess to cherish her new husband as she adored her savior. Other exhortations and lectures delivered from ingeniously decorated platforms marked Catherine's passage through London to St. Paul's Cathedral. One outstanding oration, overheard by the king, who apparently stationed himself for the purpose, provides a sense of the entire proceedings. St. Catherine's tentative equation in the initial scene had developed into a rather shocking similitude. As Catherine received the blessing of a man, "goodlike apparailed representyng the Ffader of heven," another man, as "Prelacy," compared the wedding arranged for Arthur with that arranged by God for his son. Hence Arthur was like Christ. Now Prelacy added that Arthur's father was no ordinary terrestrial king. If, to make mysteries more intelligible, it had once been said that heaven's lord was like an earthly king who prepares a wedding for his son, pageants were permitted—in order to raise history to a higher register—to intimate that the king who had redeemed a realm once cursed with baronial wars (and who would therefore leave his son a tamed and tranquil kingdom) could be little less than a celestial lord. Royal family and heavenly family were joined by analogies that virtually amounted to the dynasty's apotheosis.[21] The families' fortunes had been coupled in speeches scripted for the northern festivities (fifteen years earlier), wherein "politike providence" made the Tudors special agents of divine will. Catherine's entry and Prelacy's remarks were staged for a more stridently confident monarch and to fasten collective sentiments, political and devotional, to the personal-

---

[20]For the pageants, see *CL*, 234-48; *GC*, 297-310; and Anglo, *Spectacle*, 53-97. The London entry marked the first of the three matrimonial contracts about which the 1508 commemorative commentary later boasted.

[21]*CL*, 246-47; and *GC*, 308. The chronicler enigmatically placed Prelacy with Honor and not in the tableau that immediately preceded, with God and Church. BL Cotton MSS Julius B XII, 7 (f. 18b) has positioned Prelacy's speech correctly.

ities of the king and his heir. Celebrations such as this provoked Thomas More's sarcasm, but the pageant's deeper purpose must not escape us, as it apparently escaped him.

Holiness had been metaphorically ascribed to monarchs for millennia. Political failure and conflict, however, regularly attenuated the conviction that royal power was somehow preternatural. In fifteenth-century England, for example, decades of civil war produced doubts about the effectiveness of "the royal touch," the king's ability to cure scrofula and related afflictions, so Henry VII's deputies increased the value of alms distributed to the diseased who came to court in search of royal magic. On one level, this incentive was a rather clever but coarse gimmick. But the more profound objectives were to make the king something of a pilgrimage center—a "national" shrine in a realm that was not yet a nation—and to place him above factions as the ruler of all his peoples, including the lowest and the lame.[22] Prelacy's speech functioned similarly to associate the new dynasty with the very headwaters of divine power. To some degree, this probably encouraged faith in the king's incorruptibility and, of course, it fattened the Tudor myth and cult with yet another bale of superlatives. But the hyperbole also removed the king from territorial rivalries. To preside over the solidarity generated by the pageants as a social ideal (and as a reflection of England's true identity, realized once dissensions and diffidence had been ritually exorcised), the king must be more than an ordinary man in an embroidered robe. Otherwise, he would be likely to hold the realm's fate hostage to provincial and purblind policies.

Prelacy exalted the king because the pageant had transfigured the people. The church offered no opposition; instead, as the acknowledged purveyor of transcendence and agent of transformation, it collaborated with the Crown. The ideals of religion and those of political culture were congenial and carefully braided in municipal and royal pageants. When the public ceremonies concluded and spellbound citizens returned to their practical affairs, it remained for the sovereign and several of his ecclesiastical collaborators to translate these ideals into the language of "national" recovery.

---

[22]Marc Bloch, *Le rois thaumaturges* (Strasbourg: Publications de la Faculté des Lettres de l'Université de Strasbourg, 1924) 113-14; and Keith Thomas, *Religion and the Decline of Magic* (New York: Scribner's, 1971) 204-206.

Chapter 8

POWER:
RICHARD FOX
AND JOHN MORTON

It is impossible to overlook the contributions made to earliest Tudor administration by ecclesiastical civil servants. But it is equally impossible to chronicle them precisely. Sufficiently detailed records of Henry VII's council simply have not survived. Its deliberations remain mysterious. Had detailed memoranda been preserved, however, one might still have difficulty evaluating the church's contributions dispassionately. Earliest Tudor critics' complaints about worldliness have settled like clouds over the issue of clerical participation and leadership in government. Each of our first two parts explored a particular aspect of this historiographical problem. We may now move toward a solution by reconstructing, in two cases, the clergy's reliance upon political power and political culture's reliance upon the church.

Of the clerics who joined Henry VII in exile and thereafter shared his good fortune, Richard Fox and John Morton lay greatest claim to attention. Both returned with Henry and swiftly succeeded to positions of authority. Morton became chancellor of the realm and archbishop of Canterbury. Fox was appointed keeper of the Privy Seal, and bishop, consecutively, of Exeter, Bath and Wells, Durham, and Winchester. Both managed to earn the respect of idealistic critics as well as the admiration of diplomats and foreign princes.

Fox, with whom I shall start, endeared himself to Andreas Ammonius, who wrote effusively of the bishop's virtues, and he befriended Polydore Vergil, who thought highly of his statesmanship. From Vergil, one learns of the Scottish king's affection for Fox and of the prelate's visits in the north that induced James IV to forget festering grievances against English neighbors. According to Vergil, James was apt to share with Fox his most intimate thoughts.[1] The bishop's private thoughts and ambitions remain unspoken. He composed no revealing self-explorations that in-

---

[1] "Statuit secretiora sui pectoris aperire consilia," *AH*, 112. For Ammonius's tribute, *Andreae Ammonii carmina omnia*, ed. Clementi Pizzi (Florence: L. S. Olschki, 1958) esp. 25.

vite us behind the lists of offices and diplomatic assignments. Infrequent personal remarks, such as his expression of regret that public life kept him from pastoral responsibilities, delight his admirers and enliven thumbnail sketches of his career. Biographical entries generally agree that Fox was diligent about his political obligations and, after retirement from court in 1516, faithful in the performance of his diocesan duties.[2] But it is misleading to stage his life in two such separable acts. Fox was versatile and thought administratively about religion and religiously about earliest Tudor political culture. To recover some sign of this, one must follow the bishop to the north of England, to the diocese of Durham, the first in which he resided. His episcopal register and the cursitor rolls, which have been deposited in the Public Record Office, testify to the interpenetration of religious and political life.

"Rugged" defines the land, climate, and inhabitants of the diocese and also the challenge that faced Fox. The territory's stubborn refusal to return great profit for labor invested must have seemed an insult to the gritty farmers, shepherds, and miners. Trading in lead, which had been hauled from northern mines for centuries, was unregulated, unpredictable, and only slowly coordinated during the last half of the fifteenth century. The rapid development of mines and markets for coal that made Newcastle a commercial center was still decades in the future.[3] Newcastle was, in fact, the slowest of the kingdom's cities to recover from the effects of plague and depopulation. Rents and property values declined there years after other municipalities had started on the mend.[4] News from the fields and farms could have been little better. Northern wool was so coarse and its export yielded so little tariff revenue that the government waived the requirement that all English shipments pass through Calais. Newcastle and Berwick merchants could deliver their sacks directly to those Netherlands ports that specialized in the manufacture of cheap cloths and return with the prices they fetched.[5]

For all this, however, the bishop of Durham's estates were extensive. In fact, returns made the incumbent the realm's second-wealthiest prel-

[2]"The Episcopate of Richard Fox," published as the intro. to *The Register of Richard Fox, Lord Bishop of Durham*, ed. Marjorie Peers Howden (Durham: Surtees Society, 1932); and "Richard Fox of Winchester," in Francis Oakley, *The Western Church in the Later Middle Ages* (Ithaca: Cornell University Press, 1979) 285-94.

[3]Arthur Raistrick and Bernard Jennings, *A History of Lead Mining in the Pennines* (London: Longmans, 1965) 37-39.

[4]A. F. Butcher, "Rent, Population, and Economic Change in Late Medieval Newcastle," *NH* 14 (1978): 69-75; and R. S. Schofield, "The Geographical Distribution of Wealth in England, 1334-1649," *Economic History Review*, 2d ser. 18 (1965): 508-509.

[5]Peter J. Bowden, *The Wool Trade in Tudor and Stuart England* (London: Macmillan & Co., 1971) 107-109.

ate, if calculations exclude pluralism and other sources of income.[6] But the post was no sinecure. Northerners were unruly and particularly suspicious of remote authority. Henry VII had traveled as far as York in 1486 but, perhaps wisely, no farther. His predecessor, Richard III, had been a favorite among northerners and had lived among them as his brother's lieutenant before he became king.[7] The intractable upland was reluctant to accept the finality of the Tudor victory. Notwithstanding York's 1486 ritual of submission, the countryside was still unreconciled in 1488 when Henry VII levied taxes in preparation for war with France. Trying to collect them, early in 1489, the earl of Northumberland was killed by a mob of dissidents after he had been deserted by his retainers.[8]

The challenge to royal authority in the north became increasingly important. Henry's nemesis, Perkin Warbeck, had been courting James IV of Scotland, who gradually warmed to the prospect of having the English pretender in his realm. Scotland was restless, hostile, and likely to invade. In December 1494 Richard Fox was translated to Durham and, early the next year, tenants were notified that the temporalities had been restored to their bishop and landlord. Within twelve months, Warbeck arrived across the border.[9]

Bishops of Durham and Carlisle generally shared responsibilities for the territories' defense and internal government with leading northern barons. In the fourteenth century, bishops were frequently commissioned as wardens of the Marches, but the great border families—the Percies, the Scropes, and the Nevilles of north Yorkshire—steadily improved their positions and often in the fifteenth century claimed regal power. Naturally, rivalries made peace-keeping problematic. Henry VII was tempted to try other measures and eventually to reassert episcopal authority. Episcopal civil servants usually were men of proven administrative talents. Bishops of Durham, for example, governed a large secular franchise that was nominally independent of the king. A series of fifteenth-century charters confirmed the bishops' rights to appoint justices of the peace and coroners, to maintain and deliver prisons, and to expropriate the goods and chattels of all outlawed residents.[10] Arguments for order in the north—whether they were weighted with forecasts of Scottish invasions or with promises of a new Tudor dispensation, a reprieve from anarchy—were irrelevant without the tools to craft and enforce law

---

[6]Felicity Heal, *Of Prelates and Princes* (Cambridge: Cambridge University Press, 1980) 55-56.

[7]*Rot. Parl.* 6:204-205.

[8]M. A. Hicks, "Dynastic Change and Northern Society: The Career of the Fourth Earl of Northumberland, 1470-1489," *NH* 14 (1978): 94-100.

[9]PRO *Durh.* 3.60, m.1, 1.

[10]*Charter Rolls,* esp. 5:454-55; and 6:104-105.

and order. At least in Durham, late-medieval incumbents developed (and Richard Fox inherited) invaluable liberties and conciliar machinery.[11]

Still, it would be foolish to expect a tidy result since the north was not an especially tidy place. Indeed, it is misleading to write about the region as if it were homogenous. For one thing, the contours of economic life in the cathedral cities were vastly different. By the end of the fifteenth century, York was a busy, though not a spectacularly prosperous commercial center, with more than ten thousand inhabitants and a diverse merchant class. Durham and Carlisle housed fewer than two thousand people each and, in size, ranked below other northern cities, notably Newcastle and Beverley. The economies of Durham and Carlisle depended largely on their respective cathedral chapters, which often found it necessary to make many of their purchases from markets in southern districts.[12]

The character of lawlessness also altered as one moved from York northward through Northumberland. York officials worried chiefly about urban unrest and violence, commonly sparked by municipal elections.[13] As bishop of Durham, Fox demonstrated considerable anxiety about disobedience among miners and laborers and, in 1497, he empowered Leonard Forster to arrest spirited miners who seemed likely to shovel more trouble than coal.[14] Crime seemed most irrepressible, however, in the sparsely populated regions of Redesdale and Tynedale, which had rep-

---

[11]For general studies of the territory's disorder and Durham's palatine liberties, which are distinct yet related topics, see Gaillard T. Lapsley, "The Problem of the North," *AHR* 5 (1900): 440-66, reprinted in *Crown, Community, and Parliament in the Later Middle Ages,* ed. Helen M. Cam and Geoffrey Barraclough (Oxford: Basil Blackwell, 1951) 375-405; Lapsley's *The County Palatine of Durham* (Cambridge: Harvard Historical Studies, 1900) esp. 68-70, 155, 209-16, 308; R. L. Storey, *Thomas Langley and the Bishopric of Durham, 1406-1437* (London: Surtees Society, 1961) 52-163; and Storey's "The North of England," in *Fifteenth-Century England, 1399-1509,* ed. S. B. Chrimes, C. D. Ross, R. A. Griffiths (Manchester: Manchester University Press, 1972) 129-44. Relationships between palatine immunities and wardens' powers have never been completely clarified, but consult R. R. Reid, *The King's Council in the North* (London: Longmans & Co., 1921) 78-84; 92-94; and R. L. Storey, "The Wardens of the Marches of England towards Scotland, 1377-1489," *EHR* 72 (1957): 593-615.

[12]R. B. Dobson, "Cathedral Chapters and Cathedral Cities: York, Durham, and Carlisle in the Fifteenth Century," *NH* 19 (1983): 15-44; J. N. Bartlett, "The Expansion and Decline of York in the Later Middle Ages," *Economic History Review,* 2d ser. 12 (1959): 28-32.

[13]*YCR* 2:39-40, 192-94.

[14]PRO *Durh.* 3.61, m.4, 10.

utations for frustrating law enforcement that were often rehearsed for late-medieval parliaments.[15]

A *Monitio contra latrones*, which was copied into Fox's episcopal register, describes the situation that prompted the bishop to use ecclesiastical sanctions against border criminals. It explains that thieves from Redesdale and Tynedale not only terrorized their own districts, but frequently strayed into the neighboring areas. Wherever they went, they spread destruction. Fox was scandalized by the fact that, after larcenous excursions, raiders could cross back into, and then pass through, their own territories with their victims' property yet without fear of punishment.[16] Scoundrels lived as heroes. Unrepentant criminals publicly and loudly boasted of their atrocities. Whole households were devoted to crime and children were encouraged to learn the family "business" as though it were a perfectly respectable profession.[17] The impeccably evil collective life of Redesdale and Tynedale seems too completely cruel and criminal to be anything other than fiction, but Fox's outrage and urgency compel belief.

---

[15]*Rot. Parl.* 3:662; 4:21, 143. Also *SC* Leadam 2:72-74, where the mayor and aldermen of Newcastle alleged in 1509 that the prior of Tynemouth salaried men from Tynedale and Redesdale in an effort to disrupt the city's business. Either the prior actually recruited border ruffians or town officials added the accusation to the names of forty-one local troublemakers in order to dramatize Newcastle's peril and embroider their case before the king's council.

[16]*Reg. Fox*, 80: "Quia fama quam facti notorietate referentibus, ad aures nostras delatum est quod nonnulli villas, villulas, hamelectas et alia loca de Tyndalle et Ryddisdalle inhabitantes, nec divina nec humana jura timentes quibus se illaquiatos esse (quod summopere dolemus) intelligunt aut saltem intelligere debent, de eisdem villis, villulis, hamelectis ad et in episcopatum Dunelmensem et comitatum Northumbrie aliaque loca, dictis locis de Tyndalle et Ryddisdalle confinia et adjacentia, latronum, rapientium, ac depredantium more, per diuturna tempora saepe, saepius, et saepissime, publice, et manifeste, noctu dieque incurrentes, prout adhuc indies, cotidie, saepe, saepius, et saepissime, noctu dieque, publice et manifeste, sic incurrunt, furta, latrocinia, rapinas, et depredationes passim committentes, pecora et catalla in eisdem inventa furati depredatique fuerunt, et ab eisdem ad partes et territoria de Tyndall et Ryddisdalle predictis, aliaque loca eisdem confinia, ad libitum suarum voluntatum asportaverunt, fugaverunt, et abigerunt, prout adhuc indies nulli equidem alii rei quam, hujusmodi furtis, latrociniis, rapinis et depredationibus, dediti, furantur, depredantur, fugant et abigunt."

[17]*Reg. Fox*, 81: ". . . suosque liberos, servientes, atque famulos in hujusmodi latrociniorum, furtorum, depredationum et rapinarum perpetratione, quod maxime detestandum est, educant, et excercitant, adeo ut furtum, latrocinium, depredationem, rapinam, aut robberium hujusmodi committere, aut eidem consentire non solum non vereantur, sed crassam, [im]mo verius quesitam ignorantiam pretendentes, et dictas rapinas, furtum et depredationes, tanquam artem unde victum suum querant, publice et manifeste profitentes, crimen esse non agnoscunt."

The bishop's comments probably also reflect his frustration, his inability to scrub crime from the troubled border districts, which did not fall within the boundaries of his secular franchise. Parliament had removed Tynedale from the jurisdiction of the archbishop of York in 1495, attaching it to the shire of Northumberland and not to the County Palatine of Durham.[18] Therefore, Fox's authority there was essentially pastoral. His power, however, was both pastoral and political.

Matters might have taken a different turn had local barons in Northumberland's border regions been willing to organize resistance. But Fox was aware that the machinery for the maintenance of order, or what little there was of it in the extreme north, had altogether broken down. Nobles reportedly conspired with thieves and lined their own pockets with a share of the plunder. According to Fox, outlaws bragged that they could count on the collusion of leading landholders who cared little to hide their partnership from the public. "Openly and shamelessly, they allow these thugs and the cattle they have rustled to cross their lands and pass safely through their territories."[19] The bishop charged that barons even received and entertained hoodlums in their homes. All this made the north's "respectable" citizens as culpable for the widespread defiance of law and for the defeat of order as those who made a living through larceny and manslaughter. "If there were no one to shelter and comfort those who commit such violence, no one would venture the violence."[20]

Crime and baronial complicity drove Fox to issue the *Monitio* and to threaten excommunication. But there was also an ecclesiastical dimension to the problem in Redesdale and Tynedale. Outlaws and their patrons predictably preferred less than scrupulous priests. They either controlled provisions to vacant livings or influenced abbatical presentations. If Fox and his sources are to be believed, border felons and their friends were contaminating the church with crude, illiterate priests, many of whom had been suspended or excommunicated before they received their northern benefices. Particularly these "sham priests" disgraced the sacraments.[21] They were powerless to absolve anyone, and when they pretended to do so, they did great disservice to Christianity throughout the region. The criminals' aggrieved victims, Fox said, were tremen-

---

[18]*SR* 2:575 (11 Henry VII, c.9). The statute notes that the proliferation of crime necessitated the change.

[19]*Reg. Fox*, 81: ". . . expresse consentientes, fures ipsos, latrones, et depredatores per eorum terras et districtus cum rebus, pecoribus et catallis, quae furati sunt, liberum habere transitum scienter tolerant et permittunt."

[20]*Reg. Fox*, 81-82: "Nam si non esset, qui foveret, reciperet, et comfortaret, nullus rapinam, latrocinium, depredationes hujusmodi commiteret committereve auderet."

[21]*Reg. Fox*, 82: ". . . nonnullos etiam non ordinatos, sed sacerdotii effigiem duntaxat pretendentes."

dously dispirited when told that the sacraments had been administered to their uncontrite persecutors and that notorious thieves were forgiven, though unrepentant, and eventually buried in consecrated ground. Fox himself can be forgiven for thinking that the signs were not good for the future of Northumbrian Christianity.[22]

Border crime, then, was a religious problem. It was a problem for which the gallows rope was no solution. Fox was fighting for control of his clergy as well as for order, property, propriety, and sacramental purity. The issue of episcopal control may be investigated in greater depth if I digress for a moment. While Fox tackled Durham's difficulties, Bishop Mayew of Hereford was locked in combat with the prior of St. John of Jerusalem. By 1505 the bishop forwarded to Canterbury charges that bailiffs had wrongfully withheld the small sum due upon his triennial visitation of the parish church of Garway. The Hospitallers claimed exemption from the procurations, and the case dragged on for years. All this lodges in the early folios of Mayew's register and, prima facie, seems to be an example of a ruthlessly avaricious prelate's infatuation with the courts, a case tailored for the satires of idealistic critics.[23] To possess a few pennies, the bishop appeared ready to spend lavishly and to risk enduring hostilities. But Mayew's relentless insistence on his fees was, in fact, part of an episcopal *contrecoup* undertaken to reassert episcopal control.

By 1511 a full account of the case, along with a scorching indictment of the Hospitallers' activities in Hereford and elsewhere in England, was sent directly to Rome. Apparently, the order held episcopal sanctions in contempt. Parishes ostensibly in the Hospitallers' care did not submit to episcopal supervision. The inventory of official complaints, in this instance, resembles that compiled by Fox and his deputies. It was said that corpses of excommunicates were admitted to the Hospitallers' cemeteries, and "if the bodies . . . inadvertently rest in Catholic gravesites, [members of the order] frighten away curates who attempt to disinter them." Many apostates and fugitives from justice who had flocked to the order were appointed chaplains. "The tainted [and unordained] chaplains defiantly administer the sacraments, . . . absolving whomever comes to them" from properly assigned penances. In essence, the order not only shielded sham priests from episcopal oversight, but also enabled those

---

[22]*Reg. Fox*, 82: ". . . sicque eos, sine cautione de restituendo, ecclesiastice sepulture, cum ex sacrorum canonum et sanctorum patrum institutis haec facere districte prohibentur, passim committunt, in animarum suarum grave periculum, aliorumque Christi fidelium exemplum perniciosum, plurimorumque spoliatorum et privatorum bonis, rebus, pecoribus et catallis suis hujusmodi damnum non modicum et gravamen."

[23]*Reg. Mayew*, 20-34.

counterfeit clerics to subvert church discipline and to place the reform of lay conduct beyond the reach of legitimate authority.[24]

This sample is really too small to support the weight of a great conclusion. Still, one inference seems likely: while scholars pressed—more urgently as the sixteenth century wore on—to make Christianity doctrinally coherent, episcopal administrators labored against immunists and renegades to make the church institutionally and administratively coherent. Actually, the quest for control was everywhere apparent. Episcopal registers are packed with injunctions prohibiting absenteeism without license.[25] Collegiate churches warned members not to proceed from inferior to holy orders until the chapter examined them and endorsed their promotion.[26] In Lincoln, the bishop's vicar-general forbade Robert Judd from assuming pastoral responsibilities (*"non custodiet curam animarum"*), though Judd was deputed to the chapel of Fleckney by the abbot of Selby. While the abbot was being consulted, Judd administered rites to Alice Coltman, *in extremis*, and he was sternly scolded for such temerity and threatened with suspension.[27] The response to Judd's indiscretion, like Bishop Mayew's militancy, may seem irrational, yet tactics of intimidation were elements of episcopal programs aimed at achieving order from the center to the circumference of troubled dioceses. A single maverick could unsettle the campaign. The de facto autonomy of Redesdale and Tynedale made a mockery of episcopal government.

Fox simply wanted to revive episcopal authority and arrest the spread of disorder. He concluded his *Monitio* with a directive for those clergy still loyal: they were instructed to threaten outlaws and their Northumbrian patrons with excommunication.[28] The force of his final remarks is somewhat diminished by circumlocution; yet his attempts to tackle the prob-

---

[24]*Reg. Mayew*, 51: "Excommunicatis insuper et hiis qui sibi ipsis manus nefarie consiverunt hospitalarii illi non solum licenter exhibent sepulcra sua sed etiam, si forte ipsorum excommunicatorum corpora per inadvertenciam intra catholicorum cimiteria humata fuerint curatos exterrent ne ipsa eiciant. Hii sunt qui per eorum capellanos, omnes abjectissimos sacerdotum qui ut frequenter litteras ordinum suorum nullas habent, apostatas quidem enim regulariter interdictos, omnem suis exemptis capellis in aliorum parochianos transfugas seu fugitivos ecclesiasticam potestatem in utroque foro exercent, sacramenta omnia, maxime, penitentiae, eucharistiae, et matrimonii, ministrando absolvendoque quoscumque ad se venientes quacumque sententia a jure vel ab homine lata ligati extiterunt." For the exemptions in question, consult Laurent Dailliez, *Les Templiers: gouvernement et institutions*, vol. 1 (Nice: Alpes-Méditerranée Édition, 1980) 252-55.

[25]E.g., for Fox's Durham pontificate, *Reg. Fox*, 97-110.

[26]*Ripon*, 257-58.

[27]*Lincoln*, 4-6.

[28]*Reg. Fox*, 83-84.

lems must have provoked some crisis in the border communities, because a subsequent document, dated 1498, lists fifteen criminals eager for absolution and reconciliation. Fox ordered them to desist from criminal activity and required them to relinquish their sturdiest horses as well as their arms and armor so that they might not be tempted to any further wrongdoing. To squeeze every advantage from this mass penance, the bishop told his priests to announce the absolution on the next feast day, when their churches were certain to be full. But it was not simply the publicity value of the affair that dictated this portion of Fox's *mandamus*. The terms and conditions of the absolution were to be detailed publicly so that all the faithful might shun relapsed offenders, as if they were again excommunicated.[29]

In tribal society, ostracism is a dreadful penalty. As deterrents, excommunications and conditional absolutions relied on the social pressure that they could bring to bear. Fox seems to have made no attempt to apprehend offenders, that is, to obtain writs *de cursu* (without independent investigation) that would have empowered sheriffs to assist the church against its more obstinate enemies. The bishop may have despaired of finding cooperative local officials, but it also seems likely that Fox was relatively indifferent to the prospect of the outlaws' capture. Instead, he probably hoped swiftly to reassert episcopal control over the region's spiritual life and command over its balance of power.[30]

The absolution copied into Fox's register, then, hints that the bishop was successful. Years later, it was implied that, to great effect, he had excluded entire families from their parish churches.[31] But the border regions underwent no miraculous transformation. Two months after the absolution had been issued, two of the fifteen forgiven were again in

---

[29]Ibid., 111: "... ut non parentes ab omnibus christifidelibus tanquam excommunicati evitari possint."

[30]For the prestige of spiritual sanctions, note Thomas, *Religion and the Decline of Magic*, esp. 44; but also see the discussion of their indiscriminate use and declining influence, in Rosalind Hill, "The Theory and Practice of Excommunication in Medieval England," *History* 42 (1957): 11: "If the church imposed its supreme penalty too freely, it was not because the senior clergy were too slack but because they were too thorough, and in their determination to maintain law and order they used the sentence of excommunication so freely that at last it degenerated from a tremendous spiritual sanction into a minor inconvenience." Also in this connection, see Storey, *Thomas Langley*, 113-16; and the parliamentary endorsement of episcopal conduct and sanctions, *Rot. Parl.* 4:421. It should be mentioned that in 1500 Fox did appeal for the *"advocatio brachii secularis"* in order to rid Redesdale of a notorious sorceress (*Reg. Fox*, 129-30). With respect to such writs *de excommunicato capiendo*, review F. Donald Logan, *Excommunication and the Secular Arm in Medieval England* (Toronto: Pontifical Institute of Mediaeval Studies, 1968) esp. 86-87.

[31]*LP Henry VIII* 3:464 (1125); 3:822 (1920); and 4:6 (10).

trouble with authorities for having violated England's truce with Scotland and for murdering several of their northern neighbors.[32] The Durham documents, nonetheless, reflect Fox's readiness to use the most extreme spiritual sanctions, and they underscore the religious dimensions of the problem of social control as well as the church's stake in administrative order. "Sham priests," who were within, yet vexatiously beyond, the bishop's jurisdiction, were an embarrassment. They were also, according to Fox, a menace to souls who came to depend upon fraudulently administered sacraments. The documents communicate this and in other ways suggest how important it was for a northern bishop to have the allegiance of all his priests. Fox relied upon them to publicize his injunctions and prohibitions and, what was equally if not more strategic, to monitor obedience and enforcement. If conditions attached to his absolutions went unfulfilled, local clerics were to denounce the impudence and to warn Christians against associating with the offenders. Without the presence in the parishes of priests who were above certain provincial pressures, their bishops' pontifical pronouncements, though full of sound and fury, signified nothing.[33] It was politically and pastorally sensible to have an obedient priest in every parish. For Fox, it was politically and pastorally necessary to shatter the cozy arrangements negotiated between border criminals and their "kept" clergy.

This gives greater resonance to the common requirements that absentees supply and salary suitable substitutes. Collegiate chapters frequently cooperated.[34] When they did not, bishops might engage sequestrators to claim the income of prebends on the grounds that nonresident canons had failed to maintain a vicar in situ. Understandably, bishops were reluctant to deprive priests for incontinence if they otherwise served faithfully.[35] Staffing problems in Durham were somewhat alleviated by rushing candidates through inferior orders. Letters dimissory and ordination lists for Fox's pontificate, though incomplete, testify to the alacrity with which men advanced into holy orders and on to the priesthood. William Graye was ordained a priest in March 1499, exactly two years after he was made subdeacon at Alnwick, yet many of his colleagues pressed ahead more rapidly. Parish arrangements, however, often tested the patience and energy of the church's most diligent servants. At Fox's behest, they might suddenly become law officers or, upon a Scottish incursion and during border skirmishes, military chaplains. At Norham, on the Scottish border, George Berriswode (Bryswoode) resigned

---

[32]*CPR*, 1494-1509, 160.

[33]*Reg. Fox*, 111-12.

[34]E.g., *Ripon*, 310.

[35]*LRF*, 150-51.

his cure in 1497, after only eighteen months, and his successor, Richard Colson, lasted little less than a year before he too withdrew.[36]

Scotland's shadow was particularly terrifying. By 1488 James IV's victory over his father's forces and allies was complete. Unlike Henry VII, he had no stubborn rivals to disturb the early years of his reign. Foreign observers commented on the ease with which the young and impetuous Scottish monarch could put an army in the field, and for some time, enmity against England had been undisguised. Border raids were nothing new. "Thou haste brente Northumberlonde, and done me grete envy" was a plaint composed for Percy in *The Ballad of the Battle of Otterburne*, which commemorated a late-fourteenth-century conflict, but subsequent generations of northern nobility could justifiably echo its accusation.[37] Animosity, then, owed its survival to the nearly unbroken state of war that pitted Scotland against England's border territories. Even in York, persons identified as Scots had good cause to fear for their safety.[38] The bishops of Durham derived some advantage from diplomatic uncertainties, for their sovereigns were reluctant to endorse immunists' claims against them as long as the region required strong leadership. As a result, before Fox's pontificate, the city's convent and cathedral chapter had been tamed and chained to the bishops' will.[39] But bishops, in return, were expected to be prepared and prompt when their kings called for northern troops and productively amiable and statesmanlike when the realm seemed better served by restraint and appeasement.

Negotiations during 1496 concentrated on the prospect of uniting Tudors and Stewarts through marriage. Though he had only recently assumed his episcopal responsibilities, Fox was already involved deeply— if not yet decisively—in the commissions and deliberations. At this stage

---

[36]*Reg. Fox*, 50-51, 74, for the Norham resignations; and for a sample of letters dimissory "ad omnes tam minores quam majores etiam presbiteratus ordines," ibid., 84, 115, 126. For Graye and several of his colleagues, ibid., 43, 48, 63, and 85. Also see Heath, *Parish Clergy*, 12-18. The relative obsolescence of minor orders in the later Middle Ages is considered in Jo Ann Hoeppner-Moran, "Clerical Recruitment in the Diocese of York, 1340-1530: Data and Commentary," *JEH* 34 (1983): 35.

[37]Reprinted in John Hodgson, *A History of Northumberland*, pt. 2, vol. 1 (Newcastle: Society of Antiquaries, 1827) 126. For reports of James IV's popularity and military ambitions, *CSP, Spain*, 1485-1509, 174-75; and Sneyd, *True Account*, 31-32.

[38]*YCR* 1:169.

[39]See Frank Barlow, *Durham Jurisdictional Peculiars* (Oxford: Oxford University Press, 1950) 51-52; and also consult R. B. Dobson, *Durham Priory, 1400-1450* (Cambridge: Cambridge University Press, 1973). The general tenor of Fox's relations with the prior, Thomas Castell, is probably reflected in Castell's tentative reservations—and the cautious and respectful way they were expressed—when the bishop made an apparently unorthodox appointment, *LRF*, 24-25.

the sticking point was Perkin Warbeck's visit to Scotland and James IV's hospitality.[40] Even after the pretender left his kingdom, however, the belligerent Scottish monarch crossed the border and besieged Norham castle for two weeks in 1497. James's offensive disintegrated when word reached Norham, Fox's administrative center in the far north, of the approach of a considerable army commanded by Thomas Howard, earl of Surrey. Surrey shared with Fox and several others the power to act for young Prince Henry, who had been since 1495 the north's warden-general. He chased James back into Scotland, and soon afterward a seven-year truce was concluded. The Scots apparently were inexpert in maneuvers that would have enabled them to take and hold their neighbors' fortifications. Nonetheless, their regular raids must have panicked some northerners and have steeled others to a violent, uncertain existence.[41] Richard Cholmley, Norhamshire's justice of the peace, kept the castle well provisioned, but Fox continued to take a special interest in Norham's defense.[42] Cholmley was knighted for his part, and John Hamerton and Thomas Garth were awarded lucrative annual stipends "for seeing to the safety of the castle."[43] Fox's episcopacy was his reward but, as noted, it was a rather dubious one. Before the truce, Scottish belligerence as well as border crime, and the deleterious effects of both on order and church discipline in the north, placed considerable stress on the bishop and his administrators.

Richard Fox was resourceful, and one suspects that he would have been glad for the opportunity to fashion a wholly new order for the north, especially for Redesdale and Tynedale. But the question of control was not simply prevenient; it was paramount. And the struggle for control takes on nearly heroic proportions if placed in relief against the scuffles, sieges, rumors of war, and initiatives for peace that cluttered Fox's pontificate. Of course, the imputation of heroism is disputable. To refer the issue of control exclusively to political opportunism and episcopal self-indulgence, however, is unquestionably inappropriate. No short narrative can encompass Fox's own perspective. One can only suggest that his challenge and response were complex and hybrid. Moreover, until the church was his, lay impiety must have seemed permanently beyond reformation, and sinful souls, without a proper and properly regulated ministry, no doubt appeared beyond reclamation.

---

[40]Gairdner, *Letters*, 1:104-105; *Rot. Scot.* 2:520-22; and *CDS* 4:327.

[41]For tax relief granted "ad resistendum Scotos aut alios hujus Regni Angliae inimicos vel ad eorundem invasionem propulsandam in personis suis propriis vel ad aliquem vel aliquos viros armatos . . . ," *Reg. Fox*, 34.

[42]PRO *Durh.* 3:62, m.11, 88; *Durh.* 3:63, m.1, 2 and m.5, 20.

[43]"Pro salus et secura custodia et defensione castelli nostri de Norham contra insidias et obsidionem quas Jacobus Scotorum rex in propria persona sua cum ingenti exercitu . . . ," PRO *Durh.* 3:61, m.5, 22 and m.12, 55.

Chief among Fox's loyalists and officials, Richard Nix (or Nykke) was the bishop's vicar-general in Exeter and in Bath and Wells before both men moved to Durham. Attending constantly to his king's business, Fox found it impracticable personally to oversee matters in his first two dioceses and he was often away from Durham as well; therefore Nix, who held doctorates of canon and civil law from Bologna, exercised enormous authority. His commissions as vicar-general and official principal were much the same as similarly intended documents sealed in other dioceses. They may be read as episcopal manifestos, declaring the degree of centralization and control to which late-medieval bishops aspired.[44]

Inventories of Nix's duties were preceded by a gingerly worded note about his bishop's absence: "We are unable continually to reside in our diocese, for the king's and the kingdom's many affairs and the defense of the church universal [preoccupy us]." Nix was told that he must preside over the consistory court, though he was likely to have done so—and much else mentioned here—during the incumbent's residence as well. The vicar-general supervised appointments and elections to all ecclesiastical stations. If he found a defect in procedures or in the candidates, he must annul the action and prescribe appropriate penances and penalties. Inquiries were to be made at each candidate's presentation to a benefice and the rights of patronage were to be reestablished. This could be quite useful when the bishop or his deputy wished to wrest control of the clergy from disagreeable baronial patrons.

The vicar-general was commissioned to deprive persons of benefices or offices that they held illegitimately (*illicite occupantes*), be they parish priests or influential priors and abbots. If clerics pleaded their "clergy" before a secular court, the vicar-general, on behalf of the bishop, was to take custody and to supervise purgation. He watched over the progress of the clergy through orders and he was empowered to issue letters dimissory to hasten it. If he spied excess or heresy, the vicar-general was to correct the culprits' conduct and convictions. Where irregularities might be concealed from view by convents' high walls, he was delegated the bishop's power to visit, examine, admonish, and reform the regular clergy. The license was, at the very least, a literary outlet for episcopal ambition. Doubtlessly, in many cases it was also representative of an administrative order achieved, preserved, and passed on.

In 1501 Nix was appointed bishop of Norwich, presumably as a reward for faithful service to, and at the instigation of, Richard Fox, who was transferred to Winchester that same year. As bishop of Durham, Fox increasingly took an interest in diocesan government, but Winchester was to see even more of him. William Sever, bishop of Carlisle, inherited Dur-

---

[44]For what follows, see *Reg. Fox*, 3-6; *The Register of Richard Fox* (Bath and Wells), ed. Edmund Chisholm Batten (London: privately printed, 1889) 1-5; and Thompson, *Clergy*, 47-48, 53-54.

ham and Fox's managerial challenges and responsibilities.[45] In the second year of his pontificate, Sever gave John Heron custody for life of Durham's manor house in London, close to the royal palace (*"juxta regium"*). Quite plausibly, Sever thus signaled his intention to remain in the north and to devote himself completely to its pacification.[46]

Bishops were rather frequently moved from see to see during the first Tudor regime. Between 1499 and 1505—shortly before and soon after Fox moved to Winchester, Sever to Durham, and Nix to Norwich—seventeen of the other eighteen English and Welsh sees were vacant and refilled at least once. Death removed elder statesmen from the most lucrative dioceses. Their juniors were usually promoted and their places, in turn, were held for others who were perhaps just starting their episcopal careers, men who were especially diligent civil servants or who, like Nix, had distinguished themselves as diocesan administrators. With few exceptions, royal nomination was tantamount to appointment. Cathedral chapters' consent or "election" was a formality, and papal participation in selection had been considerably reduced. In some cases the king restored temporalities to a new bishop before approval arrived from Rome.[47] So it was with John Morton, who was named both chancellor of the realm and archbishop of Canterbury within two years of Henry VII's accession.[48]

With virtual control over episcopal promotion and translation, Henry VII had ample opportunity to reward the Crown's diligent and trustworthy servants, to match versatile executives with challenging assignments, and to keep valued advisers salaried, satisfied, and closely connected with the new dynasty's policies. The first factor, reward, figured in most episcopal appointments.[49] Only at great risk did one leave shrewd politicians unrewarded. The second factor was almost certainly behind Fox's switch to Durham, and the third suggests itself as one rea-

---

[45]See the exaggerated expressions of esteem in Sever's commission to survey the estates of the earl of Westmoreland, PRO *Durh.* 3:64, m.1, 1; but also consult W. C. Richardson, *Tudor Chamber Administration, 1485-1547* (Baton Rouge: Louisiana State University Press, 1952) 135-40.

[46]PRO *Durh.* 3:64, m.17, 57.

[47]For general papal rights and acquiescence, Guillaume Mollat, *La collation des bénéfices ecclésiastiques sous les papes d'Avignon, 1305-1378* (Strasbourg: Université de Strasbourg, 1921) 187-226, 249-69; and John A. F. Thomson, *Popes and Princes, 1417-1517: Politics and Polity in the Late Medieval Church* (London: Allen & Unwin, 1980).

[48]Emden, *Oxford*, 2:1318-20; Thompson, *Clergy*, 31.

[49]Review Joel Thomas Rosenthal, *The Training of an Elite Group: English Bishops in the Fifteenth Century* (Philadelphia: American Philosophical Society, 1970).

son, among others, why Morton was rushed to the top of the ecclesiastical hierarchy. Idealistic critics might speak derisively of sycophants and of the general pollution of court life, but they would never have encouraged their sovereigns to chase all counsel from court, and Morton struck several "court-watchers" as a man of remarkable prudence.[50] He had acquired a reputation for faithful and imaginative service to the Crown. Fox's career was launched along with his king's, but alongside Morton, Fox and Henry VII were upstarts, relative newcomers.

Morton's career extended back through two previous dynasties and through the reigns of four previous monarchs. He owed his initial appointments to the Lancastrians, to whom he was pledged until the party's prospects collapsed after the battle of Tewkesbury. Edward IV took a fancy to him, reversed his attainder, and made him master of the Rolls in 1474.[51] Thereafter Morton was preoccupied with Edward's affairs on the Continent and divided his time largely between the French and Burgundian courts.[52] Paths toward lasting alliances were mined and impassable, but Morton's efforts and skill did not go unappreciated. In 1479 he was made bishop of Ely.

Ely was one of the realm's wealthier dioceses, so Morton could afford to surrender most of his previous preferments. For a time he disappeared from court, but it is impossible to say whether he spent prolonged periods in his diocese. His predecessor and successor left detailed registers, but nothing survives from Morton's term (1479-1487). Collateral evidence contributes next to nothing. One can tell, for instance, that the priory of St. Radegund in Cambridge was trapped in a tradition of decline by the time Morton became bishop. Can its subsequent economic and moral bankruptcy conceivably be blamed on Morton's presumed unwillingness to visit, detect, and correct?[53]

Just when one thinks Morton lost, he resurfaces in London, that is, in the history of Yorkist conspiracies, and in the conspicuously unenviable position of having been branded, with Hastings, a traitor to Richard III. His arrest and subsequent confinement in the duke of Buckingham's custody are the best-known chapters in Morton's life. To be sure, Richard's controversial execution of Hastings—perfidious murder or preemptive strike?—grabs most attention, but neither Polydore Vergil nor Thomas More permits us to forget that Morton, "who dyd farre excede them all

---

[50]BL Arundel MS, f. 2 (*Joannis de Giglis . . . Libellus de canonizatione sanctorum*); *CWTM* 2:91 (More's *Richard III*); and *CWTM* 4:58 (*Utopia*).

[51]*CPR*, 1467-1477, 261, 334, 516.

[52]E.g., see J. Calmette and G. Perinelle, *Louis XI et l'Angleterre* (Paris: Société de l'École des Chartes, 1930) 194-95, 218-25.

[53]Arthur Gray, *Priory of St. Radegund* (London: Cambridge Antiquarian Society, 1898) 39-47.

in wysdom and gravytie," was there, steadfastly if helplessly, on the right side.[54] If the early accounts can be believed, Buckingham, Morton's prisonkeeper, was soon captive to his captive. The duke changed sides and led an insurrection against his sovereign.[55] The uprising was to have been timed to coincide with a Tudor invasion, but everything went badly. Buckingham fell into Richard's hands and the fifth column crumbled. Henry Tudor's fleet narrowly escaped to Brittany and Morton fled to Flanders. A few years later a second assault was successful, whereupon Morton returned and, at sixty-five, became the new government's chancellor and chief administrator.

Morton survived political convulsions that permanently dislodged other prelatical civil servants. He has also survived Ricardian historians, like Clements Markham, who spared no effort to villify him. And he has generally worn quite well such epithets as "supple" and "wily," which hang more heavily on lesser men.[56] This is largely because Morton is most often heard speaking to students of earliest Tudor political culture from the towering platform constructed of Thomas More's admiration. By 1516 More had come to think that there was something admirable about a shrewd politician who was amenable to compromise and receptive to new ideas. In *Utopia*'s first book, the new ideas belonged to Raphael Hythloday, but the author made him a somewhat abrasive and inflexible romantic. Morton, though, was the picture of *prudentia*—artful, perceptive, and irenic. More was not surprised that Henry VII had once attached great weight to his counsel, and one should not be shocked that More, with Morton's example before him, gave unmistakable signs, at the first book's end, of his own readiness to counsel Henry VIII.[57] By present standards, however, More's sketch of Morton is lean, and the newsreel character of entries in biographical dictionaries adds little more than a sampling of dates and offices. Nonetheless, Morton's place in earliest Tudor political

---

[54]Ellis, *Three Books*, 179-82; *CWTM* 2:46-49.

[55]The insurrection, of course, is a matter of record. Morton's seduction of Buckingham, however, is not. For doubts about the duke's incredible susceptibility to the bishop's pandering, see Carole Rawcliffe, *The Staffords: Earls of Stafford and Dukes of Buckingham, 1394-1521* (Cambridge: Cambridge University Press, 1978) 32; but also consult *CWTM* 2:lix-lxxii, 90-93; and Ellis, *Three Books*, 194.

[56]See Markham's *Richard III: His Life and Character* (London: Smith, Elder & Co., 1906) esp. 205-27; and Charles Ross, *Richard III* (London: Eyre Methuen, 1981) 80, 113.

[57]*CWTM* 4:98: "Sic est in Republica sic in consultationibus principum. Si radicitus evelii non possint opiniones pravae, nec receptis usu vitiis mederi queas, ex animi tui sententia, non ideo tamen deserenda Republica est, et in tempestate navis destituenda est, quoniam ventos inhibere non possis." Also note *CWTM* 4:58-60, 80; Logan, *The Meaning of More's* Utopia, 45-47; Fox, *Thomas More*, 62-63; and ch. 6.

culture and in English church history is now becoming clearer, thanks to Claude Jenkins, David Knowles, and most recently, Christopher Harper-Bill.[58]

Knowles seems to have set the tone. He suspected that "at root" Morton's religious reforms were administrative measures undertaken to increase the prelate's personal authority. On motives (here, "roots") historians often speculate, but rarely can they pronounce with complete confidence. And problems of power and jurisdiction, with reference to late-medieval religion, are easily misconstrued when historians, like Knowles, echo the censures of earliest Tudor idealistic critics. In this case, reappraisal of Morton is reminiscent of Colet's insinuation that Warham's archiepiscopal efforts *"in causis peccati correctionum"* were more opportunistic and self-serving than authentically religious.[59] To be fair, one should note that Knowles steered clear of the critics' overstatements, yet he came close at points to accepting the idealists' premise that authentic religious reform was contaminated when mixed with political objectives. Reconsideration of Morton's battles for authority with several of the realm's other ecclesiastical officials, contests that were Knowles's chief concern, may correct misapprehensions.

Convents ranked among the critics' favorite targets. Numerous parish churches had been appropriated by the larger religious houses, so dereliction and corruption, such as they were, were thought to have started in the cloisters and then to have spread through the countryside. Reformers realized that it was often necessary to jolt monastic administrators in order to have regulations enforced and revelry, indolence, and disruptive behavior penalized. Such intervention ostensibly entailed periodic inspection or visitation. Bishops were obliged to visit their dioceses' monasteries, yet when either death or transference created a vacancy in his province, Archbishop Morton set his own agents to the task.[60] The *sede vacante* visitation of Worcester in 1498, for instance, brought the Mid-

---

[58]Claude Jenkins, "Cardinal Morton's Register," *Tudor Studies*, ed. R. W. Seton-Watson (London: Longmans, Green & Co., 1924) 26-74; David Knowles, *The Religious Orders in England*, vol. 3 (Cambridge: Cambridge University Press, 1959) 76-80; and Christopher Harper-Bill, "Archbishop John Morton and the Province of Canterbury, 1486-1500," *JEH* 29 (1978): 1-21. Also see Knowles's "The Case of St. Albans' Abbey in 1490," *JEH* 3 (1952): 144-58; and two other papers by Harper-Bill, "Bishop Richard Hill and the Court of Canterbury, 1494-1496," *Guildhall Studies in London History* 3 (1977): 1-12; and "A Late Medieval Visitation—The Diocese of Norwich in 1499," *Proceedings of the Suffolk Institute of Archaeology and History* 34 (1977): 34-47.

[59]*Concilia* 3:655.

[60]*Reg. Morton*, e.g., 1:78, the *Commissio* for a *sede vacante* visitation of Winchester (1492).

land's most influential houses within his compass.[61] Charges of larceny
and of sexual license were occasionally aired, but Morton's deputies ordinarily saw little more of the purported breakdown of monastic discipline than the fretting and fussing about sanitation, foul food, and
restricted access to books. Their intrusion, in most cases, was unlikely to
provoke controversy, but some convents possessed immunities from
episcopal and archiepiscopal visitations, exemptions that Morton wished
to eliminate.

The abbot of St. Albans, William Wallingford, got wind of Morton's
plans and tried to keep control of his house well away from Canterbury.
Morton could ill afford to lose any leverage if he hoped to expand his role
in the enforcement of clerical discipline, yet Wallingford petitioned the
pope for extraordinary powers for himself and for the abbey's courts.[62]
Knowles described the abbot as an able and ambitious administrator. Indeed, in the controversy, his talents and perseverance proved sufficient
to stall the archbishop's progress. Defeat seemed imminent when, in June
and July 1487, Wallingford's representative failed to wring concessions
from Pope Innocent VIII, whereas in August Morton's proctor persuaded
the pope to abrogate all immunities from visitation—save for those of the
Cistercians.[63] Undaunted, the abbot resisted and showered Rome with
appeals. The struggle dragged on until Morton played his trumps, issued
a scorching memorandum, and silenced St. Albans.[64] Morton's memo
itemized improprieties at the monastery, but it was less a researched cat-
alogue than a threat. The general problem, as Morton revealed it, was one
of leadership. For illicit behavior at St. Albans was said to have spread,
"publice, nortorie, et impune," right under the abbot's nose. Allegedly,
Wallingford had lost control before Morton advanced to take it.[65]

Any of three implications could be drawn: the abbot was inept and
therefore powerless to brake discipline's downhill run, too thoroughly
infected by the disease to administer the cure, or too narrowly preoccupied with his own scuffle for authority to exercise the authority he indis-
putably possessed. Possibly Morton drew the first or the second of the
three, but he seems to have been satisfied when the abbot tacitly acknowledged the third and when attempts to undermine archiepiscopal
supervision disintegrated.

---

[61]Ibid., 171 (v). Worcester depositions, however, were not copied into the
register.

[62]"Instructiones pro causis Domini Abbatis," in *Registra Johannis Whetham-
stede, Willelmi Albon, et Willelmi Wallingforde*, ed. Henry Thomas Riley, vol. 2 (London: Longmans & Co., 1873) 288-89.

[63]*Reg. Morton*, 1:5 (reissued in 1490, 1:21); and *Concilia* 3:630-32.

[64]Cf. David Knowles, "The Case of St. Albans," 153-58.

[65]*Reg. Morton* 1:122; *Concilia* 3:632-34.

"Actualiter visitare intendimus," Morton's memorandum announced, stressing the archbishop's determination to take St. Albans' matters into his own hands. Nonetheless, his deputies kept their distance after Wallingford's appeals to Rome had ceased. Apparently, the abbot had learned his lesson: the way to preserve de facto autonomy was to set and enforce standards of conduct and to reconcile himself to de jure subjection to Canterbury.

A second struggle prompted Morton's efforts to sever relationships between foreign prelates and several of the realm's monastic foundations. By 1473 the priory of La-Charité-sur-Loire had launched a campaign to recover control over three English houses, which centuries of Anglo-French hostilities had attenuated. The priory of St. Andrew at Northampton was the principal prize, but the prior there flatly refused to relinquish his post to La Charité's vicar-general, William Brecknock. Eight years later, however, Brecknock prevailed on the reluctant incumbent to settle for the priorate of Wenlock, another of the houses over which La Charité claimed hegemony. But tensions were only temporarily relieved.[66]

Though quiet for a time, the dislodged prior, Thomas Sudbury, was inconsolable. The accession of a new dynasty gave him fresh incentive to renew his fight for Northampton. He acquired from Henry VII letters patent that vindicated his right to return, yet chancery endorsed the letters patent that Edward IV had issued to Brecknock. The government's conflicting responses are mystifying, and they must have made the mess even more unmanageable.[67] In 1487 Morton was informed that discipline had all but dissolved. He summoned Sudbury and Brecknock to appear before him, but Brecknock went into hiding, presumably because he feared that Yorkist favorites and French agents would get little sympathy from the new archbishop. The situation in Northampton deteriorated further, and in 1489 the priory's predicament became a public embarrassment. Monks complained to parliament that both pretenders were squandering the convent's wealth. Annuities and leases had been recklessly distributed to buy support. Jewels, vestment, and plate—even pots and pans—were exchanged for partisanship. Whether accurate or exaggerated, reports of the monastery's impoverishment stirred the archbishop, but it took him two more years to extort resignations from both rivals.[68]

Archiepiscopal neutrality or detachment was a luxury that Morton thought unaffordable. Mayhem too closely followed division, and divisions precipitated by foreign prelates were particularly intolerable. In

---

[66]For this and much of what follows, see Rose Graham, *English Ecclesiastical Studies* (London: S.P.C.K., 1929) 85-87; and Knowles, *Religious Orders*, 76-77.

[67]*CPR*, 1485-1494, 66, 110.

[68]*Reg. Morton* 1:29; *Rot. Parl.* 6:434-45.

France, for instance, quarrels between Citeaux and Clairveaux had long plagued the Cistercians. A clamor was raised when one of the contenders proposed to visit England. Several of the order's English abbots were convinced that the invitation issued to Citeaux was a mistake. The others charged them with delaying the order's reform. The defense seems to rest with the abbot of Conway's remarks to Marmaduke Huby, who had been lobbying at court for a safe conduct for Citeaux. Speaking for the cautious English Cistercians, Conway argued that Citeaux's appearance would only inspire dissension. The government saw things his way: the king's councillors were reluctant to import more trouble.[69]

One cannot be certain of Archbishop Morton's opinion. The story of Cistercian unrest, like the others I have retold, has gaps that the most carefully mortared narratives would be unable to conceal with guesswork. But signs point, if not to the archbishop's aggressive intervention, at least to his acquiescence, which unquestionably would have been influential. Morton's presence in the other stories is more conspicuous, yet there as well his thoughts often slip through history's sieve, as do the motives and schemes of Wallingford and Brecknock. Scholars nonetheless seem to have reached a consensus. "At root," Morton's initiatives were administrative transactions "motivated solely by a desire to extend [his] jurisdiction."[70]

A final example should underscore my disagreement. The London chronicles include an opaque account of accusations and arrests that resulted from Bishop Richard Hill's controversial visitation of the Augustinian priory of Holy Trinity, Aldgate.[71] Jurisdiction over the priory belonged to the Canterbury cathedral, and the register there enabled Christopher Harper-Bill to draw a full and accurate picture of the perplexing affair. The point at issue was Hill's usurpation of Canterbury's prerogatives. The bishop of London not only visited the Aldgate priory, he deposed and imprisoned the prior, Thomas Percy, and installed his own candidate. Morton answered by demanding Percy's reinstatement and Hill's unconditional submission. Were it not for one curious development, Harper-Bill would have been entirely justified in concluding that the archbishop was "willing to maintain an unworthy prior at Aldgate

---

[69]Talbot, 128-29.

[70]In full, Harper-Bill's statement ("Archbishop Morton," 10) reads: "Morton's concern for monastic reform was *not* motivated solely by a desire to extend his jurisdiction." Yet the passage is appropriately reset here without the negative, because the remark refers to a discussion of relatively disinterested reforms, a discussion that follows the statement in Harper-Bill's paper. Clearly the implication is that the examples that precede "not motivated solely," examples studied again in this chapter, were "aggressive assertions" of Canterbury's prerogative made to improve Morton's political position.

[71]*GC*, 250-51, 256; *CL*, 199-203.

because his position had become inextricably interwoven with the maintenance of the jurisdictional privileges of the church of Canterbury." However, the fact is that less than a month after Hill's submission, Percy resigned and Hill's replacement was recalled.[72]

What might this mean? Perhaps Morton had no wish to obstruct reform, yet he was well aware that his own prerogatives had been preempted. As archbishop, he was titular abbot of the cathedral chapter. He may have concurred with Hill that Aldgate was in an awful state, but his suffragan had violated proper procedure. Morton may appear small-minded, yet he was persuaded that the erosion of order and archiepiscopal supremacy was tantamount to ecclesiastical disintegration. Whenever final authority was shared or inconclusively disputed, the wrack and ruin of reform closely followed, whereas to defend primatial power was to preserve the preeminent means to reform.

Speculation about Morton's meanings and motives is by no means offered here as a crippling qualification to current assessments. In one sense the shift in emphasis complements rather than contradicts Harper-Bill's image of the archbishop's "reform by centralization." Yet it is important to emphasize that ecclesiastical decisions about jurisdiction were moral and religious as well as political choices, with moral, religious, and political repercussions. To say this is to conflate the issues of control and reform. The pontificates of Fox and Morton yield evidence that licenses precisely this approach. The conflation, I believe, will never achieve the status of fact or founder as fiction, for the complete story of early Tudor ecclesiastical reform is irretrievable. Nevertheless, the survival of tantalizing fragments, some of which I have retrieved and presented here, should at least disincline scholars to agree with J. C. Dickinson that "Criticism *and Complacency*" (my emphasis) is an appropriate heading for narratives that include generalizations about the first Tudor decades.[73]

---

[72]Harper-Bill, "Bishop Hill," 6, 12.

[73]See Dickinson's *An Ecclesiastical History of England: The Later Middle Ages* (London: A. & C. Black, 1979) esp. 335-39.

Chapter 9

PRIVILEGE

Ecclesiastical complacency fits perfectly into the popular picture of early Tudor political culture, which was redrafted in this book's historiographical chapters. Despite the fine work of Bowker, Heath, Lander, and Harper-Bill, prelates are still thought to have remained idle and accommodating while government made away with the church's liberties and privileges. The association of this theft with the early Tudors has achieved a conspicuous and formidable respectability, as has the assumption of clerical complacency. Both the association and the assumption stand in need of further revision.

As for the Tudor "attack" on the church, most attention is justifiably lavished on Henry VIII, but the plural is stubborn. Henry VII is paired with his son, frequently in connection with the purported abrogation of ecclesiastical rights and with the "notable encroachments" on ecclesiastical privileges.[1] If one can uncouple the first two Tudors, one can easily acquit Henry VII's council and courts. And if one is thereupon compelled to drop the charge of larceny, one might also see the church's "complacency" in a very different light. Without sacrificing important immunities, the earliest Tudor church cooperated with the new government and

---

[1] S. B. Chrimes alleged that earliest "encroachments" were rather unremarkable, but he has not persuaded his colleagues. For the "attack" on sanctuary, see Baker, *Reports* 2:341; E. W. Ives, "Crime, Sanctuary, and Royal Authority under Henry VIII: The Exemplary Sufferings of the Savage Family," in *On the Laws and Customs of England,* ed. Morris S. Arnold et al. (Chapel Hill: University of North Carolina Press, 1981) 303; and John Bellamy, *Crime and Public Order in the Later Middle Ages* (London: Routledge & Kegan Paul, 1973) 111; as well as Chrimes's *Henry VII,* 240, 244. Bellamy borrowed the term *notable encroachments* from Isabel Thornley's "The Destruction of Sanctuary," in *Tudor Studies,* ed. R. W. Seton-Watson (London: Longmans, Green & Co., 1924) 200. Thornley's few pages on Henry VII are impenetrably ambivalent. They catalog measures passed against the privilege as if they were confident strides toward Henry VIII's sweeping condemnation and grand achievement ("to level liberties to make the foundation for liberty," 185). Yet, to emphasize the amplitude of the later developments, Thornley also suggested that earlier efforts were inconsequential. What follows in this section is an adaptation of arguments first offered in my "Henry VII and Sanctuary," *Church History* 53 (1984): 465-76.

adapted its own prerogatives and privileges to the king's "war" on crime and domestic disorder.

John Fortescue calculated that late-medieval England executed more men for robbery and homicide in a single year than France put to death for similar violations in seven years. The context makes it clear that Fortescue was not simply congratulating his countrymen for efficient law enforcement. He was complaining about the frightful pervasiveness of crime.[2] In fact, he and his colleagues were disturbed that so many English felons regularly dodged persecution and penalty, a situation for which the church was partly to blame. Some lawbreakers had taken orders in the church in order to escape the king's courts. Others could claim the same immunity by demonstrating their literacy (presumably signifying their intention to take orders). Criminals, after pleading their "clergy," were transferred to their bishop's custody, there to remain until exonerated by acquaintances prepared to testify under oath to their good character and plausible innocence.[3]

Other felons found refuge in local churches. Their safety was predicated on their pledges to leave the realm within forty days of their arrival in sanctuary. Church officials mapped émigrés' routes from each temporary asylum to the nearest ports, prescribed uniforms and provided crosses by which protected fugitives could be identified, and required certain rituals of their felons should they fail to embark promptly and have to await transport.[4] Around 1500 one Venetian visitor recorded this odd protocol and puzzled over the gravity and grief with which culprits contemplated exile from the chilly island kingdom.[5]

Exile of a different kind was possible within the precincts of several monasteries chartered to provide permanent or perpetual sanctuary. There, criminals joined penurious debtors and were safely beyond the reach of sheriffs, summoners, and creditors. The charters were forged, but the privileges that they awarded were nonetheless jealously guarded by priors and abbots, who waved their documents as weapons whenever immunities were violated or threatened. In many instances, persons seized from sanctuaries were returned. Such seizures, however, were exceptions because the privileges were ordinarily respected. Charters were packed with pious guarantees ascribed to previous monarchs who were

---

[2]See Fortescue's *The Governance of England*, ed. Charles Plummer (Oxford: Clarendon Press, 1885) 141; and for related matters, consult J. A. Sharpe, "A History of Crime in Late Medieval and Early Modern England: A Review of the Field," *Social History* 7 (1982): 187-203.

[3]Gabel, *Benefit of Clergy*, 31-87; and ch. 4.

[4]André Réville, "L'Abjuratio Regni: histoire d'une institution Anglaise," *Révue historique* 50 (1892): 1-42.

[5]Sneyd, *True Account*, 35.

said to have forbidden all persons, even their successors, from invading sanctuaries in search of their prey. Aggressors were warned to keep their distance rather than dishonor the holy relics deposited with each sanctuary's keepers. Ostensibly, privileges and immunities had been granted as homage to saints, who somehow were thought to be present posthumously in these protected pockets along with felons and debtors who quickly discovered that the bones of the blessed dead were more companionable than their pursuers and predators.[6]

A word should be added here, insofar as the influence of the dead tends now to be underestimated. Relics were once tokens of considerable power—political as well as religious and redemptive power. Aelred of Rievaux expressed the medieval consensus that miracles would multiply wherever relics of deceased saints were honored; and from a contemporary perspective, it does seem rather miraculous that the pursuits of justice or vengeance, otherwise unrelenting and sometimes reckless, should have halted abruptly when fugitives reached refuge. Aelred, of course, referred to miracles most closely related to the church's *ordo salutis* or *ordo pastoralis*, that is, to the conversion of those seeking sanctuary. In fact, surviving evidence indicates that some pressure for penance accompanied the offer of protection. In most cases, fugitives' petitions for admission and immunity candidly and almost eagerly conceded guilt, named accomplices, specified weapons, and stipulated the nature and location of victims' wounds—all as if the interviews were conducted in a confessional. And to say that asylum was tantamount to absolution or amnesty is only a slight exaggeration.[7]

Close confinement was the exception rather than the rule. Many sanctuaries afforded inmates a nearly normal life among neighboring townsfolk. At St. John's, Beverley, they were welcome in the village within the sanctuary's precincts, where they could practice their trades without relinquishing their immunity.[8] The same was true in the tenements and

---

[6]E.g., see the charter of King Edgar, printed in John Flete's *The History of Westminster Abbey*, ed. J. Armitage Robinson (Cambridge: Cambridge University Press, 1909) 51: "Libera et absoluta ab omni invasione vel inquietudine omnium hominum cujuscunque ordinis vel potestatis." Also consult Frank Barlow, *Durham Jurisdictional Peculiars* (Oxford: Oxford University Press, 1950) esp. 149-51.

[7]*SDB*, 3-90, for a sampling of petitions. For Aelred's assurances, *De sanctis ecclesiae Haugustaldensis*, printed in *The Priory of Hexham*, ed. James Raine, vol. 1 (Durham: Surtees Society, 1864) 174: "Hinc est quod sancti patres nostri, quorum reliquiarum praesentia gloriamur, antiqua miracula novis cumulare non cessant." Also note R. H. Forster, "Notes on Durham and Other North-Country Sanctuaries," *JBAA*, n.s. 11 (1905): 120-21.

[8]*SDB*, 114-18; Norman Maclaren Trenholme, *The Right of Sanctuary in England* (Columbia: University of Missouri Press, 1903) 49-51; and Charles Cox, *The Sanctuaries and Sanctuary Seekers of Medieval England* (London: Allen, 1911) 135-41.

streets protected by privileges granted to Westminster and to St. Martin-le-Grand in London.[9] The economy of Beaulieu, near the Channel coast, relied so heavily upon the presence of sanctuarymen and their families that citizens asked Thomas Cromwell to extend their immunities, notwithstanding the dissolution of the monastery.[10]

Mention of Cromwell takes one well beyond 1516, but one must venture there if one wishes to distinguish earliest Tudor policy toward ecclesiastical privilege from initiatives engineered by Cromwell and endorsed by Henry VIII after 1530. Sanctuary survived the reformation legislation of 1534, yet sanctuary's days must have seemed numbered when parliament eliminated the last of the English palatine jurisdictions two years later. The language employed to describe and dismantle Durham's immunities could have applied equally to sanctuary's liberties: the statute's preamble insisted that "sondrye gifts of the king's most noble progenitors" had been used "to the hinderance and great delay of justice." Actually Cromwell had marked sanctuaries for extinction, incorporating their "utter destruction" into his program for "the dissolucion of all franchyses."[11] The act of 1536 did not live up to his expectations, though other legislation that year pruned ecclesiastical privileges. Sanctuary itself, however, narrowly escaped. Cromwell continued to press for "a determination" of the issue, and in 1540 a more comprehensive statute deprived felons of all immunities.[12] As a concession to "the lawe of mercy," parliament designated eight cities that might receive and harbor destitute debtors, but confusion replaced custom.[13] Legislators in 1566 were still discussing "how sanctuary persons shall be compellable for payment of their debts."[14] By then immunities had long, and often, been debated and pared. All of that was but an extended epitaph for irrecoverable ecclesiastical exemptions.

Nothing in the courts and councils of Henry VII foreshadowed such developments, though naturally, if one consults the king's enemies, one

---

[9]E.g., see Alfred John Kempe, *Historical Notices of the Collegiate Church or Royal Free Chapel and Sanctuary of St. Martin-le-Grand, London* (London: Longman, Hurst, Rees, Orme, Brown, and Green, 1825).

[10]The petitions were collected by W. H. St. John Hope and Harold Brakspear and were printed in "The Cistercian Abbey of Beaulieu in the County of Southampton," *The Archaeological Journal*, 2d ser. 13 (1906): 176-78. Five years earlier Beaulieu was crowded with fugitives and forced to turn fresh applicants away, PRO, *KB* 27, 1086, m.4.

[11]See the memorandum calendared among Cromwell's "Remembrances," *LP, Henry VIII* 10:93. Also review *SR* 3:551 (27 Henry VIII, c.19); and *SR* 3:555 (27 Henry VIII, c.24).

[12]*LP, Henry VIII* 15:180.

[13]*SR* 3:756-58 (32 Henry VIII, c.12).

[14]*Journals of the House of Commons* 1 (1566): 73-74.

is likely to hear otherwise. In 1489 Perkin Warbeck and his associates accused the king of trampling the church's liberties. They compared the first four years of Henry VII's reign to the reign of Henry II, who, it was thought, would have slugged the church into submission had not the martyrdom of Thomas Becket gloved his fist. Three hundred years had passed, but the pretender's party knew that the comparison could evoke memories, fears, and old animosities. Consequently, Warbeck charged that early Tudor advisers had compressed into policy "such unlawfull poyntes as Seynt Thomas of Canterbury dyed for," that is, "dyed" to forestall.[15]

The indictment could only have referred, if referent it had, to the taking of Humphrey Stafford from the sanctuary at Culham. Stafford's unwavering opposition to Henry VII certainly endeared him to the rebels in 1489. He himself had once left sanctuary in Colchester to join a Worcestershire insurrection, but this, his second attempt to overthrow the Tudors, failed miserably. Stafford was again forced to seek sanctuary. From there, however, he was forcibly removed in May 1486, and he begged the courts to return him.[16]

A writ *scire facias* brought the abbot of Abingdon's counsel to the King's Bench to display the Culham charters, which were in the abbot's custody. The proof was less impressive than Stafford's counsel had led the court to expect. One charter was signed but unsealed. Another was pleaded *per inspeximus;* it apparently had disappeared, as had evidence of papal confirmation, which Stafford's appeal cited, but the abbot had been unable to produce. Since the case seemed so slender, justices required Stafford to show that other courts, in cases of high treason, had allowed fugitives to take sanctuary at Culham. This added stipulation was hardly a sign of early Tudor belligerence. As a response to Stafford's feeble efforts to corroborate Culham's immunities, it was reasonable, cautious, even conservative. Stafford's failure to satisfy the justices and his subsequent execution for treason lend no weight to fanciful claims about Henry VII's war on the church.[17]

Henry's "war on crime" is another matter altogether, particularly his grim determination to purge the realm of subversives, to stifle sedition, and thus to clamp the new dynasty more securely to England's history. To the extent that fugitives sought sanctuary for crimes against the government—that is, for high treason—friction between earliest Tudor authorities and certain defenders of ecclesiastical privileges was unavoidable. Two traitors were dragged from Hexham in 1487 and four more from St.

---

[15]*Paston* 6:131.

[16]*AH*, 12; and C. H. Williams, "The Rebellion of Humphrey Stafford in 1486," *EHR* 43 (1928): 186-87.

[17]*SC* Hemmant 2:115-24.

Martin's in 1493, but the stormy times and the nature of their crimes, rather than any ascertainable royal resentment of sanctuary's privileges, conditioned the fugitives' fate. Indeed, in each instance, authorities were deferential. A letter from the king, copied into Thomas Rotherham's archiepiscopal register, admits that Thomas and Herbert Redshawe were forcibly removed from Hexham, yet it also promises to attempt nothing further "against the privileges and franchises."[18] At St. Martin's, officials permitted Thomas Bagnall, the only one of the four captives to have pleaded his sanctuary, a separate trial, while the other three risked a plea on the actual charges and lost. Bagnall's fate is unknown, but six years later George Sawyer was restored to sanctuary when he attempted a similar maneuver and contested the removal (*"contra voluntatem suam"*) rather than the actual charges.[19] Perkin Warbeck, the king's most implacable enemy, was cornered twice, yet each time he was teased rather than taken from asylum. Too much can be made of Francis Bacon's remark, which referred to the government's reluctance to snatch Warbeck from sanctuary, saying that the king was "tender" toward the church's privileges.[20] Still, the record certainly indicates, if not countenance of immunists' pious pretensions and unctuous submission to charters and bones, at the very least, considerable restraint.

Restraint must have seemed politically advantageous. But this supposition leads nowhere, for conclusions cannot confidently be drawn from the few remaining fragments of information. Save for common sense, there is little that works as a brake on speculation; yet what is known of late-medieval political culture suggests a hypothesis that seems to drive speculation toward a highly plausible reconstruction of the coalition between government and church. The hypothesis is simply this: sanctuary's unpopularity made the privilege hostage to the government. Rather than extinguish immunities, authorities tried to reform abuses and to absorb practices and privileges into a program for the realm's recovery. The "polytyque churche" was not so much a victim as a collaborator.

The first step is to prove unpopularity, and it is an easy one. The Commons petitioned the king twice, early in the fifteenth century, to have allegedly widespread abuses of sanctuary's privilege corrected.[21] The speech composed for the duke of Buckingham in Thomas More's *History of King Richard III* reveals that calm had not settled by the second decade of the sixteenth century. More's villainous Richard was a composite drawing, pieced together from partisan chronicles, from friends' reminiscences, and

---

[18]*Reg. Rotherham* 1:220.

[19]PRO *KB* 27, 953 Rex m.4 (Sawyer); John Stow, *The Annales of England* (London: R. Newbery, 1592) 796 (Bagnall).

[20]Bacon, *History*, 239-40.

[21]*Rot. Parl.* 3:503-504 (1402); 4:291 (1425).

from Tacitus's life of Tiberius, which had become something of a text-book tyranny. Tacitus had scattered references to the Roman practice of sanctuary in his own work, but Thomas More was, without doubt, prompted to take up the issue more by the contemporary debate on ecclesiastical immunities than by antiquarian interest. Richard III's reputed problems in luring one of his nephews from sanctuary at Westminster provided the occasion for the dramatist to deliver himself of opinions shaped by late-medieval arguments against asylum.

Buckingham was a perfect spokesman. Though he acted as Richard's agent, he died collecting impeccable Tudor credentials during Henry VII's initial attempt to return from exile. More's sources disagreed about the duke's part at Westminster. One chronicle failed to place him at the scene.[22] Another implied that he proposed to assault the sanctuary and seize its helpless young fugitive, *"cum gladiis et fustibus."*[23] Thomas More, however, made Buckingham a man of gentle yet telling reason. His *porteparole* conceded that creditors, destitute and turned into debtors, and politicians, capsized by dynastic upheavals, found the immunities useful.[24] But Buckingham could only manage a tepid and qualified endorsement because he believed that fugitives unworthy of their acquired privileges far outnumbered legitimate sanctuarymen.

His contention, and More's argument, is that "without sin" persons might take from sanctuary those with no good cause to be there, felons and fraudulent debtors. Squads of recidivists left sanctuary to commit fresh crimes and then returned with impunity. Pitiless capitalists, who periodically and arrogantly repudiated their debts, abused sanctuaries' hospitality. All impiously echoed the church's unequivocal claims about sanctuary's inviolability.[25]

From those very claims one learns of sanctuary's unpopularity, particularly when the stress under which they were formulated speaks more loudly than the words. Thomas More had a good ear for this. The desperate declaration, which he scripted for the privilege's apologist in the *History of King Richard III* ("Godde forbydde that anye manne shoulde for

---

[22]*GC*, 230.

[23]*Historiae Croylandensis continuatio*, in *Rerum anglicarum scriptorum veterum*, vol. 3 (Oxford, 1684) 566.

[24]*CWTM*, 2:30: "Yet will I not saye naye, but that it is a deed of pitie, that such menne as the sea or theyr evil dettours have broughte in povertye, shoulde have somme place of libertye, to keep their bodies oute of danger of their cruell creditours. And also yf the Crowne happen (as it hathe done) to come in questyon, whyle eyther parte taketh other as traytours, I wyll well there bee somme places of refuge for bothe." More's Latin *Historia Ricardi,* perhaps composed with the English, adds for clarification, "ubi dubiis aut afflictis rebus, pendente adhuc victoria, sint in tuto."

[25]*CWTM* 2:29.

anye thynge earthlye enterpryse to breake the imunitee"), caught the spirit
that haunts the capacious *Objectiones et argumenta contra et pro privilegiis
sanctuarii Westmonasterii*, a valuable but largely forgotten account of the
late-medieval debate.[26] After gathering armloads of Old Testament anecdotes for sanctuary's defense, the *Objectiones* tendentiously reviews arguments pro and con. Occasionally it discloses dimensions of the
controversy left unexplored by other literature, as when it insists that
perpetrators of unpremeditated crimes deserve asylum.[27] Generally,
however, the *Objectiones* confirms that issues raised in remonstrances reflected complaints that were parts of a prolonged and involved discussion. One opposing argument repeats that sanctuary, as an alternative to
punishment, encouraged crime. Another shares with parliamentary petitions and More's Buckingham an impatience with deceitful debtors
shielded by the church's privileges.[28] Ultimately, however, the *Objectiones* budgets most of its ink for defense. Sanctuary's administrators are
said to have monitored admission and to have inventoried fugitives'
property. Extorted and (temporarily) concealed assets were returned to
rightful owners and to creditors. When appropriate, inmates were assigned penalties ranging from public humiliation and flogging to expul-
sion.[29] The opposition's charge that criminals enjoyed a scandalously
carefree life financed by the fruits of their crimes was, according to the
Objectiones, a gross distortion.

　　If, as I suspect, the refutation testifies to the importance of the accusation, then the *Objectiones* is a token of sanctuary's unpopularity. But
there is more to be said. Composed late in the fourteenth century, when
sanctuary's privileges were hotly contested, the treatise exists only in a
late-fifteenth-century hand. The copyist, William Ebesham, was in sanctuary at Westminster in 1470, and he was a visitor, if not a resident, as
late as 1497. Officials at Westminster presumably commissioned the
work.[30] If one wishes greater specificity, conjecture must carry the bur-

---

[26]Cf. *Obj*, ff. 18r-21v, a repetitive yet peculiarly forceful staging of the imperative that "sanctuary's liberties not be sacrificed for the sake of some imperma-
nent political advantage," *propter temporale commodus adquirendum*; and *CWTM* 2:27.
Also note Thornley, "Destruction," 196-97.

[27]*Obj*, f. 97r.

[28]Ibid., ff. 96v, 124r.

[29]Ibid., ff. 130r-132r.

[30]*Paston* 5:1-2; and A. I. Doyle, "The Work of a Late Fifteenth-Century Scribe,
William Ebesham," *Bulletin of the John Rylands Library* 39 (1957): 319-21. I am indebted to Miss Jane Fowles of Longleat House for additional information on the
Objectiones' composition, culled from Lawrence Tanner's unpublished notes of
1933. I am also grateful to Mr. Dan Breen of the University of North Carolina for
assistance with parts of the manuscript.

den of the argument about the transcription's date and purpose. Conjecture, however, need not be uninformed. As noted, the *Objectiones* collected scriptural justifications for sanctuary's inviolability and attempted to build a case—more extensive than Buckingham's—for the privilege's social utility, often perhaps by suppressing evidence of mismanagement. Yet the treatise also introduces considerations that would have appealed to the king's justices. It asserts that custom (*"diuturna consuetudo"*) assumes the force of law when not contradicted explicitly by existing legislation.[31] More to the point, it repeatedly returns to Westminster's charters and, in a hand other than Ebesham's, it amplifies their insistence that immunities be administered without interference, *"de curia regali [et] de civitate."*[32]

Such observations are made more meaningful when one learns that Abbot John Estney appeared before the king's council to defend Westminster's charters in 1485. Estney was told quite rudely that he would be wiser to enforce the sanctuary's regulations than to parade its exemptions.[33] Whether the *Objectiones* copied by Ebesham was part of the preparations for Estney's appearance or a response to his abrupt dismissal, the manuscript seems to have been a symptom of late-fifteenth-century anxieties about the fate of sanctuary, anxieties prompted by a wave of complaints that crested during the first year of Henry VII's reign.

Unpopularity generated opportunity for the Crown. By reiterating complaints, Breton officials earlier had obtained papal consent to enactments that essentially closed sanctuaries to felons.[34] Though Henry had spent much of his exile in Brittany with several supporters who, upon their return to England, became the king's closest advisers, early Tudor government followed a significantly different course. England relayed grievances to Rome, but English authorities adopted more moderate remedies than those tried across the Channel.

There are indications that, had he been pressed, Pope Innocent VIII would have been wholly accommodating. Upon request, he swiftly sent Henry confirmation of his succession and a dispensation for his marriage. The pope also advised the clergy in no uncertain terms that those who collaborated with the Tudors' enemies henceforth would forfeit all claim to papal protection. Innocent urged continental authorities to deny comfort and aid to English rebels who fled for safety to their territories. But Henry VII soon informed Rome that sanctuaries in his own realm screened enemies who remained in England. In 1487 the king reported

---

[31]*Obj*, ff. 141r-142v.

[32]Ibid., particularly f. 228r, but also ff. 59r and 194.

[33]*Reports*, Hilary term, 1 Henry VII, plea 11, p. 10.

[34]See Barthelemy A. Pocquet du Haut-Jusse, *Les Papes et les ducs de Bretayne*, 2 vols. (Paris: Bibliothèque des Écoles Francaises d'Athènes et de Rome, 1928) 2:647, 720.

that fugitives had abandoned their asylum at Westminster and ransacked the properties of his followers when it was rumored that insurgents had defeated the Tudor army in the north. When rumors proved false, the mob returned to the London sanctuary, which harbored the fugitives as before.[35]

Innocent VIII authorized three reforms. Fugitives, having once left their refuge to make mischief, should be prohibited from again enjoying immunities. Rome also reaffirmed creditors' and victims' rights to restitution. Finally, the pope allowed the government to post guards within sanctuaries' precincts to prevent troublemakers from escaping.[36]

Only the third provision was new. Articles against recidivism had been passed earlier in the century. Efforts to protect creditors' and victims' rights were familiar as well. But an earlier effort to introduce guards was thwarted successfully in 1453 by the dean of St. Martin-le-Grand, Roger Cawdry. Cawdry had marched to the courts with his charters when William Oldhall had been kidnapped from sanctuary. The government restored Oldhall to Cawdry's custody, but Henry VI's agents suspected that Oldhall engineered Yorkist conspiracies, notwithstanding his confinement. They installed four guards to monitor his every act and liaison. Cawdry again played the gremlin. He imperiously removed the invaders and demanded the penance of those who had planned their intrusion. Oldhall put an interesting interpretation on the episode. In order to reverse forfeitures that followed his failure to appear in court and contest his outlawry, he argued that the guards had transformed his asylum into a prison.[37]

Pope Innocent's concessions did not exactly empower the government to make prisons of the church's sanctuaries. Nevertheless, they enabled officials to absorb immunities into a program for the detention and isolation of malcontents that one might call, without seeming unpardonably anachronistic, early Tudor penology.[38] The program culminated in 1504 with the "statute of negligent escapes." Parliament therein restated, in a vocabulary of fines and penalties, late-medieval English interests in

---

[35]Gairdner, *Letters*, 1:94-95. The king also reminded Innocent that he had previously written Rome about similar abuses (*"pro reformanda hujusmodi enormitatibus"*), so pressure for more sweeping reforms may have been even greater than surviving evidence permits us to suppose. The letter that preceded that report in 1487 possibly retold the story of Humphrey Stafford's exit from and return to sanctuary (1486) in order to vindicate the Culham decision.

[36]*Concilia* 3:622-23.

[37]J. S. Roskell, "Sir William Oldhall, Speaker in the Parliament of 1450-1452," *Nottingham Medieval Studies* 5 (1961): 104-106.

[38]Cf. Michel Foucault, *Surveiller et punir* (Paris: Gallimard, 1975) 233, with reference to procedures *"a l'extérieur de l'appareil judicaire,"* for redistributing and quarantining criminals.

effective incarceration. Neither Henry VII's council nor his courts found reason to discontinue assessments against clerical wardens whose prisoners had disappeared.[39] Abbot Islip of Westminster was twice fined for permitting the escapes of criminous clerics remanded to his custody. Bishop Oliver King tried to have similar penalties passed on to an escapee's accomplice after the council had rendered judgment against him.[40] Justices even contemplated charging the abbot of St. Albans for the carelessness of his deceased predecessor.[41] Though fines were considered useful deterrents, to my knowledge they were never levied against sanctuary's administrators. Other preventive measures were tried. In one instance, the courts restricted immunities and fugitives were protected only if they remained within the more easily policed environs of a sanctuary's main buildings.[42] To be sure, the presence of royal guards would have been the best precaution against escape, but there is no record that the government ever sent them. Possibly the threat of their intrusion compelled many administrators more diligently to enforce their own curfews and regulations. As the question now stands, no shred of evidence encourages dispute of Grafton's contention that Henry VII, after 1487, was able to "kepe the gates of all sanctuaries . . . shut and well locked."[43]

This success was probably due to pressures applied at several levels. By 1490 the pope licensed Archbishop Morton to review sanctuaries' various rules and prohibitions. As I have already remarked, Morton's register, in places, marks his conquests of jurisdictions that had once been shelved beyond Canterbury's reach. In this case the register contains a papal writ that authorized Morton to appoint and direct a panel with vast powers virtually to redraft charters and alter immunities.[44] Whether guards were introduced into sanctuaries' precincts or only (and hypothetically) into discussions of sanctuaries' management, their "therapeutic value" would have been enormously enhanced by Morton's

---

[39]*SR* 2:654-55 (19 Henry VII, c.10); and also note *YCR* 1:139-40. Review Ralph B. Pugh, *Imprisonment in Medieval England* (Cambridge: Cambridge University Press, 1968) esp. 218-37; and, for an early controversy about fines, see the "Gravamina prelatorum et cleri," in *Rotuli Parliamentorum hactenus inediti*, ed. H. G. Richardson and George Sayles (London: Historical Society of Great Britain, 1935) 107, item 4.

[40]*SC* Bayne, cxlix (King); and Herbert Francis Westlake, *Westminster Abbey*, 2 vols. (London: P. Allan & Co., 1923) 1:177 (Islip).

[41]Baker, *Reports* 1:122.

[42]*Reports*, Hilary term, 9 Henry VII, plea 15, p. 20.

[43]Richard Grafton, *Chronicle or History of England*, 2 vols. (London: J. Johnson, 1809) 2:225. The remark, intended as a tribute, was composed six decades after Henry's death.

[44]*Reg. Morton*, f. 20r.

commission. Immunities did not dissolve, but they seem to have been extended and administered more responsibly and in keeping with earliest Tudor concerns for dynastic security and for the realm's peace. The little we know permits us to assume some degree of intimidation based either on the papal concessions to the king in 1488 or on powers of review and reform given to the archbishop in 1490.

Did all this constitute an "attack" on sanctuary that ended, and could only have ended, decades later with the "utter destruction" of ecclesiastical privileges planned by Thomas Cromwell?

The *Objectiones* should be reintroduced here because it so helpfully draws lines that conclusively divide sanctuary's friends and enemies. According to the manuscript, the latter were persuaded that cancellation or some other decisive qualification of the privileges (*"per subtractionem et revocationem aut aliam congruam interpretationem"*) would deter crime and yield abundant, though unspecified, rewards for the realm. To this, the treatise replies that previous violations, which were tantamount to periodic suspensions of the immunities, had never led to lasting advantage and that persons who risked such damnable actions were eventually repaid with misfortune. Sanctuaries' enemies countered that indecision by governments that recognized how perilous it was to shield lawbreakers from the law courted greater political misfortune and ruin (*"ex illis cotidie regis et regni ruina timetur"*).[45]

Sanctuary's friends judged these warnings alarmist and historically unfounded. If they were uttered at all by Henry VII's councillors, the Jeremiah was probably John Fineux, who from 1495 was chief justice of the King's Bench. Fineux, however, expressed his opposition most forcefully after death removed Henry and Morton from the stage.[46] This is not to claim that the king and archbishop were adamant immunists. Earliest Tudor government seems to have settled on an agreeable tertium quid. To the extent that sanctuaries were porous, they were to be sealed. It was not unthinkable that such a remedy for recidivism could be adopted without suppressing time-honored privileges.

Buried beneath this restraint, the conviction that guided Bracton's discussion of sanctuary centuries earlier appears to have affected the shape of policy until Cromwell had his way. "Sword should aid sword" in the maintenance of order and justice, Bracton had said of the temporal and spiritual estates.[47] To be sure, sanctuary's place in Tudor penology was undermined in 1536 and collapsed in 1540, but that decade began differently. Fearing that abjurers were taking their skills and services as well as England's secrets abroad "so that . . . the strength and power of this

---

[45]*Obj*, ff. 61r-62r.

[46]Keilwey, *Reports*, f. 189.

[47]*De legimus* 2:383.

realme ys gretely mynyshed," Parliament ordered criminals to abjure only their liberty and to proceed from temporary to permanent sanctuaries where they were to remain for life or until they were needed for military service.[48] This, and not Cromwell's "utter destruction" of privileges, is the best epilogue to earliest Tudor efforts to integrate ecclesiastical immunities and territorial interests.

---

[48]*SR* 3:332-34 (22 Henry VIII, c.14).

Chapter 10

THE "POLYTYQUE CHURCHE" AND THE ENGLISH PEOPLE

Thus far the "polytyque churche" may seem composed entirely of ecclesiastical and government functionaries, who redistributed power and protected privileges, along with those few literate impresarios who scripted pageants. If, as a bonus, glimpses of the social field or setting have been available, and one hopes that they have, the narrative is stronger and more valuable for it. But Natalie Zeman Davis, among others, has served notice that this will no longer do. Studies that appear to adopt the producer/consumer model of church history, whereby a handful of articulate prelates doled out doctrine to ostensibly inarticulate laymen, lately have been anathematized as historiographical heresy. Davis emphatically pronounced that the laity was not a "passive receptacle." Historians of popular piety have issued something of a manifesto, which one ignores to one's peril: Even scenes from clerical life must henceforth yield more than fleeting impressions of lay loyalties.[1]

This having been said, however, the fact remains that the makers of bread and ale are not as accessible as the makers of doctrine and public policy. The nearly inexhaustible stocks of parish records and probated wills furnish researchers with cracks through which parts of parish life can be watched rather closely. The view is certainly better than that provided by exclusivist histories of elites or by idealistic critics, and no student of the "polytyque churche" can afford to neglect opportunities to exploit what other colleagues have seen. Nonetheless, aspirations to rewrite late-medieval history from the bottom up are unrealistic. Methodological difficulties plague the enterprise and urge caution on those of us who wish to draw the observations of sociologists, anthropologists, and popular historians into more conventional studies. It would be useful, to say the least, to learn how ordinary people experienced their church and how parish priests perceived their duties. But to tease experiences and

---

[1]See Davis's "Some Tasks and Themes in the Study of Popular Religion," in *The Pursuit of Holiness in Late Medieval and Renaissance Religion*, ed. Charles Trinkaus and Heiko A. Oberman (Leiden: E. J. Brill, 1974) 309. Also in this connection, see Peter Laslett, *The World We Have Lost*, 2d ed. (London: Methuen, 1979) 207-208.

perceptions from behavior and to tease behavior from surviving and often formulaic documents is very tricky business. Ethnographers generally avoid it. Historians of late-medieval culture, "popular" or elite, have no choice but to forge ahead and gingerly to forage for clues to their subjects' pieties.

Inevitably certain kinds of evidence must be selected and "privileged" as indicators of sentiments that cannot be directly monitored. But W. G. Runciman's warning bears repetition even at the earliest stages of selection, for "theoretically pre-emptive inferences" frequently prejudice decisions and discredit conclusions drawn thereafter.[2] I have already suggested that Lollard abjurations are inappropriate indicators of widespread lay resentment. They were relatively few, regionally concentrated, and largely formulaic. What makes the inferences of most historians of dissent theoretically preemptive, however, is that abjurations are assumed to have been signs of defiance and impiety and not the first symptoms of contrition. According to J. J. Scarisbrick, who has chased Lollards and their abjurations from his history of *The Reformation and the English People*, lay fraternities' registers and probated wills are better indicators of the population's loyalties and perceptions. The fraternities were "lay dominated structures lying alongside and within the old church." They rested on a bedrock of traditional beliefs about the mass, about saints' intercession, and about purgatory. Their popularity in late-medieval England, in Scarisbrick's judgment, proves that "lay religion" was respectful, not resentful—conservative, not contentious.[3]

---

[2]*A Treatise on Social Theory*, vol. 1 (Cambridge: Cambridge University Press, 1984) 139-43.

[3]The fraternities in question were funeral associations formed under the patronage of particular saints, or the Trinity, or the heavenly host. Brothers could rely on their associates for relief from economic hardships or for support in disputes and lawsuits against outsiders as well as for requiems. The greater guilds owned property, distributed charity from their bulky bequests, and sponsored annual pageants with opulent processions. Though many fraternities were joined by clerics and hired chaplains, "they were lay controlled," and Scarisbrick makes much of this in order to argue more persuasively that the Reformation, with its dissolution of chantries, "caused the pendulum of influence to swing *against* the layman" (his emphasis). The timely intervention of John S. Henderson permitted me to test Scarisbrick's findings against a competent and compendious analysis of the penitential devotions of Florentine lay confraternities. See Henderson's as yet unpublished dissertation, "Piety and Charity in Late Medieval Florence: Religious Confraternities from the Middle of the Thirteenth Century to the Late Fifteenth Century" (University of London, 1983); and J. J. Scarisbrick, *The Reformation and the English People* (Oxford: Basil Blackwell, 1984) 19-39, 168. Also note Joel T. Rosenthal's remarks on chantries and lay control, *The Purchase of Paradise: Gift Giving and the Aristocracy, 1307-1485* (London: Routledge & Kegan Paul, 1972) 31-52.

The laity's wills seem to indicate this more compellingly. They illustrate extensive attachment to the church, which commonly received custody of an appreciable portion of the deceased's disposable wealth along with custody of the body. Funds were normally left to pay for obits and masses, yet wills also regularly designated money, livestock, and property as additional gifts. Naturally, one wonders whether the parish priest's appearance locked every failing number of his flock in a deathbed dilemma. At such a delicate time, could the most indifferent Christians afford to alienate their pastors? Would the stoutest and most self-sufficient testators be susceptible to their priests' self-serving advice? How much would be enough to compensate for the frivolity or impiety that sometimes stains a life lived with the best intentions? How much would be required to quiet profound regrets, to cover damaging and damnable lapses? These questions point toward the decisive one: are wills reliable indicators of lay churchliness, or are they hostage, in the course of this argument, to theoretically preemptive inferences that offend scholarly sensibilities?

A small crop of reservations about the conditions under which wills were composed clearly complicates efforts to read them as tokens of unfaltering lay devotion to the church. But then, as now, wills were not always contemplated with death's scythe in sight. Priests were not always present to play upon—or to prey upon—testators' regrets and sympathies. Still, the suspicion that thoughts of death brought Christians closer to their church is virtually ineradicable. To frame this as a telling objection, however, would require a rather implausible presumption, namely, that death ordinarily precipitated dramatic conversions. Alternatively, though no more plausibly, one might hold that legacies camouflaged irreverence. When the courtship between legitimate suspicions and dogmatic skepticism produces such progeny, for which no warrant can be found, one regrets having fathered the suspicions in the first instance. Reservations about death's influence on testators' piety must stand, but they do not stand as an interpretation that supersedes the most direct reading of testamentary evidence. The question of clerical influence, or, as Scarisbrick dubs it, "clerical ventriloquism," is another matter: when one reads lay wills, perhaps one hears the parish priest and not the testator.

Should there be reason to question authorship in this way, wills would hardly be trustworthy indicators of lay piety. The documents, however, incline one to minimize the clerical contribution. Preambles are patterned by convention to which most scribes, clerical and lay, would have subscribed. Priests were likely to remind testators of "routine payments" to the parish (for tithes in arrears) and to the cathedral church of the diocese. Beyond that, bequests were probably made at the testators' discretion. They often stipulated several parish churches as beneficiaries—a tactic difficult to explain if the local priest were eager to extort legacies and if he dictated terms rather than took dictation. Gifts to the regular clergy are even harder to reconcile with parish priests' interests. When added to the idiosyncratic character of other provisions, these considerations amount to a conclusive case against "ventriloquism." But other arguments could be incorporated. For instance, were a ruthlessly enterprising priest presiding, Thomas Palmer, a Stortford butcher, would probably not have been allowed to give his lay executor plenary powers to distribute his properties for the sake of his soul and for the souls of all the faithful. But the point is that parish clergy really had no need to tamper with testators' intentions. The notion that priests extorted legacies rests on the supposition that laymen were reluctant to volunteer them. Testamentary evidence suggests that an altogether different thesis more competently accounts for expiatory benefactions. Laymen were concerned for their salvation and satisfied that their church offered them chances to obtain it. Possibly they welcomed clerical intervention, even if they occasionally received more directions than they solicited.[4]

Bernd Moeller's study of late-medieval German piety raises a similar possibility with reference to the market for indulgences, which the Catholic clergy are thought to have manipulated, much as they are thought to have engineered deathbed philanthropy. Moeller did not dispute the church's financial interest in death, purgatory, and penitential endowments. He noted only that consumer pressure, so to speak, contributed to the active indulgence trade. He inspected testamentary evidence as well, and he also assembled other indicators of lay sentiments, all of which led to a somewhat startling conclusion—startling at least to those who have long supposed the German reformations to have been heralded by pervasive lay discontent. To the church's material advantage, prelates, it seems, responded with consolation to the demands of lay piety so successfully that piety was characterized by a remarkably "consistent churchliness" ("geschlossene Kirchlichkeit").[5]

Moeller's findings are not automatically transferable, yet Scarisbrick's research has certainly facilitated passage from Germany to early Tudor England. "Churchliness" is actually the lesser part of Scarisbrick's concern. (When he inventories bequests, he lingers over expiatory benefac-

---

[4]For Palmer's will, *London Consistory Court Wills, 1492-1547*, ed. Ida Darlington (London: London Record Society, 1967) 151. Scarisbrick uses testamentary evidence to counter arguments that there had been general disenchantment with the church before the Reformation (*Reformation*, 1-18). He claims to have examined twenty-five hundred wills, only a random sample of extant documents. Nonetheless, Scarisbrick's generalizations seem sober and sound, and they certainly stand the test of the few printed collections that I had consulted before publication of his *Reformation*.

[5]Bernd Moeller, "Frömmigkeit in Deutschland um 1500," *ARG* 56 (1965): 5-15; trans. Joyce Irwin, in *The Reformation in Medieval Perspective*, ed. Steven E. Ozment (Chicago: Quadrangle Books, 1971) 51-56.

tions that appear to have been "secular," such as endowments left to schools and almshouses.) But a flood of gifts to churches—cloth for vestments, plate for liturgical use, property for income—attests to the laity's predominant institutional allegiance, as does the sporadic provision of otherwise unspecified, "emergency" funds (*"lego ad opera ejusdem ecclesiae ubi major necessitas est"*).[6] This does not vitiate my earlier remarks about lay criticism. Moeller recognizes that "general churchly devotion of the late fifteenth century did not entail unqualified and uncritical endorsement of prelates' pretensions." But he submits that exegesis of complaints tends toward overevaluation. Scarisbrick agrees and adds that practices that caused idealistic critics to shudder were "not occasions of serious disquiet" for most laymen. They were irritated at times by ecclesiastical taxes and compulsory offerings. Yet, despite outspoken opposition to mortuaries, many wills obligingly provided for the fees "as is accostomed." Laymen usually were inclined to pay for the clergy's intercession.[7]

Laymen were most annoyed when they failed to get services they paid for, particularly when parish priests disappeared. Rectorial incumbents, who collected tithes but who elected not to reside, were required to subcontract for the services of unbeneficed clergy. Priests who wished temporary leave had to obtain licenses and often replacements. Nonetheless, rules were broken, and fears for their souls mobilized aggrieved laymen to present their problems in consistory courts or during episcopal visitations. The records are used to document the pervasiveness of nonresidence. This theme is used frequently by historians confessionally disposed to reconstruct pastoral care in the pre-Reformation church as a mixture of sinful neglect and slapstick comedy. Peter Heath's fine review of absenteeism should certainly put an end to that, and Heath's supposition that records of lay concern are dependable indicators of lay dedication to the church's ministry fits neatly into this reevaluation of the evidence.[8]

Other signs of pastoral care's importance surface in some surprising places. When the case against negligent rectors was carried to convocation, one preacher presented a full and unconditionally favorable account of the benefits that derived from effective parish service.[9] *Miracula postuma* attributed to Henry VI contain a curious account of Richard Swet-

---

[6] *Buckingham*, 155-56 (from the will of Lawrence Wycombe of Iver).

[7] E.g., *Ripon*, 257-58, 285, 304, 330. Also see Moeller, "Frömmigkeit," 23 (my translation); Scarisbrick, *Reformation*, 41-42; and Christopher Haigh, *Reformation and Resistance in Tudor Lancashire* (Cambridge: Cambridge University Press, 1978) 58-62, 76-86.

[8] Heath, *Parish Clergy*, 49-69.

[9] *Oratiuncula*, 70-74.

tocke, a deaf Suffolk priest. After his impairment miraculously vanished, he was again able to hear confessions and, we are told, he subsequently set about his customary duties with fresh and exemplary determination, which strengthened the devotion of all who witnessed his restoration of "the ministry of divine works."[10] Of those works, the mass was the most regular and arguably the most influential. By the later Middle Ages, parishioners expected priests to celebrate at least once each day. Thrice-weekly celebrations were insufficient, and the infrequency was considered cause for official protest.[11] Without statistics on attendance, however, little more can be made of this unless the study of symbolic strategies in group organizations proceeds to a more theoretical level, at which the mass may be related to the generation and preservation of community solidarity. The religious dimensions of civic pageants claimed attention at the start of this part. The field of inquiry now extends to the social and political functions of religious ritual.[12]

Having filed provocative papers on baptism and on the mass, John Bossey has seasoned the study of the sacraments with some rather exotic ideas. He places great stress on the socially integrative powers of religious ceremonies and symbols.[13] Bread consecrated as Christ's body, for example, inspires accommodation and corporate identity—a sort of community disarmament—among Christians assembled at communion or among citizens following the *corpus christi* processions through their cit-

---

[10]Grosjean, *Miracula Postuma*, 2:128: "Revera etenim, quod et fidem ac devotionem roboravit plurimorum, die dominica adveniente jam proxima, omnis illa surditatis obtusitas acumine auditus quodammodo commutata, ita hominem effecit sanum et hilarem ut nequaquam antehac perspicatiorem se habuisse organi illius usum et publice fateretur et effectu monstraret liquidissimo, siquidem ad omne mox sive divini operis ministerium, sive humane sollicitudinis curam, ille sicut ceteri reddebatur aptissimus."

[11]Heath, *Parish Clergy*, 5-6.

[12]See, e.g., Abner Cohen, *Two-Dimensional Man: An Essay on the Anthropology of Power and Symbolism in Complex Society* (London: Routledge & Kegan Paul, 1974) 82: "An ideology will function only if it is maintained and kept alive by continuous indoctrination, conditioning of moods and sentiments, and affirmation of belief. This is achieved mainly through ceremonials, in the course of which symbols are continuously charged with meanings that are relevant to the current problems of the group." In addition to Cohen's analysis of "symbolist man," (18-89), see Trexler, *Florence*, 43, 56-57; and discussions of "the cultural model of public religion" in John F. Wilson, *Public Religion in American Culture* (Philadelphia: Temple University Press, 1979) esp. 150-51, 157-59, 172-74.

[13]John Bossey, "The Mass as a Social Institution, 1200-1700," *Past and Present* 100 (1983): 52-59. Also consult Bossey's "Blood and Baptism: Kinship, Community, and Christianity in Western Europe from the Fourteenth to the Seventeenth Centuries," in *Sanctity and Secularity: The Church and the World*, ed. Derek Baker (Oxford: Ecclesiastical History Society, 1973) 129-43.

ies' streets. Much as royal entries, these processions were rituals of reconciliation whereby Christ's body, the host, was ceremonially associated with the body politic and the city was transformed into an ideal or transcendent "communion." Municipal clergy and lay fraternities played notable parts in the festivities, yet regimentation and the final regulation of productions fell to the craft guilds and to city government.[14] The mass, however, was an uncontested ecclesiastical province.

Earliest Christian authorities conceived of church unity as a necessary precondition for the celebration. Medieval prelates, according to Bossey, liturgically induced the dispositions that previous celebrants had taken for granted. Of course, Christ's sacrifice was at the center of devotion and gave meaning to the whole mass.[15] But the relationship between sacrifice and ritual solidarity is a particularly close one. External circumstances may not alter perceptibly, that is, prayers for health, precipitation, or conquest may go unanswered. But the act of sacrifice encompasses and achieves its more recondite objective. Ritual theorists seem to agree that sacrifice revitalizes the communities that offer it, that sacrifice gives symbolic expression to common aspirations, which everyday language only imperfectly expresses.[16] Bossey is convinced that there was no late-medieval sacred symbol as powerful as the host and that the "mystically unitive emotions attending it" had significant consequences. The ritual surrounding its consecration and recapitulation of Christ's sacrifice extended peace from its source in the savior's atonement to the community of Christians, both through the forgiveness that *liturgi* tendered in Christ's behalf and through the repentance and mutual forgiveness that the celebration inspired.[17]

In the mass the celebrant commemorates Christ's sacrifice, proclaims its meanings, and gives communion. *Liturgi*, from earliest times, explained their ceremonial functions by associating sacrifice and solidarity, usually by asserting that Christ was inseparably joined to his unified and harmonious church.[18] For all this, ritual theorists most highly prize or-

---

[14]Review Charles Phythian-Adams, "Ceremony and the Citizen: The Communal Year at Coventry, 1450-1550," in *Crisis and Order in English Towns, 1500-1700*, ed. Peter Clark and Paul Slack (London: Routledge & Kegan Paul, 1972) 57-85; Alexandra F. Johnston, "The Guild of Corpus Christi and the Procession of Corpus Christi in York," *Mediæval Studies* 38 (1976): 372-84; James, "Ritual, Drama, and Social Body," 8-11, 24-27; and Bossey, "The Mass," 50.

[15]Bossey, "The Mass," 34.

[16]Consult, e.g., R. Godfrey Lienhardt, *Divinity and Experience* (Oxford: Clarendon Press, 1961) 265, 291-97; and idem, *Social Anthropology* (London: Oxford University Press, 1964) 185-86.

[17]Bossey, "The Mass," 29-30, 59-60.

[18]*Missarum Sollemnia*, e.g., 2:48-49.

dinary participants' formal behavior as a sign of shared, profound, socially constructive (or socially integrative) commitments. To recover a "social conception" of the mass, theorists use the people's prayers and postures as avenues to otherwise unspoken and inaccessible dispositions. Footing is always treacherous on this route from observation to generalization. But something akin to a romantic impulse pushes ritual theorists past externals to sensations and onward toward their "social conception."

What is mildly surprising—and fortunate for these purposes—is that the same destination can be reached by a less treacherous and less speculative route. Medieval forms of popular participation in the mass were prescribed explicitly to achieve and sustain community among the faithful and conformity between the faithful and the celebrant. The explanatory power of Bossey's propositions, therefore, does not rely exclusively on ritual theory, which some field researchers and social historians may consider badly grounded ethnography. The liturgy itself forges connections between sacrifice and solidarity, so one might presume that laymen insisted on their masses not only to honor their God, but also to bring unity and peace to their communities.[19]

There is no sense hammering this point, for the mass itself is an obstacle to deeper penetration. Mystification was crucial to the mass's complex achievement. ("It is indeed the very essence of the symbolic process to perform a multiplicity of functions with economy of symbolic formation. The more meanings a symbol signifies, the more ambiguous and flexible it becomes, the more intense the feelings that it invokes, the greater its potency, and the more functions it achieves."[20]) Late-medieval susceptibilities to mystery are not comparable to those of most empirical, verbocentric historians, who are heirs of the sixteenth-century reformers to whom mystification in rituals of reconciliation was highly objectionable. Nonetheless, from time to time, traces of nostalgia breed some sympathy with laymen who once gravitated toward the church, toward the transcendental, in order to find ritual expression for social ideals.

"The Reformation simplified everything," J. J. Scarisbrick reported with evident melancholy. "It effected a shift from a religion of symbol and allegory, ceremony and formal gesture to one that was plain and direct: a shift from the visual to the aural, from ritual to literal exposition, from the numinous and mysterious to the everyday."[21] Reformers were convinced that guileless, credulous laymen were trapped in and dazzled by

[19]Cf. ibid. 1:306-20 with Bossey's rather uncritical application of controversial material from Rene Girard's *Violence and the Sacred* (Baltimore: Johns Hopkins University Press, 1977), "The Mass," esp. 51-53.

[20]Cohen, *Two-Dimensional Man*, 32.

[21]Scarisbrick, *Reformation*, 163.

delusion. Mystifying ceremonies kept them from the good news of their liberation. Protestant gospelers would set them free, but how grateful would the English people be? Close to the soil, so to speak, the reform of worship made only gradual and grudging progress.[22] The later Tudors and many of their subjects had an inveterate attachment to their ceremonies and sacraments. If ever the question of gratitude is finally settled, the resolution will most likely intensify appreciation for late-medieval lay churchliness in England.

This brings me well beyond my thesis, but the Reformation's preference for exposition over mystification has obvious relevance to humanist and idealistic criticism, which can be assimilated far more easily to the mood of subsequent reform than to the parish piety and to the other scenes of clerical life I have been sketching. Much of late-medieval English humanism was rather puritanical about ritual and display.[23] Though Erasmus treated Catholic sacramentalism with tact, he was more concerned with virtue than with ceremony. He accorded supreme importance to clerical education.[24]

During the thirteenth century, the English church set minimal standards for clerical education, and thereafter the canons were often republished. Bishops and archdeacons were to insure that priests could recite the seven deadly sins and the seven principal virtues as well as give a passable account of the seven sacraments. However committed high officials may have been to this part of their administrative responsibilities, they could not mastermind an impressive advance. Loyal clergy, barely literate, mystified but could not analytically clarify their religion. Lest critics make too much haste in evicting all parish priests from the company of the learned, Peter Heath scoured clerical wills in Norwich for evidence that their authors owned books. He discovered that one-fifth of the bequests mentioned modest libraries. This is a rather remarkable proportion if one remembers that less than two percent of these testators were university graduates. Heath, however, quickly intercepts colleagues ready to usher clerical bibliophiles back among the learned. Priests who bothered to itemize their volumes generally left only service manuals, mis-

---

[22]In this connection, consult the work of Keith Thomas on *Religion and the Decline of Magic,* cited in ch. 7; and that of Christopher Haigh on "Some Aspects of the Recent Historiography of the English Reformation," discussed in ch. 2.

[23]Walter F. Schirmer, "Der englische Humanismus," *Kleine Schriften* (Tübingen: M. Niemeyer, 1950) esp. 20-21.

[24]See Fritz Caspari, *Humanism and the Social Order in Tudor England* (Chicago: University of Chicago Press, 1954); but also note my "John Colet and Erasmus' *Enchiridion,*" *Church History* 46 (1977): 296-312, and *Augustinian Piety and Catholic Reform,* 121-33.

sals, and processionals. Heath bluntly concludes that "if they read at all, they read the wrong books."[25]

If one turned the coin, it might be said that the parish clergy's reading proves that literate priests took their liturgical obligations most seriously. Elsewhere in his review of parish life, Heath confirms precisely this. When he assumes "the view of the humanists" as his own, however, Heath is less generous and savagely censures clerics for their "astoundingly conservative and narrow tastes." Erasmus was his principal model, though Heath turned initially to William Melton's *Sermo Exhortatorius*.[26] Something of a "pep talk" for ordinands and their examiners, Melton's presentation did protest against clerical illiteracy. It blamed candidates for holy orders for underestimating the value of education and it blamed authorities for failing adequately to test candidates' intelligence. What Heath seems to have forgotten is that Melton started his sermon with an evocation of the mystery of the eucharistic sacrifice. He stipulated that the most learned candidates (*"eruditissimus . . . et exercitatissimus sanctarum scripturaram"*) should disqualify themselves if they have less reverence than artless parishioners for the mysteries with which they are about to be entrusted.[27]

Melton bargained that mystery dictated modesty and veneration. There was no place in the ministry for the arrogance spawned and perfumed by erudition. The power with which humble parish priests summoned Christ to their altars and transformed their communities into communions defied explanation. Though their intellectual prowess be undoubted, candidates unprepared to subject themselves to that power ought to be rejected: *"istis licet litteratissimis sacer ordo conferendus non est."*[28]

Melton's abiding respect for mystery thus tempered his attack on illiteracy. It would be a mistake to reduce his faith to the level of lay credulity or to draw from it an apology for the existence of devout yet uneducated priests who honorably performed their sacramental duties. Plainly, however, Melton was not one to put education entirely above mystification. Heath apparently has different ideas. He presumes that lay

---

[25]Heath, *Parish Clergy*, 87-91. Also cf. Roy M. Haines, "Education in English Ecclesiastical Legislation of the Later Middle Ages," in *Councils and Assemblies*, ed. G. J. Cuming and Derek Baker (Cambridge: Cambridge University Press, 1971) 161-75; and Dorothy M. Owen, *Church and Society in Medieval Lincolnshire* (Lincoln: Lincolnshire Local History Committee, 1981) 132-42.

[26]Heath, *Parish Clergy*, 70-71.

[27]Melton, *Sermo*, iv. Tests for reverence, understandably, are unspecified. But Melton has much to say about examiners' carelessness in administering tests for literacy. He claims that ordinands quite easily duped examiners, some of whom were prone to pass unskilled petitioners (". . . latinam linguam perperam legunt vel qui legendo a justa saepe titubant serie verborum"). Also see ch. 5.

[28]Melton, *Sermo* vi(r).

literacy made great strides during the later Middle Ages and that the parish clergy could not keep pace. One gets the image of swarms of literate laymen buzzing about the latest volumes from England's first printing presses. And all these avid readers were ill served by "the unreading priest [who] would have little of personal reflection, insight, and experience to offer his people; he would be a man only sufficient to keep dogmas alive, and not able to make them move; a man who, in the language of the Christian humanists of that time, was better equipped to proclaim the 'Law' than to induce 'faith.' " Heath's disapproval (as he himself would agree) is "Erasmian," yet Erasmus and his humanist colleagues might not have attributed the tragedy to the church's high officials. Heath, however, accused them quite directly. Officials had advanced "no concerted plan and no blueprint" for clerical training; according to Heath, this was a costly omission.[29]

Heath's ruling stands in contrast to what is known of general episcopal and archiepiscopal government. On the whole, bishops were conscientious stewards of their properties. They often scaled immunities when regular clergy defied episcopal regulation and supervision. They tirelessly chased their quarry when renegade parish priests ran for cover and settled among border criminals. Diocesan courts extended the reach of bishops and their energetic deputies. The court's officers grappled with regional crime and rebelliousness, but also enforced contracts and arbi-

---

[29]Heath, *Parish Clergy*, 73, 91. But when it served his purposes, Heath forgot the lay literati and illustrated with vivid anecdotes the rough-and-ready character of parish life (e.g., 8-12). Without directly countering Heath's censure, one might nonetheless reconsider episcopal patronage. Fox, Fisher, and Alcock were particularly kind to Cambridge colleges. Bishop Smyth of Lincoln was Oxford's great benefactor. In 1507 alone, he founded a fellowship at Oriel, packaged a generous gift for Lincoln, and pressed ahead with plans to endow Brasenose. That same year he completed arrangements with the monks of Laund and mayor of Chester whereby the church agreed to subsidize instruction at the school that Smyth himself had established in his native parish. See Ralph Churton, *The Lives of William Smyth and Sir Richard Sutton, Knight* (Oxford: Oxford University Press, 1800) 231-45. Also see Rosemary Masek, "The Humanistic Interests of the Early Tudor Episcopate," *Church History* 39 (1970): 5-17; and Felicity Heal, *Of Prelates and Princes* (Cambridge: Cambridge University Press, 1980) 89, 96, 330-33. Humanistic interests and assorted endowments may not "a concerted program" make, but they would fill a recipe for rebuttal with respect to clerical indifference to learning. The only course open is to suppose that episcopal administrators did not perceive the problem as Heath and the humanists did, but that course is briefly pursued in the text.

trated civil disputes.[30] If authorities seem irresponsible to Heath, it may be because they simply did not share humanist ideas about the aims of clerical education. As Margaret Bowker pointed out, diligent administration of the sacraments was thought sufficient before the Reformation. Theologically informed explanations were required only after the crisis. Until then, lay complaints rarely concerned clerical ignorance, so diocesan investigators justifiably concentrated on clerical misconduct during visitations.[31]

At nearly every corner, this inquiry seems to collide with lay complaints. By now, it must be clear that they were not cranks' complaints, but neither should they be considered unequivocal indicators of pervasive lay disaffection. Perhaps here I can set criticism and disaffection in proper perspective. Modest measures against clerical ignorance and more impressive efforts to reduce clerical immorality left much undone. Worldliness, as the critics usually defined it, was part of clerical life. Rectories' account books were stuffed with *venditurs*, an eloquent testimony to local churches' economic entanglements.[32] It must have seemed to some that the church had adjusted too comfortably and perhaps too eagerly to the ways of the world. Yet laymen commonly clamored for their sacraments and left legacies for clerical support. If some failed to keep their chancels in repair, other laymen dutifully reported the neglect to their archdeacons.[33] Indeed, if church repair and decorative improvements are admissible evidence of lay churchliness, the case for widespread devotion is strengthened, if not sealed. Renewed architectural activity after 1480 marks the earliest Tudor period as a time of revival and recovery.[34]

Of course, disaffection and devotion are not irreconcilable: ecclesiastical culture was capacious enough to contain both. But emphasis on one attitude often induces amnesia with respect to the other, and this historiographic lapse is not unrelated to another problematic disposition, which I have sought to correct by summoning conclusions from the study of Tudor pageant, power, and privilege. J. H. Hexter calls this disposition "the

---

[30]In addition to chs. 4 and 8 of this study, see F. R. H. Du Boulay, *The Lordship of Canterbury* (London: Nelson, 1966) 197-237, 303-305; A. Daniel Frankforter, "The Reformation and the Register: Episcopal Administration of Parishes in Late Medieval England," *Catholic Historical Review* 63 (1977): 204-24; and Thompson, *Clergy*, 41-49.

[31]See Bowker's *The Henrician Reformation: The Diocese of Lincoln under John Longland, 1521-1547* (Cambridge: Cambridge University Press, 1981) 38.

[32]BL. Add. MSS 34.786 ("Compotus . . . rectoris de Helmingham").

[33]*Buckingham*, 210-11, 222-23.

[34]Platt, *Medieval England: A Social History and Archaeology*, 205; and Hoskins, *Age of Plunder*, 158-59. W. K. Jordan's figures on building and repair after 1490 (*Philanthropy*, 317) substantiate the subsequent observations of Platt and Hoskins.

assumption of the conservation of historical energy" and "the seesaw theory." His clever captions animate his dispute with A. F. Pollard and others who believe that increased secular activity in a given society—Tudor society, to be specific—must betoken diminished religious commitment. The seesaw is a simple, graphic metaphor: one end cannot rise unless the other falls. But Hexter counters that the seesaw is best dismantled because levels of activity, intensity, or commitment could increase at both "poles" simultaneously. Contemplate, for instance, the hypothesis that the character and extent of lay churchliness so alarmed dissidents that they doubled their efforts to expose scandal, ridicule superstition, and de-ecclesiasticize political culture. But one suspects that Hexter offers his alternative explanatory model for disruptive rather than for constructive purposes. He wants principally to unsettle Pollard's seesaw and perhaps to present history as a playground full of possibilities. The supposition of simultaneity, however, suggests one possibility that Hexter appears unwilling to ponder, because he insists on thinking that religion and "secular" political culture are polar phenomena. Though he concedes that "clear-cut distinctions" are occasionally difficult to maintain, he proceeds as if they were not. I submit that earliest Tudor history gives a new twist to simultaneity.[35]

"National recovery" is a dreadfully anachronistic way to refer to the target of earliest Tudor policy. Strictly speaking, there was no nation to recover. But when W. C. Richardson borrowed the phrase from more contemporary political rhetoric and joined it to the late-medieval reformation of revenue administration and to the Tudors' preoccupations with peace and social order, I believe he came very close to that government's perceptions of the imperative that braced most policy decisions.[36] More to the point, the need to recover political control over subordinates and the need to develop a sense of shared destiny were common to both church and court. Ecclesiastical management and reform required institutional control; and whenever Fox, Morton, and their colleagues tried to achieve this, their efforts to redistribute *power* in the church intersected compatible dynastic interests in political centralization. When the government tried to consolidate its authority, officials were apt to integrate ecclesiastical *privilege* with their own purposes. The social aims of religious and political *pageant* were, as John Stevens found, nearly identical. Stevens's study of music and poetry looked again at the polarities that characterized binary explanatory models and pronounced them artificial and misleading. "There is no easy distinction to be made between religion and state ceremonial any more than between a 'sacred' and a 'secular' song. There was no domain of life into which religion did not enter,

---

[35]Cf. Hexter's *Reappraisals in History* (Evanston: Northwestern University Press, 1962) 40-42.

[36]See Richardson's *Tudor Chamber Administration*, 442-46.

no activity that was not thought of as part of God's purpose."[37] But readiness to relinquish traditional distinctions so often depends on the presentation of persuasive reconceptualization.

The interpenetration of religious and political life, which these sketches of earliest Tudor pageant, power, and ecclesiastical privilege have illustrated, cannot be presented as easily and as seductively to the historical imagination as Pollard's seesaw and Hexter's simultaneity. "Civil religion" is a category that has achieved notoriety in the United States. At first, it may seem tailored for my purposes, yet its usefulness in this context is limited because it generates a fresh distinction between "a religion of the body politic" and the religion of churches and denominations. Current sociological and theological redefinitions of civil religion constitute little more than a reminder that Christianity repeatedly made political authority one mediator of divine grace and it esteemed political culture as a reflection of divine order.[38] As so often is the case, however, it is easier to criticize predecessors than to construct alternatives. On this count, The "Polytyque Churche" is something of a preamble, inasmuch as the introduction of theoretical refinements must await further "medlyng with worldly maters."

The scenes from clerical life with which this preamble concludes are bridges between propaganda and practice as well as rejoinders to the idealistic critics of clerical worldliness. Connections between providential design and political destiny, which form the formidable cell structure of Tudor ideology, were readily recoverable from publicists' pronouncements and prescribed prayers. I have tried to explore ways in which those ideological connections shaped civic pageants, ennobled episcopal and royal power, preserved ecclesiastical privileges, and touched parish life. All this amounts to a partial retrieval of the "polytyque churche." It is a traveler's tale; stories of the tracks covered should generate discussion that will illumine the way ahead.

---

[37]John Stevens, *Music and Poetry in the Early Tudor Court* (London: Methuen & Co., 1961) 236.

[38]See, e.g., R. Bruce Douglass, "Civil Religion and Western Christianity," *Thought* 55 (1980): 169-83.

ABBREVIATIONS

Acts and Monuments *The Acts and Monuments of John Foxe*, ed. Josiah Pratt, vol. 4 (London: Religious Tract Society, 1877).

AH *The* Anglica Historia *of Polydore Vergil, A.D. 1485-1537*, ed. Denys Hay (London: Royal Historical Society, 1950).

AHR *American Historical Review*

Allen, *OE* *Opus epistolarum Des. Erasmi Roterodami*, 12 vols., ed. P. S. Allen, H. M. Allen, and H. W. Garrod (Oxford: Clarendon, 1906-1958).

ARG *Archiv für Reformationsgeschichte*

Bacon, *History* *The History of the Reign of King Henry the Seventh*, ed. Fred Jacob Levy (New York: Bobbs-Merrill, 1972).

Baker, *Reports* *The Reports of Sir John Spelman*, 2 vols., ed. John Hamilton Baker (London: Selden Society, 1977-1978).

BL British Library
    Add. MSS Additional Manuscripts
    Arundel MS Arundel Manuscript 36
    Cott. MSS Cottonian Manuscripts

Buckingham *The Courts of the Archdeaconry of Buckingham, 1483-1523*, ed. Elizabeth M. Elvey (Aylesbury: Buckinghamshire Record Society, 1975).

CDS *Calendar of Documents Relating to Scotland*, ed. Joseph Bain (Edinburgh: H. M. General Register House, 1881-1888).

Charter Rolls *Calendar of the Charter Rolls Preserved in the Public Record Office*, ed. Henry Churchill Maxwell-Lyte, vols. 5 and 6 (London: PRO, 1916-1920).

CL *Chronicles of London*, ed. Charles Lethbridge Kingsford (rpt.; Dursley: Sutton, 1977).

Concilia *Concilia Magnae Britanniae et Hiberniae*, 4 vols., ed. David Wilkins (rpt.; Brussels: Culture et Civilisation, 1964).

Conv The Sermon of Doctor Colete, Made to the Convocacion at Paulis, appended to Joseph H. Lupton, *Life of Dean Colet*, 293-304 (London: G. Bell and Sons, 1909).

CPR Calendar of the Patent Rolls Preserved in the Public Record Office, ed. J. G. Black et al. (London, 1891-).

CSP Spain Calendar of Letters, Despatches and State Papers, Relating to the Negotiations between England and Spain, ed. Gustav Adolph Bergenroth, 2 vols. (London: PRO, 1862).

CSP Venice Calendar of State Papers and Manuscripts Relating to English Affairs Existing in the Archives and Collections of Venice, ed. Rawdon Lubbock Brown et al. (London: PRO, 1864).

CWTM The Complete Works of St. Thomas More, 14 vols. (New Haven: Yale University Press, 1963-).

De legibus Henry de Bracton, *De legibus et consuetudinibus Angliae*, ed. George E. Woodbine, 2 vols. (Cambridge: Belknap Press, 1968).

EEC John Colet, *Enarratio in primam epistolam S. Pauli ad Corinthios*, ed. Joseph H. Lupton (London: G. Bell, 1874).

EER-a John Colet, *Epistolae B. Pauli ad Romanos: expositio literalis*, in *Opuscula quaedam theologica*, ed. Joseph H. Lupton (London: G. Bell and Sons, 1876).

EER-b John Colet, *Enarratio in epistolam S. Pauli ad Romanos*, ed. Joseph H. Lupton (London: Bell and Daldy, 1873).

EHR English Historical Review

Ellis, *Three Books* Three Books of Polydore Vergil's English History, ed. Henry Ellis (London: The Camden Society, 1844).

Elton, *Studies* Geoffrey Rudolph Elton, *Studies in Tudor and Stuart Politics and Government: Papers and Reviews, 1946-1972*, 3 vols. (New York: Cambridge University Press, 1974).

Emden, *Oxford* Alfred Brotherston Emden, *A Biographical Register of the University of Oxford to A.D. 1500*, 3 vols. (Oxford: Clarendon, 1957-1959).

Ench Erasmus, *Enchiridion Militis Christiani*, in *Ausgewählte Werke*, ed. Hajo Holborn and Annemarie Holborn (Munich: Beck, 1933).

Epigrams Thomas More, *Latin Epigrams,* ed. Leicester Bradner and Charles Arthur Lynch (Chicago: University of Chicago Press, 1953).

EWTM *The English Works of Sir Thomas More,* ed. William
E. Campbell, 2 vols. (New York: The Dial Press,
1931).

Gairdner, Letters *Letters and Papers Illustrative of the Reigns of Richard
III and Henry VII,* ed. James Gairdner, 2 vols. (Lon-
don: Longman, Green, Longman, and Roberts,
1861-1863).

GC *The Great Chronicle of London,* ed. Arthur Hermann
Thomas and Isobel Dorothy Thornley (London: G.
W. Jones, 1938).

Heath, Parish Clergy Peter Heath, *The English Parish Clergy on the Eve of
the Reformation* (Toronto: University of Toronto
Press, 1969).

HJ *Historical Journal*

Hume, Letters *The Letters of David Hume,* ed. John Young Thomson Greig, 2 vols. (Oxford: Clarendon, 1932).

JBAA *Journal of the British Archaeological Association*

JEH *Journal of Ecclesiastical History*

JHI *Journal of the History of Ideas*

Keilwey, Reports *Reports d'ascuns cases,* ed. Robert Keilwey (London: Charles Harper, William Crooke, and Rich-
ard Tonson, 1688).

Kelly, Canterbury Ju- Michael J. Kelly, *Canterbury Jurisdiction and Influ-
risdiction ence during the Episcopate of William Warham, 1503-
1532* (Ph.D. dissertation, Cambridge University,
1963).

LB *Desiderii Erasmi Roterdami Opera Omnia,* ed. J. Cler-
icus, 10 vols. (Leiden: Peter Vander Aa, 1703-1706).

Leland John Leland, *De rebus Britannicis collectanea,* ed.
Thomas Hearn, vol. 4 (London: Richardson, 1770).

Lincoln *An Episcopal Court Book for the Diocese of Lincoln,
1514-1520,* ed. Margaret Bowker (Lincoln: Lincoln
Record Society, 1967).

LP, Henry VIII *Letters and Papers, Foreign and Domestic, of the Reign
of Henry VIII, 1509-1547,* ed. J. S. Brewer, J. Gairdner, and R. H. Brodie, 21 vols. (London: Longmans, 1862-1932).

THE "POLYTYQUE CHURCHE"

LRF *Letters of Richard Fox, 1486-1527*, ed. Percy Stafford Allen and Helen Mary Allen (Oxford: Clarendon, 1929).

Medwall, Plays *The Plays of Henry Medwall*, ed. Alan H. Nelson (Cambridge: D. S. Brewer, 1980).

Melton, Sermo *Sermo exhortatorius Cancelarii Ebor. hiis qui ad sacros ordines petunt promoveri*, ed. William de Melton (London, 1494).

Memorials *Memorials of King Henry VII*, ed. James Gairdner (London: Rolls Series, 1858).

Missarum Sollemnia *Missarum Sollemnia: Eine genetische Erklärung der römischen Messe*, ed. Josef Andreas Jungmann, 2 vols. (Vienna: Herder, 1952).

NH *Northern History*

Obj *Objectiones et argumenta contra et pro privilegiis sanctuarii Westmonasterii*, Longleat MS. 38, Longleat House.

Opera Erasmi Erasmus, *Opera Omnia* (Amsterdam: North-Holland Publishing Company, 1969-).

Oratiuncula Eduard Fueter, *Oratiuncula ordinata*, printed as "Die 'Predigt von 1483,' " in *Religion und Kirche in England in fünfzehnten Jahrhundert*, 68-78 (Tübingen: J. C. B. Mohr, 1904).

Paston *The Paston Letters*, ed. James Gairdner, 6 vols. (New York: AMS Press, 1965).

PL *Patrologia cursus completus* (Series Latina), ed. J. P. Migne, 221 vols. (Paris, 1844-1885).

PRO Public Record Office
   KB *King's Bench*
   Durh *Cursitor Rolls, Durham Diocese*

PSD John Colet, *Super opera Dionysii*, ed. Joseph H. Lupton (London: Bell and Daldy, 1869).

Reg. Fitzjames *The Register of Richard Fitzjames, Bishop, 1506-1521/ 2*, MS 9531.9, in *Bishops of London Registers*, The Guildhall Library (London).

Reg. Fox *The Register of Richard Fox, Lord Bishop of Durham, 1494-1501*, ed. Marjorie Pears Howden (London: B. Quaritch, 1932).

Reg. King *The Registers of Oliver King, Bishop of Bath and Wells, 1496-1503, and Hadrian de Castello, Bishop of Bath and Wells, 1503-1518*, ed. Henry Churchill Maxwell-Lyte (London: privately printed, 1939).

Reg. Mayew *Registrum Ricardi Mayew, episcopi herefordensis, A.D. 1504-1516*, ed. Arthur Thomas Bannister (London: Canterbury and York Society, 1921).

Reg. Morton *The Register of John Morton*, MS, *Registers of the Archbishops of Canterbury, 1486-1500*, Lambeth Palace Library (London).

Reg. Myllyng *Registrum Thome Myllyng, episcopi herefordensis, A.D. 1474-1492*, ed. Arthur Thomas Bannister (London: Canterbury and York Society, 1920).

Reg. Rotherham *The Register of Thomas Rotherham, Archbishop of York, 1480-1500*, ed. Eric E. Barker, 2 vols. (Devonshire: Canterbury and York Society, 1976).

Relation *A Relation, or Rather a True Account, of the Island of England*, ed. Charlotte Augusta Sneyd (London: Camden Society, 1847).

Reports *Les Reports des Cases (Yearbooks)*, ed. John Maynard (London, 1678).

Ripon J. T. Fowler, *Acts of Chapter of the Collegiate Church of St. Peter and Wilfrid, Ripon* (Durham: Andrews and Company, 1875).

Rogers, *Correspondence* *The Correspondence of Sir Thomas More*, ed. Elizabeth Frances Rogers (Princeton: Princeton University Press, 1947).

Rot. Parl. *Rotuli parliamentorum et petitiones*, 6 vols. (London, 1767-1777).

Rot. Scot. *Rotuli Scotiae in Turri Londinensi et in Domo Capitulari Westmonasteriensi asservati*, ed. D. Macpherson, I. Caley, and W. Illingworth, 2 vols. (London, 1814-1819).

Sac John Colet, *Opus de sacramentis ecclesiae*, ed. Joseph H. Lupton (London: Bell and Daldy, 1867).

SC, Bayne *Select Cases in the Council of Henry VII*, ed. C. G. Bayne and William H. Dunham (London: Selden Society, 1958).

SC, Hemmant *Select Cases in the Exchequer Chamber before All the Justices of England*, ed. Mary Hemmant, vol. 2 (London: Selden Society, 1948).

SC, Leadam *Select Cases before the King's Council in the Star Chamber, Commonly Called the Court of Star Chamber, A.D. 1477-1544*, ed. Isaac Saunders Leadam (London: Selden Society, 1903-1911).

SDB *Sanctuarium Dunelmense,* in *Sanctuarium Dunelmense et sanctuarium Bevenlacense,* ed. James Raine (London: Surtees Society, 1837).

Skelton, *Poems John Skelton: The Complete English Poems,* ed. John Scattergood (New Haven: Yale University Press, 1983).

SR *Statutes of the Realm,* 11 vols. (London: 1810-1828).

Talbot *Letters from the English Abbots to the Chapter at Citeaux, 1442-1521,* ed. Charles H. Talbot (London: Royal Historical Society, 1967).

Thompson, *Clergy* Alexander Hamilton Thompson, *The English Clergy and Their Organization in the Later Middle Ages* (Oxford: Clarendon, 1947).

Thompson, *Newarke* Alexander Hamilton Thompson, *The History of the Hospital and the New College of the Annunciation of St. Mary in the Newarke, Leicester* (Leicester: E. Backus, 1937).

TRHS *Transactions of the Royal Historical Society*

YB see *Reports*

YCR *York Civic Records,* ed. Angelo Raine, 8 vols. (Wakefield: Yorkshire Archaeological Society, 1939-1954).

INDEX